FOOD IN
ROMAN BRITAIN

FOOD IN
ROMAN BRITAIN

JOAN P. ALCOCK

The
History
Press

First published in 2001 by Tempus Publishing

Reprinted in 2010 by
The History Press
The Mill, Brimscombe Port
Stroud, Gloucestershire GL5 2QG
www.thehistorypress.co.uk

Reprinted 2014

British Library Cataloguing in Publication Data.
A catalogue record for this book is available from the British Library.

ISBN 978 0 7524 1924 4

Typesetting and origination by Tempus Publishing.
Printed and bound in Great Britain by
Marston Book Services Limited, Oxfordshire

Contents

List of illustrations   7

Acknowledgements   11

1   Background evidence   13

2   Cereal products   17

3   Meat, game and poultry   33

4   Fish, shellfish and other crustaceans   47

5   Dairy products   57

6   Vegetables, fruits and nuts   63

7   Herbs, spices, salt and honey   69

8   Olive oil and liquamen   77

9   Wine, beer and water   83

10   The kitchen   99

11   The dining room   119

12   Shops and markets   137

13   Army diet   149

14   Diet and nutrition   161

Classical authors mentioned in the text   169

Bibliography   174

Index   183

List of illustrations

Text figures

1   Soldiers cutting corn
2   Modern relief showing reconstructed *vallus*
3   Mosaic of man with a corn measure, Ostia
4   Rotary quern
5   Reconstruction of mill
6   Graffito of a mule working a donkey mill
7   Loaf baked in the form of Roman bread
8   Unleavened bread
9   Forms of Roman *testum*
10 A Roman bakery
11 The tomb of the baker, M. Vergilius Eurysaces, Rome
12 Dexter cattle, Little Butser Demonstration Iron Age Site
13 A Soay ram
14 Figurines of goats
15 Relief of man butchering a pig, Aquileia
16 Sacrificial scene on the Bridgeness Distance Slab
17 Hunting dog from Lydney
18 Bronze figurines of boars
19 Hunting scene on a relief found near Bath
20 Mosaic depicting Winter in the Chedworth Roman villa
21 Winged *amorino* fishing, relief from Chester
22 Figured mosaic depicting fish, Lufton Roman villa
23 Cheese presses, Longthorpe fort
24 Round cheese press
25 Pottery, Lullingstone Roman villa
26 Reconstructed scene of pottery and food arranged in the Verulamium Museum
27 Brine evaporation to produce salt
28 Tarraconensis amphora dredged from the River Thames
29 Types of amphorae imported into Britain
30 Pottery jars carried on a cart, early twentieth century
31 Mosaic of man carrying amphora on his shoulder, Ostia
32 Amphorae, Mainz
33 Wine barrel, Silchester
34 Boat transporting wine barrels, Moselle Valley, Germany

35 Altar set up by M. Aurelius Lunaris at Bordeaux
36 Scene from sarcophagus of Cupids playing amongst vines
37 Fountain at the crossroads, Pompeii
38 Water pipes, Fishbourne villa
39 The Corbridge Lion
40 Reconstructed Roman kitchen
41 Trivet, Great Chesterford; gridiron, Silchester
42 Roman kitchen
43 Little Butser Iron Age Demonstration Site Farmstead
44 Round house, Little Butser
45 Model of Boscoreale Villa
46 *Dolia* in courtyard, Ostia
47 Cauldron chains from Silchester and Great Chesterford
48 Roman frying pan from Egypt
49 Detail of brackets supporting Roman frying pan
50 Folded frying pan
51 Handle of *patera*
52 Baking pan, Pompeii
53 Water heater, Pompeii
54 Combined ladle and flesh-hook, Great Chesterford
55 Knife handles, Silchester
56 Roman balance
57 Roman steelyard
58 Steelyard weight, Old Carlisle
59 Steelyard weight, Silchester
60 Black burnished ware
61 Severn Valley and Savernake ware
62 Pottery, Verulamium Museum
63 Glass vessel, Caerleon, later used as container for a cremation
64 Table seating arrangement
65 Some of the contents of the so-called 'child's grave', Colchester
66 Tombstone of Curatia Di(o)nysia, Chester
67 Tombstone of Julia Velva, York
68 The family meal
69 Funerary relief, Neumagen, showing a family gathered round a table
70 A dancing girl entertaining after a banquet
71 Cologne beaker with hunting scene, Verulamium Museum
72 Rhenish ware beakers, Verulamium Museum
73 Glass vessels
74 Glass vessel with chariot race, Colchester
75 Glass bowl, Wint Hill
76 Bronze strainer
77 Handle of skillet, Capheaton
78 Bacchic platter, Mildenhall Treasure

79   Coffin from Simpleveld, Holland
80   Relief of a wineshop, Dijon
81   Baker's shop
82   Counter of baker's shop, Pompeii
83   Rear of wineshop counter, Herculanium
84   Shop, Herculanium
85   The innkeeper and the departing guest
86   Bill of fare
87   Wine shop and bar, Herculanium
88   Carbonised dates, Colchester
89   Poulterers' shop
90   Apple stall, Arlon
91   Relief of bakers weighing bread, tomb of M. Vergilius Eurysaces
92   Steelyard weight in use, Trier
93   Plan of macellum attached to the Baths, Wroxeter
94   Granary, The Lunt fort, Baginton
95   Bronze cooking vessels and gridiron, Newstead
96   Bases of circular oven, Caerleon
97   Legionary bread stamp
98   Unleavened bread and North African style brazier.
99   Pulverising food in a pestle and mortar
100 Adult skeleton with flagon, Pepperhill Roman cemetery, near Gravesend, Kent
101 Mosaic of skeleton with wine jugs, Pompeii

Colour plates

1   Grain gathered ready for winnowing, Nepal
2   Woman winnowing with a wooden riddle, Nepal
3   Corn measure, Carvoran, Hadrian's Wall
4   Man pounding corn with pestle and mortar, Pakistan
5   Bakery in the Via di Stabia, Pompeii
6   Fresco of the bakers of Pompeii
7   Leather bag containing milk, Mongolia
8   Coarse ware pottery, Newstead in National Museums of Scotland, Edinburgh
9   Tarraconensis amphora found in the Thames
10 Reconstruction of Chieftain's grave, Welwyn
11 Fountain at crossroads, Herculanium
12 Experimental Roman domed oven
13 Table with pottery and food reconstructed in Museum of London
14 Steelyard in use, Gyantse, Tibet
15 Reconstruction of reception room at the Roman villa site at Castle Hill, Ipswich Museum
16 An intimate dinner party

17 Tombstone of Gaius Julius Maternus
18 Reconstruction of Roman living room, Museum of London
19 Samian ware from Newstead
20 Samian bowl with gladiatorial scene
21 Table set with samian ware and cupboard, in reconstructed room, Museum of London
22 Roman glass, first-third centuries, Ospringe, Kent
23 Butcher's shop
24 Shop at Herculanium showing remains of shuttering
25 Reconstruction of baker's shop, Poultry, London
26 A Roman legionary preparing a meal
27 Soldiers of re-enactment group, Cohors V Gallorum, with bread and North African style brazier

Acknowledgements

I am most grateful to the staff of the museums, libraries and organisations mentioned below who have helped me to obtain the photographs necessary for this book. The following museums and organisations, to whom copyright belongs, have kindly given permission for the following photographs to be reproduced: Cadw: Welsh Historic Monuments. Crown Copyright (**96**); The Grosvenor Museum, Chester (**66**); Colchester Museums (**65, 74**); Colchester Archaeological Trust (**88**); Ipswich Borough Council Museums and Galleries (**colour plate 15**); The Museum of Antiquities of the University and the Society of Antiquaries of Newcastle upon Tyne (**colour plate 3**); The Museum of London (**colour plates 13, 18, 21 & 25**); The National Maritime Museum, London (**28 & colour plate 9**); The Trustees of the National Museums of Scotland (**16, 95, colour plates 8 & 19**); The National Museums and Galleries of Wales (**63**); The Trustees of the British Museum (**colour plate 10**);The Warburg Institute (**22, 75, 77 & 78**); St Albans Museums (**26, 62, 71, 72 & colour plate 20**); Union Railways (South) Ltd (**100**); The National Museum of Antiquities, Leiden, Holland (**79**); Crown Copyright Material NMR reproduced by permission of English Heritage acting under licence from the Controller of HMSO (**20, 25, 67** & **colour plate 22**).

Somerset County Museums Service, to whom copyright belongs, most generously gave permission for the photograph of the East Coker mosaic to be displayed on the cover and I am grateful to Stephen Minnett, Assistant County Museums Officer, for arranging this.

Copyright also belongs to the following who provided photographs and drawings. Alex Croom, Tyne and Wear Museums, generously allowed me to reproduce photographs of Cohors V Gallorum (**98, 99, colour plates 12 & 27**). Eileen Wright, with whom I explored Nepal and Bhutan, provided **colour plate 2** and Hilary Dalke, South Bank University, provided the drawing of the reconstructed kitchen (**40**). Charlotte Fawley, with exemplary patience, undertook the drawings of artefacts and implements (**4, 9, 14, 17, 23-24, 29, 33, 41, 47-54, 56-58, 60-61, 73, 76, 93 & 97**) and recreated scenes of Roman life (**10, 13, 19, 21, 27, 42, 64, 68, 70, 89, 92, colour plates 16, 23 & 26**). The author provided the other photographs and drawings.

The research for this book has been undertaken for several years and I am grateful to Peter Kemmis Betty who undertook publication. Equally encouraging was the help given by friends and colleagues, which enabled me to complete the book. In particular I should like to acknowledge the courteous assistance given to me over many years by the staff of the Library of the Institute of Classical Studies, University of London. John Marchant, Head of the National Bakery School, South Bank University, gave valuable advice on milling of flour and baking of bread. Vivien Swan improved the sections on the types of pottery and provided information on the North African pottery and the exploits of Cohors

V Gallorum. Andrew Costin of the National Bakery School, South Bank University, made experiments with bread to produce Roman style loaves, which were both authentic in shape and palatable when consumed.

Amongst others who provided helpful discussion and encouragement in a variety of ways were Mark Hassall, Institute of Archaeology, University of London, Helen Glass, Senior Archaeologist, Rail Link Engineering, Helga Pihlakas, Margaret Roxan, Associate Fellow, Institute of Classical Studies, University of London, and Maureen Walshe. Phyllis Kern yet again meticulously checked the manuscript and proofs. Lastly I owe an enormous debt to Bryan Reuben, Professor Emeritus, South Bank University, whose detailed reading and constructive advice was invaluable in producing the final version of the text.

1 Background evidence

Most historians of food are familiar with the Roman cookery book of Apicius, a book perhaps more often quoted than read. It was not the only cookery book in the classical world. According to Athenaeus, there were others including *Cookery* by Simus, *On Cakes* by Iatrocles and *Bread making* by Chrysippus of Tyana. Apicius is unique in that his book has survived as a complete cookery book and one where the recipes can be adapted to modern tastes, as they have been in the translations by Barbara Flower and Elizabeth Rosenbaum, and John Edwards. This has given the book a commanding position so that there is a tendency, when discussing food and food supplies in Britain, to transfer Roman or Italianate methods of cookery to the habits of Romano-British society. It is as if a large proportion of the population dined *à la Apicius,* but there is no evidence whatsoever that Apicius' recipes were followed in Britain. His book may have been known to the cooks who came to Britain with administrators and other officials and it is possible that some food was cooked in accordance with his recipes. Examples can be given indicating to what culinary use food could be put, and what might have been eaten in this somewhat remote province of the empire. There is also no evidence that gourmets such as Trimalchio gave gargantuan feasts in the province. Dining in a Roman style was, no doubt, natural to administrators and other officials and this practice would be copied by persons who adopted Roman lifestyles. Others might continue to follow Celtic practice, especially if they lived on a subsistence diet.

The cookery book of Apicius is a mystery in itself. The one bearing his name is not the work of one person; possibly there were three men engaged in the compilation. The first Apicius seems to have lived in the first century BC, being mentioned by Posidonius for his love of luxury. The second, Marcus Gavius Apicius, was a renowned gourmet living in the reign of the Emperor Tiberius (AD 14-37), who is believed to have written two books, one a general recipe book, another on sauces. The work which has come down to the present time is neither of these. Rather it is a compilation of over 500 recipes made in the late fourth or early fifth century from both his books and snippets from books on medicine and agriculture. Into this has been interposed a short collection of recipes, possibly by him or another of the same name, but collated by Vidinarius. The third Apicius lived in the reign of the Emperor Trajan (AD 98-117) and is best known for his advice on transporting oysters.

It is the second Apicius who is famous for the method of his death, recorded by the Roman poet, Martial. Apicius spent 60 million *sesterces* on food and feasting. Finding that he had only 10 million left, this 'he refused to endure, as mere hunger and thirst, and as the last draught of all, quaffed poison. You never did anything, Apicius, more gluttonous!'

The purpose of this book, *Food in Roman Britain,* is to provide evidence relating to the provision and eating of food in Roman Britain and to counteract the suggestion that the population subsisted on gourmet meals. Much of the evidence presented has been culled from archaeological excavations and to some extent is a compilation of the finds. Environmental archaeology has greatly improved in recent years so that it is possible to deduce what crops were grown, how cattle were butchered, even what was evacuated from the alimentary canal. Examination of skeletons can reveal long-term eating habits and a disease from which a person suffered, possibly due to poor nutrition.

The coming of Rome meant the beginning of an urban society. Townspeople would rely on shops to supplement what was grown in gardens and allotments and shopping patterns would establish new habits. Tastes could be stimulated by the new products imported by merchants and supplied on a commercial basis by retailers. Excavation uncovers the layout of shops and houses, of the position of kitchens and dining rooms. To some extent, it exposes the position of hearths and fires, but there is a gap between what is revealed and what may be reality. This may be bridged by interpolating the words of classical authors so that to add flesh to the bones, in a manner of speaking, archaeological evidence is supplemented by literary evidence. Cato, Varro and Columella provide evidence of food, agricultural practices, medical usages and cookery methods and Pliny the Elder's compilation of the plants and animals known to the ancient world and their medical and culinary uses is invaluable, even though the uses to which he said they were put needs careful evaluation. Classical parallels have to be made if some account of the food produced and eaten in Roman Britain is to be attempted. Reference to the work of a cook and to the pleasures of a hedonistic diner may flesh out archaeological evidence.

Reference can also be made to the customs and lifestyles of other peoples, especially those of the Celtic world. But although this information complements the archaeological evidence, classical authors, for example, focus on the customs and diet of the central Roman Empire, that is Italy, rather than the provinces. Their evidence therefore reveals culinary practices and eating habits of a Romanised people. This may illustrate the eating habits of administrators and officials who were sent from Rome to Britain or of those persons who wished to emulate their way of life. These customs would be found mainly in the urban centres or in the villas.

The Romans brought to Britain new crops, and new products were introduced through trade, many transported in amphorae. Evidence provided by sherds and graffiti can reveal the origin, the name of the shipper or the supplier, and its contents. Not only liquids were carried in these distinctive containers; a wide variety of commodities — fruits, nuts, cereals and vegetables — were conveyed from various sources. Some plants, such as turnips and cabbages, could have been brought to Britain from Gaul to be grown in a garden or on a commercial scale. Native plants were gathered from the wild but were also domesticated to increase their yield. This had been common Roman practice. Seneca implies that his friend, Fabricius, gathered food plants from wild land which he had cultivated. Some plants he left in the wild because he believed they would have more potency and therefore greater efficacy as a herbal remedy.

This is not to imply that the native Celts did not eat well before the Romans came. Celtic tales of feasting and the wide variety of native plants show that they did. But for the first time Britain experienced a greater variety of food grown on an economic basis and able to be transported by an impressive series of roads. The Romans introduced more advanced farming techniques and better breeding of animals. The changes may not have been great, but they were cumulative and, over a long period of time, were effective in bringing untilled land into cultivation. By the third and fourth centuries, large villa estates were farmed more intensively making use of new or improved agricultural tools and techniques. Food supplies, especially grain crops, had to be increased in order to provide for a large urban non-productive consumer population and a resident army.

At first the army purchased grain, if necessary by compulsion, but by the third century Britain had become subject to the annona or corn tax, which was administered and collected by officials (*frumentarii*) who made ever-increasing demand on grain producers. Yet it seems that Britain responded so well that she became a corn exporter. So much was being produced that, as Libanius, a fourth-century writer, indicates, shipments of corn from Britain became regular practice until the supply was interrupted by attacks of the barbarians. The sixth-century Greek historian, Zosimus, noted that the Emperor Julian in AD 359, determined to ensure these shipments would continue, built a fleet of 800 large boats to transport corn to supply the Rhine garrisons.

There are problems connected with a study of food in Roman Britain. First, much of the archaeological evidence is difficult to date. Where possible dates have been given, but excavation reports may not, or cannot, date all the evidence, especially if finds are out of context. Raspberry seeds found in a well, for example, may be dated with pottery dumped when the well was filled in; the precise date of eating the raspberries may not be known. Secondly, timescale has to be taken into consideration. The period known as Roman Britain covered almost 400 years. During that time people ceased to be groupings of invading conquerors and subject Britons and coalesced into a Romano-British population. A cursory reading of surviving tombstones reveals that Italians, Sardinians, Gauls, Tungrians, Batavians, Spaniards, Germans, Syrians, Palmyrenes and others settled in Britain and intermarried with each other and the native Celtic tribes. Each group brought with them their own culinary tastes, likes and dislikes and methods of cookery. This situation can be paralleled by modern analogies. The British returned from India with a preference for curry, the hotter the better, and also devised Anglo-Indian recipes, such as kedgeree. Some troops returning to Britain after the Second World War demanded pasta and pizza. Immigrants have introduced ethnic tastes, soon adopted and adapted by the native population. Given these analogies, the discovery of a Romano-British cookbook of the fifth century might reveal a revolution in culinary practices.

Thirdly, the evidence presented here for the consumption of a commodity may seem considerable but, taken as a whole, does not justify claims made for it; this occurs in the case of fish. Admittedly evidence for eating fish is harder to gather than eating meat. Excavators rely on sieving of soil samples, especially in cess pits, to find bones and scales, and on the discovery of fish hooks, netting needles and lead sinkers. Unlike animal bones many fish bones are digested. The excavators at York concluded that the distribution of chub and barbel bones proved that they had gone through the human gut. Sherds of amphorae may provide evidence for the importance of fish sauce, and debris on sites suggests processing industries.

Fourthly, it is difficult to determine what value individuals place on a product. This is partly linked to demand and availability, as well as keeping quality. Again with reference to fish, even in mediaeval York the only fish that seem to have been eaten in great quantities were herring and cod. Yet more must have been available. Partly, consumption is dependent on wealth; scarcity of fish implies higher prices. Gallant states that the nutritional value of a kilo of fish is only two-thirds that of a kilo of grain; more energy and satisfaction can be obtained from meat and bread. Fish is not a 'filler'. Today it wins approval for its vitamin content, unsaturated fatty acid and its value in a diet. Many people in Roman Britain were more concerned with staving off hunger; fish would have given satisfaction in this context, but this would depend on a supply of fresh sea fish and transportation in a reasonable condition. Bones of sea fish are found on inland sites but not in large enough quantities to indicate an overall efficient transport system.

Two other problems relate to status and regionalism. Roman Britain had a relatively defined status differentiation in the personnel of the towns, forts and villas, most having a high status, which can be set against the more remote un-Romanised settlements, some of which rejected Roman ways or did not wish to follow improved agricultural methods, and others which lived outside the range of access to Romanised foodstuffs. These areas might experience problems. If crops were requisitioned by the army as part of its food supply, or if there were a series of bad years climatically, famine conditions could apply. Regionalism can be related to dietary regionalism. The Romans had a somewhat distinct dietary identity and when they occupied other lands, they brought that identity with them. This was already breaking down because of the polyglot nature of the society which evolved in the empire. Together with contrasts of climate and landscape, this forced a modification of the original dietary identity.

In spite of these caveats, this book provides evidence for the type of food eaten in Britain both by the military and the civilian population. It is not concerned with agricultural practice, nor with trade, nor with large-scale production of food. It attempts to assess the foods available in Roman Britain and the eating, cooking and dining habits of the people who inhabited the province. It also considers the nutritional effects of the diet on some of the population. Roman Britain was not an homogeneous whole. It was home to a great variety of people, who lived in urban and country areas, in town houses, villas and huts, some of whom were eager to adopt and adapt new ideas, others who were content to follow the ways of their ancestors. Climatic conditions, habitat, wealth and poverty would affect the supply of food, which, in turn, could dictate eating habits. Good nutritional habits, so much a priority nowadays, had they ever been identified, would have given place to the provision of a sustaining and adequate food supply.

2 Cereal products

Wheat and other grains

Grain crops are the most important type of plant food, both directly as cereals and indirectly as fodder for animals. Their chief value lies in the provision of carbohydrates and as a source of B group vitamins. It is therefore not surprising that they were a staple food of northern European countries for the production of bread and pottage products.

The main wheat crop of early prehistoric history in Britain was einkorn (*triticum monococcum*), a spring sown wheat, but this was supplanted by emmer (*triticum dicoccum*) in Iron Age Britain. Spelt (*triticum spelta*), which grew well in a damp climate and had the added advantage of being a hardier plant sown in the winter, was introduced into Iron Age Britain by the Belgae. Both of these gave a high food value but like all bearded wheats they were difficult to thresh, so that often they were replaced by old bread wheat (*triticum aestivum)* and club wheat (*triticum compactum*). Emmer, a robust crop, tolerant of wet and cold summers, which had a protein value sufficient for the purpose of bread making and could also be used for pottage, became the principal bread wheat of the Roman army.

At Caerleon, where a large quantity seems to have been imported in the late first century AD, the grain had been allowed deliberately to germinate and was in process of being roasted for malting when fire caught hold and set the building ablaze. Evidence of a particularly good crop of spelt comes from Verulamium, where a fire in the second century destroyed a granary in the forum. This is an unusual place to find storage of grain, so that it must have been a temporary measure.

In London a deposit of spelt, which had been burned in the Boudiccan rebellion of AD 60-1 contained lentils and vetch seeds, which suggested that it had been imported from the Mediterranean or the Near East. This deposit may have been intended as part of a consignment for distribution as seed corn to other parts of the province. Another deposit at York was so infested with grain beetles when it was imported that the deposit had to be sealed and the building dismantled. Charred wheat grain, found in Culver Street, near the Balkerne Gate at Colchester, had no sign of fungus or insect infestation indicating that, after being effectively processed by winnowing and sieving, it had been adequately stored.

Insect contamination might be acceptable to a certain degree but in the end a foul taste, together with an unpleasant appearance, would make grain unacceptable. Roman writers disagreed on infestation. Varro was adamant that infested grain should be removed as soon as possible. Columella disagreed: it should be left because insects would infest only the top layer. Cato recommended that the grain should be sprinkled with a mixture of olive lees (*amuca*) and chaff to prevent infestation; Varro advised that the walls and floors of the granary should be covered with a mixture of cement and *amuca*. Correct storage of grain was important because even a small loss might mean famine.

Rye growing became more common under the Romans. Helbaek suggested that the crop was introduced into Britain by the Romans, but grains of rye, found in the stomach of the man found in Lindow Moss, Wilmslow in Cheshire and dated to the late Iron Age, indicate that it was part of the diet of pre-Roman Britain. Grown profusely in cool northern areas and often on poorer soil, it was prized as an early fodder crop for sheep, and its stalks were ideal for thatching. It is a crop which threshes easily without parching. At Wilderspool (Cheshire) in the third century AD, both spelt and rye were grown; other examples of rye have been found on sites in the Midlands and northern Britain. Rye was also present in the grain stored in the Verulamium forum.

Oats had also been grown in Iron Age Britain, first as a wild crop but soon cultivated for use as a basis for pottage. In Roman Britain they were grown mainly to provide the army with a fodder crop, especially in the Highland zone, as was barley. Barley does not contain the necessary protein to make a well-risen loaf. Two-rowed barley was particularly useful for malting to make beer, but its main purpose was as an excellent fodder crop because animals can digest both the husk and the grain. According to Columella, stallions could be fattened on it before mating, and brood mares given an extra allowance after foaling to build up their strength. Pliny recommended it to increase the strength and enlarge the muscles of the animals. An examination of coprolites found during excavation of the fort at Lancaster showed that the horses of the auxiliary cavalry regiment stationed there ate a great deal of barley and little wheat.

Grain was cut by gripping bunches of it with one hand and cutting it with an open-bladed reap-hook or a small sickle. Columella stated that it took a man a day and a half to reap a *jugerum*, a plot of land 73m (240ft) by 37m (120ft). Cutting corn is shown on a scene from Trajan's Column (**1**), where legionaries cut it just below the ear, and sickles have been found at Silchester and the fort of Newstead (Borders). Diodorus confirmed that this method was used in pre-Roman Britain: 'the Britons harvest their grain crops by cutting off only the ears of corn and storing them . . . each day they pick out the ripe ears to grind for a daily supply'. This allowed the long straw to be used for thatching, but it was also used as fodder and litter; if it was burned the ashes could be used as a fertilizer.

The Romans brought with them the scythe, examples of which have been found at Great Chesterford (Essex), Silchester, Newstead and the Barnsley Park villa (Gloucestershire). These cut through a larger area of the crop, but with the disadvantage that the grain falls on the ground; the ears then have to be collected by gleaning. The Great Chesterford and Barnsley Park scythes present a problem for they are 1.6m (5ft 4in) long, a difficult size for a man to handle. It is possible that they formed part of some kind of cutting machine, such as that revealed on a relief found in excavations at Buzenol in Luxembourg (**2**). A box on wheels, pushed seemingly by a mule or donkey, has a row of teeth in front cutting through the wheat; by the side is a man keeping the teeth clear by sorting out the corn. Another relief found at Arlon in Belgium shows a man placing his arms on two long shafts connected by a bar of wood. He would presumably be behind the donkey guiding the machine. The reliefs depict a mechanical harvester called a *vallus*, described by Pliny and Palladius and seemingly being used in Gaul on large estates. If the scythes in Britain were

1   Soldiers cutting corn with sickles, Trajan's Column

part of this machine, it would appear that it was used in Britain on large estates, which were either growing grain as a cash crop or were imperial domains with the money to invest in a mechanical process.

When the grain had been reaped it was conveyed to the threshing floors. There it would be trampled by oxen or mules or could be beaten by sticks as is still done in countries such as Nepal. Varro described a threshing sledge known as the *tribulum* 'constructed of a board made rough with stones or iron'; another one consisted of a toothed axle running on low wheels dragged by oxen. In parts of the Far East, threshing is done by letting a horse or mule trample it and in Tibet, rather surprisingly, it is done by placing the grain on the road and letting mechanical vehicles run over it. Possibly horses or carts could have been driven across the grain in Roman Britain. Evidence for threshing floors have been found at several villas. Langton (Yorkshire) had a rectangular area sunk five feet below ground level. A second-century circular floor, measuring nearly 11.9m (39ft) across, was found at Ditchley (Oxfordshire). Covered by a roof it would have provided an excellent threshing room. Then the grain had to be separated from the chaff by winnowing (**colour plate 1**), either throwing it up into the air so that the lighter chaff was carried away in the breeze or passing it through a wicker or metal riddle, common practices still used in the Far East and Africa (**colour plate 2**).

In Britain the damp climate necessitated the drying of corn if it was to be stored, and this was particularly essential in the treatment of spelt. Corn driers were usually in

19

2 *Modern relief showing a vallus reconstructed from Roman reliefs found at Buzenol, Luxembourg and Arlon, Belgium*

the form of a T-shaped hypocaust, that is a long flue crossed by others along its length. These have been identified at large numbers of villa sites such as Brading (Hampshire) and Park Street (Hertfordshire); the latter had an elaborate double T-shaped form with a heated platform. At Hambleden (Buckinghamshire) a large number of T-shaped flues, many filled with charred wheat, may be the result of experimental methods of drying corn on what was, according to other evidence, a large estate run with slave labour. In towns such as Silchester and Caerwent (Monmouthshire), it would seem that individual traders carried out their own drying techniques Some of the driers were multi-functional and used not only for drying corn but also for pottery. A drier at Catterick (North Yorkshire) was used for pottery, spelt and barley.

After drying, the grain was stored in granaries. This was an advance on Iron Age methods, where the grain had been stored in pits, although pit storage continued in some areas throughout the Roman period. Tacitus in the *Germania* says that the Germans hollow out cavities and pile refuse on top. In these they store their produce to keep out the winter's cold and to save it from their enemies. Such cavities or pits were used in Britain. An experiment at Broadchalk Down near Salisbury (Wiltshire) aimed to replicate the Iron Age storage system to discover whether it was possible to store corn underground throughout the winter months and extract certain amounts from it at intervals.

Four pits were dug. Two were roofed with cob, a mixture of chalk and clay, and two with clay. Two were lined with wickerwork. Two were filled with barley and two with emmer. When the pits were opened twice during the winter season, it was discovered that the grain kept reasonably well provided that the lid fitted tightly. If rodents broke through the lid or if the pit was not resealed correctly, then the grain could germinate or become mouldy. Even so, below this mouldy area, which formed a crust on the top, grain was usable. If the walls were not lined, a crust formed against them which kept the grain dry.

The details of one pit, filled in late September, show that there was reasonable capacity. This pit, 1.37m (4ft 6in) deep and 1.5m (5ft) in diameter, took two men eight hours to dig with a modern pick and shovel, whereas Iron Age people would use antler picks and wooden shovels, or shovels with an iron sheath. The capacity of the pit, 1.98 cu m (7 cu ft), was reduced when a basket weave 5.2m (17ft) long and 1.5m (5ft) wide was fitted round the inner curve. This, taking 18 hours to weave but only 30 minutes to fit, reduced the capacity of the pit to 1.6 cu m (5.5 cu ft). 44 bushels (1100kg) of barley were put in and the pit sealed. Copper pipes were put in for the aspirating carbon dioxide. The cob lid was bedded with clay and covered with rubble. When the pit was opened the following March it was noted that, although the grain had kept well, field mice had broken in and eaten the grain to a depth of 25cm (10in).

This form of pit storage continued. Evidence from Iwerne (Dorset) indicates the inhabitants were using this method until at least *c.*AD 200, as were those at Wickford (Essex), where a large second-century clay pit, 4.9m (16ft) in diameter, was reshaped and fitted with a wicker lining for grain storage. Much later this pit filled with building debris.

Grain continues to take in oxygen and give out carbon dioxide and water, so the aim of storage is to slow down this process by placing the grain in as dry a place as possible. If grain is stored while it is hot and wet, it begins to germinate and ensures the growth of bacteria. Infestation by insects also occurs if storage methods are neglected. Therefore the more advanced Roman granaries had raised floors to allow air to circulate underneath and to keep out vermin. Both Pliny and Vitruvius gave detailed instructions as to their construction, the latter stating they should be built on pillars to let air blow from all sides. Pliny summarised the main methods of grain storage, dismissing the superstition of those who believed that a toad hung up by one of its longer legs would preserve grain. He stated that the most important factor was to store grain at the right time, if possible on the ear, as then it would be least likely to suffer damage and urged that grains should be stored correctly, otherwise pests would breed in it. Even so, infestation occurred because the saw-toothed grain beetle, thought to have been brought into Britain in recent years, has been found in corn remains at Alcester, York and the Barnsley Park villa.

Grain was sometimes stored in houses. In a large townhouse at Alcester (Warwickshire) one pebble-floored room had piles of charred grain in it, while in the Sparsholt villa (Hampshire) a room with a chalk floor near to the kitchen contained carbonised grain. The Park Street (Hertfordshire) and Hartlip (Kent) villas had stored grain in their cellars, seemingly not a sensible method unless it was stored in bags. At the Chalk villa (Kent), the remains of large storage vessels associated with grains of wheat and barley were found in a room above a cellar. The grain might have been kept handy in jars ready for easy domestic use, but as villa owners adopted a more Romanised lifestyle, separation of function was undertaken and grain storage was moved to purpose-built granaries.

The imposition of the corn tribute, the *annona*, meant that some estate owners were responsible for delivering the grain to military granaries some distance away from their property. Conveyance could be by cart or packhorse. In Egypt it was the custom for drivers to manage three donkeys each of which carried three *artaba*, about 168 litres of grain; elsewhere in the empire estate owners could apply to the guilds to do the work. There is no evidence for this in Roman Britain and it is highly likely that the villa owners themselves arranged their own transport, possibly by heavy four-wheeled wagon drawn by oxen. In the fourth century the state provided this form of public

3 Man with a corn measure: mosaic in the Square of the Corporations, Ostia

carriage; the animals were fed at public expense and wagons were placed at the disposal of the landowners. The standard modius was 9kg (20lb) and the standard wagon carried close to the maximum load of 75 modii (680kg; 1500lb).

A *modius* (dry corn measure), found at Carvoran on Hadrian's Wall, was inscribed $17\frac{1}{2}$ *sextarii* (9540cm; 16.8 pints) (**colour plate 3**). However, it has a capacity of 11.33 litres (19.9 pints) which exceeds the stated capacity by almost 20 per cent. This discrepancy was at one time suggested to be a device to defraud the Britons, who were forced to contribute the tax, but close inspection reveals that the gauge, which was set lower than the rim, might be missing. John Mann has suggested that $17\frac{1}{2}$ *sextarii* is a precise measurement that can be divided into 7 x $\frac{1}{2}$ *sextarii*. The $2\frac{1}{2}$ *sextarii* was enough for a soldier's daily ration and therefore the *modius* represented one soldier's weekly ration (**3**).

Be that as it may, Tacitus reported that Agricola, during his governorship (AD 77-83) had to 'ease the levy of corn and tribute by distributing the burden fairly' and to contain the resentment of the Britons, who were often forced to deliver corn to military depots many miles from their particular tribal areas, instead of to the nearest forts, a practice imposed elsewhere in the empire. When the corn had been delivered and placed in the granaries, more resentment was felt as the Britons had to wait to buy back their own corn at what Tacitus states were 'farcical prices'.

Milling

Milling or grinding is required before wheat or any other grain can be made into bread. The process involves removing bran and grinding the exposed endosperm. When the quantity of flour yielded by this process represents 70 per cent of the original wheat grain, it is described as 70 per cent extracted flour. Flour of an even higher extraction rate can also be milled ranging up to 100 per cent extraction rate; this is known as whole wheat. Stone-ground flour is relatively high in vitamin B and this flour produces a coarse-grain sticky-crumb nutritious bread.

4   Reconstruction of rotary quern

In Roman Britain, although milling became a commercial enterprise, grain could still be ground in the household either by the saddle or the rotary quern. The saddle quern, in which an oval stone was rolled across a saddle-shaped base stone, was the oldest means of producing flour, but it crushed rather than ground the grain. As heavy pressure was required to break up the grain, the operator had to kneel to press heavily enough on the roller stone. At present, in parts of Africa, a skilled operator is said to produce about 6lb of flour an hour by this method. Another method to reduce the grain to meal was by pounding with a stone or with a pestle and mortar as done in parts of India and Pakistan today (**colour plate 4**). Pliny said this was so hard a task that an iron cap had to be fitted to the pestle and the coarse meal produced was usually used for pottage.

The rotary quern, introduced into Britain in the first century BC, was a more practical device (**4**). It entailed two stones, one placed on top of the other. Some stones were flat ground, but others were shaped, the lower side of the upper stone having a concave surface rotating over the convex upper side of the lower stone. The upper one had a vertical hole through which the grain was dribbled. The two stones, varying from 63.5-76.2cm (25-30in) in diameter and from 15-25cm (6-10in) thick, were controlled by a spindle in a central socket. The socket had to be large enough to allow the grain to be fed through it. A wooden handle to turn the mill was fixed into a groove along the top of the upper surface or into a hole at the side of the stone. The Iron Age rotary querns seem to have had the handle fixed horizontally.

The upper stone was either rotated against the lower stone or moved back and forth, thus grinding the grain. The flour produced might have grit in it, and the gritty bread produced could have two results. It could have broken or ground down the teeth, and might also have acted as a fibre laxative on the stomach. In either case, it would not have been advantageous to the health of a Roman Briton. Hence, it was the object of any miller to produce the finest sieved flour.

5   Reconstruction of small mill, used by slaves: Museo della Civiltà Romana, Rome

In Iron Age Britain the rotary quern appears to have been the norm. Some sites such as Hunsbury (Northamptonshire) have produced as many as 150 of them, all made from local stone. The Romans preferred to use more efficient material and imported large numbers from the Andernach region of the Rhineland. Silchester seems to have imported querns from the Rhineland, where the lava provided excellent grinding material. In the Gloucester-shire region, the material was of millstone grit or puddingstone; elsewhere it was of red or green sandstone. Querns could be set onto a table at waist height or, more likely, placed on the ground where women or slaves would squat to grind the grain needed for daily use. Flour bins would be needed for storage, together with large bowls or wooden troughs in which the dough could be mixed and proved. Wooden troughs were ruinous to a baker's hands because there was the risk of splinters, as well as bran, entering under and round the nails causing septic wounds.

A first-century AD poem, the *Moretum,* by an unknown author, described this form of daily milling in a poor Italianate home, with a man rising at cock crow on a cold winter's morning, fearing grim hunger in the approaching day. It is not a pastoral fantasy, but a life of poverty and struggle to combat hunger, which could replicate life in Roman Britain. The mill has first to be cleaned, then both hands do the work, one feeds in the corn, the other rotates the stone, 'each to its own task'. The operator changes hands from time to time as each hand tires. It is uncertain how long the task takes. The poet merely stated that when the task of turning has reached its appointed end, the flour is transferred into a sieve and shaken. The refuse stays at the top of the sieve, while the pure flour sinks down and filters through the holes cleansed of impurities. The operator uses warmed water to mix and knead the dough, taking care to add salt.

Experiments were made in 1950 into grinding wheat with a Romano-British quern and using two types of modern wheat, hard-type white Holdfast English wheat and soft-red English-grown, at an optimum turning speed of a hundred revolutions an hour. In prehistoric and Roman times, as indicated in the *Moretum,* the operator would be more skilled at turning and the muscles in the arm accustomed to the constant, circular motion needed to turn the upper stone. For efficient grinding the rate of feed had to be carefully controlled, otherwise the upper stone rode on the lower and no crushing occurred. The grain also needed to be put twice through the quern and the lower quernstone had to be fixed to the ground, otherwise it turned with the upper stone. It was also a tedious business to scoop the flour from the surrounding surface. The hard wheat provided a relatively high vitamin B_1, content which was lost with the soft wheat. Both flours were sieved to remove any ground product other than flour and to aerate them. In spite of the second grinding, the bran remained large and had to be sieved and reground to make it palatable.

There was, however, a limit to what could be ground. The flour was sieved through wool or linen bolting cloths, the most useful being those with an operating hole length of $\frac{1}{2}$mm. The meals produced had an extraction of 71 per cent in the case of the hard wheat and 54 per cent in that of the soft wheat. The finished experimental output (including sieving) was 450g (1lb) an hour but with a skilled operator it would be higher; obser-vation in present-day India suggests a production rate of 1.8kg (4lb) an hour. Pliny mentioned several different flours and gave the yield and possible extraction rates. Martial said that it was impossible to enumerate all the properties or the uses of flour because it was so handy for the baker and the cook.

6 *A mule working a mill, drawn from a graffito in a house on the Palatine and now in the Musei Capitolini, Rome. The accompanying inscription read: 'Work my little donkey as I have worked and you shall be rewarded for it'*

More commercial operations came with the donkey mill which the Romans introduced into Britain. This consisted of an hour-glass shaped hopper (*catillus*) supported on a spindle above a cone-shaped base (*meta*) (**5**). The hopper would be turned by means of a wooden framework inserted into the *meta,* either by donkeys or slaves; in Rome there were two slaves to each mill, one to push, the other to gather up the grain. Horses past their prime could be used if they were blinkered. Apuleius in *The Golden Ass* portrayed them pacing round, necks chafed by the yokes, ribs broken and hooves flattened (**6**).

The grain would be poured into the conical space in the top half of the mill and ground as it passed between the upper and lower millstone; the resulting flour was collected round the circular base within a wooden frame. The output would be the equivalent of 0.127 cu m ($4\frac{1}{2}$ bushels) of wheat a day rising to 0.543 cu m (15 bushels) when a horse was used. Pieces of hoppers have been found at Corfe Mullen (Dorset), Hamworthy

7 Bread baked in the form of loaves found at Pompeii

(Dorset) the fort of Clyro (Wales) and in London. Chemical and petrographic evidence has revealed recently that both the Corfe Mullen and the London examples are made of lava from different areas in the Chaîne des Puys in Central France, which suggests two different manufacturing regions. The Hamworthy mill is of Sardinian lava and on stylistic grounds is suggested to be of post-Roman date.

The best-known surviving examples are found in Pompeii, and their method of working is revealed on a relief, now in the Vatican Museums, which shows the mill being turned by a horse. One bakery in Pompeii still has a row of mills and the narrow space between mills and wall suggests they were turned by slaves (**colour plate 5**). At Silchester, a building set at right angles to the street, 13.5m (44ft) long, 10m (33ft) wide, had a series of circular platforms about 1.4m (4ft 7in) in diameter and 60cm (2ft) high, which might be bases to support the cone-shaped mills driven by animal power. A spindle from a mechanical geared mill was also found; another one was discovered at Great Chesterford (Essex).

The tedious and time-consuming process of milling was overcome by the technical development of the watermill, which soon became common throughout the Roman world. Several have been identified along Hadrian's Wall. At Chollerford a stone axle-tree was probably part of a wheel which worked a geared mill; other mills were noted at Willowford and Haltwhistle Burn, and large power-driven millstones from the former site have been placed in the Chesters museum. These millstones would have ground flour as part of a system serving the forts on Hadrian's wall. Some towns would have their own mills and bakeries capable of producing flour and bread in large quantities. Individual villas might do the same, as the large millstones found at the Woolaston villa (Gloucestershire) seem to prove. At the Gloucestershire villas of Frocester, Chedworth and Kingscote millstones of more than one metre (3ft 3in) diameter may have been turned by water power. Certainly they could not be turned by a single person. Substantial remains of a late first-early second century AD watermill and two storage barns were found at Redlands, near Stanwick (Northamptonshire) on a low sandy island on the

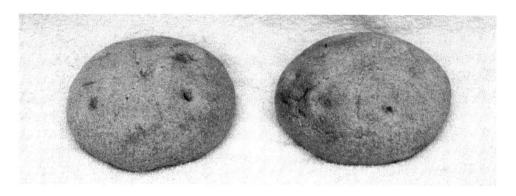

8   Unleavened bread

floodplain of the River Nene. The mill was served by two low-lying leats. Nevertheless the rotary quern continued to be used throughout the Roman period because it was the cheapest and most practical method of grinding the daily amount of corn in a household.

Bread

No organic remains of bread have been found in a Roman-British context, but carbonised remains of a flat bannock shape were found at the Iron Age site of Glastonbury. The evidence from Pompeii, both from paintings and from carbonised remains, indicated that one shape produced was round and scored into eight sections, somewhat like a bun-round today, so that it could be divided into portions (**7**). According to Athenaeus the Greeks had a wide variety of types and shapes of bread and the Romans likewise. Outside a restaurant in Pompeii was a list of 14 types of bread including *pane cibarium* (bread with bran). Twisted bread, mentioned in a trader's list at Vindolanda, was made with milk, pepper and oil or lard.

To make bread, the dough had to be kneaded thoroughly in a dough trough, such as that found on the Poultry site in London, and then left to rise before being rolled out or pulled into roundels or other shapes before baking. In the home, bread could be baked on a griddle or in a cone-shaped oven. This followed the same principle as a commercial wall oven. Charcoal or other heating material was put into it and kept alight until the oven vault became hot enough, usually after half an hour. Once the oven had reached the correct temperature, the ashes were raked out, the dough put in and the oven sealed to retain the heat. The heat of this oven produced a flat unleavened bread after 30-45 minutes baking time (**8**).

Simulus, the hero of the *Moretum*, marked his dough into equal divisions, then placed a piece on a part of the hearth cleared of ashes, heaped tiles over it and put a fire on top. Ovid mentioned a similar method of baking bread, but a better one was to put the dough onto a flat, earthenware plate and cover it with a conical pot over which hot ashes or peat would be placed to provide all-round heat. The heat engendered drew the dough

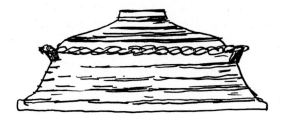

9   Forms of Roman testa. Left: a late Imperial design, right: reconstructed from Castor-ware pottery sherd (After Cubberley)

up slightly so that it cooked by a steaming process, which gave the bread a leavened appearance. Cato gave a recipe for bread made with a similar method: 'Wash your hands and a bowl. Pour flour into the bowl, add water gradually, knead thoroughly. When it has been well-kneaded, mould and bake under a crock'. This type of cover known as a *testum* would have been scorched by the fire. Possible examples have been found in some pottery assemblages such as at Castor near Peterborough (**9**). One example, in Nene Valley grey ware, showed that local industries were producing pots for home baking. Another, found at Catterick (North Yorkshire) was probably part of army property.

   This method was common in many parts of Europe until well into the present century. In Ireland the dough was turned once to give a crisp even bake and the loaf produced had a thick crust. Cato recommended that the dough be thoroughly kneaded, then rolled out and baked under a crock. The bread was unleavened, although it could be given a raising agent: a portion of dough kept from the previous day's baking, or a mixture of boiled flour and water left to go sour. Pliny commented that when grains from Gaul or Spain were steeped in beer, the 'foam which forms on the surface is used for leaven which gives a lighter bread'.

   All grains can be ground to make flour but the quality of the bread varies. Oats have no gluten content and barley has very little so they were not usually used in bread-making; oatmeal may be combined to give flavour in connection with other grains. It has a secondary use as a basis for making porridge or pottage. In an experiment resulting from finds from a ditch at the Bearsden fort on the Antonine Wall, porridge was made from spelt and emmer wheats. The spelt porridge was somewhat tasteless, but the emmer porridge, thicker, with grains well-swollen as in the best oatmeal porridge, had excellent flavour and texture.

   The Romans knew the distinction between hard and soft wheat and referred to hard wheat as *triticum* and soft wheat as *siligo*. Hard wheat gives a high protein content which is needed to bake a satisfactory bread. Soft wheat produces flour with a lower protein content which is best used for pastry or cakes. The different types of flour gave different types of bread. Spelt gave a strong flour with much gluten-forming protein in the grain so that the bread rose more than emmer bread. Bread wheat flour produced the lightest bread. Emmer flour yielded a coarse dough and a crumbly bread. This flour, when made into dough, contained enough gluten-forming proteins to hold a pitta-like bread together.

Dioscorides wrote in the first century AD that emmer bread was more nourishing and digestible than barley bread though not as good as wheaten bread. In the 1950 experiment related above, very little stone and dust remained in the flour once it had been finely sifted. The bread baked from the soft wheat flour produced a course open-grained crumb bread, not unpalatable but with little spring, indicating that the gluten was under developed. Longer fermentation would have given a more elastic dough, providing a better loaf. The bread baked with the hard wheat flour produced a coarse sticky-crumb loaf. Salt added to the loaf influences both the rate and degree of flour hydration; the correct proportion helps to retain moisture while too much results in a hard-crust loaf. Modern bakeries use between 1.8-3.2kg (4-7lb) of salt per 127kg (280lb) sack of flour.

Stone-milled flour has a characteristic flavour due to the heat generated by the milling process and bread from it contains more dietary fibre than white bread. At Bearsden on the Antonine Wall, occupied AD 142-58, the latrine had debouched into the fort ditch. Examination of the faecal remains revealed quantities of emmer and spelt pericarp together with fragments of coriander, seeds of celery, figs and opium poppy and minute remains of lentils and field beans. The two wheats could have been used to make porridge, as indicated above, but if they had also been used to make bread, the soldiers would have eaten a highly palatable, flavoured bread of a *panis militaris* type, rich in the B vitamins. A sample of the wheat fragments submitted for electronic spin resonance spectroscopy (ESR) gave a temperature between 180 and 200 degrees centigrade consistent with a temperature required to make bread. Degraded barley fragments were also found which resembled pearl barley, cooked for several hours as if they had been present in thick broth.

Literary evidence confirms archaeology. Pliny noted that wholemeal flour was flavoured with coriander and sprinkled with poppy seeds on the top crust of country loaves. The seeds had been mixed with egg to make them stick, a method still used by modern bakers. Pliny suggested that celery should be placed under bread to give a 'festival flavour' but he may have been referring to the leaves of the plant as well as seeds being put into the bread. He also commented that flavoured bread was much appreciated and that the grain could be soaked in wine to produce unleavened bread. Petronius, author of the first-century picaresque novel, *Satyricon*, sneered at one guest at Trimalchio's feast who asked for wholemeal bread because it was nourishing and prevented constipation. In the northern areas of Britain, rye flour could be used for bread. This has some gluten content, but this is inferior to wheat gluten, making the dough difficult to handle unless mixed with wheat flour. The lower protein content makes the darker bread heavier in texture, so that it becomes far more of a 'filler' than wheat bread, and one which would allay hunger more easily. When mixed with wheat flour, the bread becomes more palatable.

Barley was used mainly for animal fodder or brewing, but a bread made from it may have been eaten in Iron Age Britain. The last meal of Lindow Man was a wheat, rye and barley bread, baked in a heather fire. Roman writers made it clear that, even though barley bread had been eaten in Greece, bread made from this grain was not appreciated. Pliny said experience had condemned barley bread 'though it was anciently much used', and that it was normally fed to animals and slaves. There was a hint of poverty about it. It was

10 A Roman bakery drawn from a relief on the tomb of the baker, M Vergilius Eurysaces and his wife, Antistia. On the left workers are kneading bread, on the right, the baker puts bread into the oven using a peel

barley bread which, according to St John's Gospel, was fed to the five thousand. The miracle is enhanced by poor bread being fed (and multiplied) to the poor. An issue of barley bread could be used as a punishment, as noted by Suetonius. In his biography of the Emperor Augustus, he said that if a company broke rank in battle, the emperor ordered the soldiers to draw lots. Augustus then executed every tenth man and fed those remaining on barley bread instead of bread made from the customary wheat ration; this was the ultimate degrading punishment. Barley grain has little protein content. It has to be dried and roasted which destroys almost all the gluten content so that the bread produced is heavy with a greyish tinge and a decidedly earthy taste. It develops a heavy crust and if left it soon goes mouldy. Nevertheless, the taste can be improved by adding wheat flour and/or milk or buttermilk. Such bread if eaten with pieces of meat and fish would provide a meal of protein, fat, carbohydrate and a useful quantity of fibre and vitamin B.

Villas which had a large work force would have to produce bread on a scale comparable to a small commercial baker, which would mean the construction of large bread ovens. At Fishbourne, a large bread oven was sited conveniently close to the kitchen garden, to the building and its inhabitants, to the road, near to a water supply and the servants' quarters. Probably a large milling area was also established nearby. Commercial bread making would be the norm in towns. Each town would have its collection of bakers' shops (**10**), from which the bread could be collected each morning by the household slave, who could select from the variety of the freshly baked bread. In Pompeii a full establishment had mills, ovens, a granary for the storage of cereals and a stable for the animals which turned the mills, as well as a shop for the sale of bread.

Possible bakers' shops in Britain have been identified at Springhead (Kent), Holditch (Staffordshire), Canterbury, Silchester and Cirencester. Four mortaria of progressive size marked DECANO FECIT, found in the *vicus* of the Lancaster fort, may have been mixing

11 *The tomb of the baker, M. Vergilius Eurysaces, and his wife, Antistia, situated outside the Porta Maggiore, Rome. The relief showing the different stages of baking encircles the top. The holes represent the ovens*

bowls from the stock-in-trade of a bakery and food shop. Some mortaria in London, almost 90cm (3ft) in diameter, made in the late second century, were stamped with the name, Verecundus, whose workshop was at Soller in Germany. These were almost certainly bakery mixing bowls. At Verulamium a long iron slice has been found which could have been used to take bread from an oven. Bakers, who were also millers, adapted a flat instrument used to stir the grain on the threshing floor into a form of shovel, also known as a slice or peel. This was inserted into the oven and pushed underneath the bread so that it could be pulled out. This implement is so functional that it has continued in use in modern bakeries. A pastry cook's mould from Silchester has on it a scene representing the Emperor Severus, his wife, Julia Domna and the sons, Caracalla and Geta, all of whom seem to be offering a sacrifice. The mould may therefore have been used to mark pastries commemorating an official or a religious occasion. Bread and pastries were not only a staple food of Roman Britain, it could also play a propaganda role. Pastries could be fast food. Seneca commented on the cries from pastry makers being heard constantly below his lodgings in Rome and these may have been replicated in the streets of Britain.

Evidence from the reliefs on the tomb of the baker, M. Vergilius Eurysaces, in Rome and archaeological remains at Pompeii indicate that baking was a thriving business (**11**). One portrait survives on the wall of a building containing several ovens. This fresco, painted between AD 50-79, portrays a young couple, who may be a bakert and his wife (**colour plate 6**). He rests his chin on a papyrus scroll; his wife holds a stylus and a two-leaved writing tablet, obviously helping him with his accounts. Their business must have thrived for them to have commissioned an artist, who painted in the fashionable Greek style of the first century AD. Both are dressed formally, he in a toga, she in a red gown and long pearl earrings. Her hair is neatly arranged with curls teased out over the forehead, so fashionable at the time. Did this young couple, so solemnly gazing out, survive the eruption of Vesuvius which was to overwhelm Pompeii or were they, as Pliny the Younger so graphically put it, 'buried deep in ashes like snowdrifts'. We know nothing about Romano-British bakers. This young couple must stand as surrogates for bakers in the distant province of Britain.

3 Meat, game and poultry

Meat

Early studies on the Roman army concluded that it was mainly a cereal eating army; meat was rarely eaten. More recent archaeological evidence reveals that by the third and fourth centuries AD, meat was eaten in great quantities by both soldiers and civilians. This is understandable as meat of all kinds had been appreciated in Iron Age Britain. Better breeding of animals over the centuries has altered their shape and form, but in Iron Age Britain the main cattle are believed to have been Bos Longifrons, akin to Highland cattle, and Bos Taurus, a short-horned variety. Kerry cattle in Ireland and Welsh black cattle would be the nearest modern equivalent to the latter; in fact they may be direct descendants (**12**). Bones found at Vindolanda indicate that the cattle were almost all Celtic shorthorns with, according to the horn cores found, some huge beasts like wild auroch. Probably the unit attached to Vindolanda had a regimental grazing ground on which cattle grazed under the care of herdsmen. They could be wintered or bred on this pasture as part of the system of providing food for the garrison. If so, this would not be an isolated example. Cattle were a valuable source of meat, milk and butter, and use would be made of horns, hair, hide, bones and hooves. Large quantities of leather were required both for military and civilian use.

The Romans practised various systems of animal husbandry. They introduced more selective breeding of existing stock and imported new stock probably the result of interbreeding with native strains in other provinces. This could result in larger animals, a fact noted in studies of bones on Roman sites. Cattle were kept out-of-doors both in summer and winter, moving from pasture to pasture; in northern Britain, summer grazing took place on the higher pastures. Free grazing was the norm. There was also a problem of providing sufficient fodder to keep animals alive during the winter, because it was not until the eighteenth century that sufficient root crops were produced to stop the annual cull of stock. In Gaul, however, turnips were used as a fodder crop and the practice may have spread to Britain. Columella recommended chickpeas, vetch and beans for fodder. His writings, together with those of Cato and Varro, provided help for farmers, while Pliny described animals available to them. The number of cattle bones on Roman sites is high in relation to those of other meat animals. They are highest on military sites, less so on the early villa sites, where most of the bones are from sheep. In relation to the number of bones found, urban and military sites would have more because they had better organised butchery and distribution arrangements.

Sheep were kept for wool, skins and milk, as well as for meat. The habit of keeping them in folds at night because of the danger of wild animals helped to provide manure

12 Dexter cattle: Little Butser Demonstration Iron Age Site, Queen Elizabeth County Park, Hampshire

for the field and the garden. The nearest equivalent to Iron Age sheep are Hebridean breeds and Soay sheep (**13**), whose unique form has been preserved by their isolation on the St Kilda group of islands, 40 miles west of the Outer Hebrides. Their lithe goat-like form is covered with shaggy wool, which is plucked and not shorn. John Wild, however, suggests that breeding had produced a type of sheep more akin to the Orkney sheep of North Ronaldsay. These produced a thicker fleece than the Soay sheep and could be shorn. The Romans may have crossed this type of sheep with the ancestors of the Spanish fine woollen Merino sheep. This would have improved the wool, but not necessarily the meat of the animals, and it could have been one of the reasons for the success of the Romano-British woollen industry. The newer breeds would require more careful herding to produce better samples of wool. Evidence from Vindolanda indicates that hairy medium wools predominated, although there was some evidence of a finer medium type. Improved fleeces ensured fibres for the weaving of cloth, including the byrrus, the heavy British cloak worth 6000 *denarii*, mentioned in Diocletian's price edict of AD 301.

Domesticated goats were less common in the Iron Age and this continued to be the case in the Roman period, when they were kept as much for their hair and their skins as for their meat and milk products. Two small bronze figurines, one found at Silchester and the other in London, and a silver figurine from the Thames at London Bridge show the characteristics of fine animals (**14**).

The importance of pork to the Celts is evidenced from classical and Celtic writings. Strabo said of the Belgae in Gaul, that 'they have large quantities of food together with milk and all kinds of meat, especially fresh and salt pork'. 'Brave Warriors', said Diodorus, speaking of the Celts, 'they honour with the finest portions of meat'. Athenaeus records that, when the hindquarters were served, the bravest warrior took the thigh piece. If another warrior claimed it, both fought in combat to the death. This is confirmed in the tales of the Irish heroes, for example, that of Mac Datho's pig, where the plot is based on the ancient Celtic practice of assigning the choicest portions of the pig to the guest who could most successfully assert his superiority over the others. Cet mac Mach of Connaught claimed this right until challenged by Conall the Victorious of Ulster. 'It is true', said Cet, 'that you are a better warrior than I, but if my brother Anluan were in the house, you would be no match for him'. 'But he is', said Conall, taking Anluan's head out of a bag and throwing it at Cet, where it hit his chest with a great rush of blood. After that there could be no argument. Cet left the pig and Conall took the champion's portion.

On some late Iron Age sites in the South-East, mainly the high status *oppida*, the pig bones found reached 50 per cent of the bones of the three main animal species, indicating the value of pork in the food chain. Pigs are ideal animals to be kept in small numbers and in backyard pens as they

13 A Soay ram

can easily be fattened on household waste, turning it into meat and manure. They yield meat, lard, brawn, sausages and pigskin. Everything can be used in a pig, goes the old saying, except the squeal. A relief from Bonn shows a pig being carried by its hind legs over the back of a slave. The animal could have been meant for a sacrifice, but another scene shows the cauldron into which it is to be dropped. A relief at Dresden reveals a butcher's shop with pigs' heads hanging up ready for sale.

Suckling pig was much appreciated; Apicius gave seventeen recipes for it, either stuffed or with spiced sauces. The excavators of the Billingsgate, London, site noted that most pigs were killed between two and three years old, but 13 per cent of the bones were from pigs under one year old. At the Castle Copse villa, Great Bedwyn (Wiltshire), a large number of pigs' foot bones were found in one dump, suggesting a taste of the villa inhabitants for pigs' trotters. Pig hides can provide some of the softest leather; stone statues of warriors found in the Gard region of France are portrayed wearing leather jerkins made from pigskin. Only a few animals need to be kept to provide constant replacement as sows can breed prolifically. Once boars are castrated they become more manageable and the breed will feed in the wild, especially in oak and beech woodland, with little attention. Columella and Varro gave advice on the care of pigs including fattening on beans or grain. For prime condition, the first writer advised that they should

14 Figurines of goats found in Britain. Top: silver, found in the Thames, London (British Museum); middle: bronze, found at Silchester (Reading Museum); bottom: bronze, found in London (Museum of London)

be given feeds of apples, nuts and, if possible, grass in a good orchard. Pigsties, provided at the Pitney (Somerset) and Woolaston Pill (Gloucestershire) villas, may have been meant to keep the pigs safe or for fattening them; Boon identified other possible sties at Silchester. At Vindolanda, pork and bacon were issued as part of the military diet. There was no difficulty in keeping pigs near the fort and one of the writing tablets gives an issue of corn to Lucco for the pigs.

The Romans disliked eating horseflesh. Horses were kept for riding, pulling carriages and racing and generally not for food. Nevertheless, there is some evidence that horses were eaten in Britain. One shop at Verulamium has been identified as a butcher's shop where flesh had been stripped from dismembered horses before the bones were buried on the site. The flesh would be best eaten in the form of sausages. The excavators of the General Accident Site at York concluded that the occasional horse 'found its way onto the butcher's slab'. At Vindolanda, some bones of horses had been smashed as if to obtain the marrow, but the excavators suggested that this was for dogs rather than for human consumption. Evidence of chop marks on bones of both horses and dogs in the fourth century waterfront at Lincoln suggest that these animals were being butchered and eaten in small numbers.

Oxen were used mainly as draught animals. Cato advised that oxen should be trained to walk for a thousand paces in an orderly manner and without fear. Oxen have to be trained in pairs; when one dies the other is useless and its only value is as meat. A small bronze figurine found at Piercebridge (Co. Durham) reveals two oxen placidly pulling a plough urged on by a hooded ploughman. They may be engaged in the normal task of ploughing, although a ritual meaning has been suggested: the marking out of a land boundary. Ox-shoes found in Roman-British contexts also reveal the value of these animals in Britain. Ox meat, however, seems to have been on sale in Southwark, London, where the excavations revealed a large increase in bones discarded during the second century.

Examination of bones found on both military and civilian sites has shown that methods of butchery were different from those existing today. Modern butchery practice is to hang up the carcass, split the body down the axis, then quarter it. That this practice was known to the Romans is suggested by a mosaic from Cherchel (Caesarea) in Israel, which shows a sheep's carcass hanging from a tree and being split down its axis; the limbs are being taken off while the carcass is suspended. A relief from Aquileia in north Italy shows a butcher approaching a pig with his cleaver raised to split the animal lengthways (**15**). Modern practice places each quarter on a chopping block to allow each limb to be removed in sections.

In Roman Britain, however, a different method was used. Once the

15 Man, butchering a pig, relief from Aquileia, Museo de Verona, Italy

carcass had been placed on a table, each limb was removed as a whole before being further divided. A recent study by Maltby of bones in Hampshire suggests that different butchery techniques were used in town and country. In the towns, heavy cleavers were used to split carcasses; in villages, the limbs were disjointed with knives, a technique perfected in the Iron Age. Shave marks, like those found on bones at Silchester, had been made by a heavy cleaver shearing meat from the bones. Then the bones were chopped into small pieces. This type of butchery was common at several military sites such as Caerleon and York. Some bones, chopped axially, showed that after the meat had been removed, they were chopped and boiled, probably to make soup and to obtain the marrow and grease for cooking. The cattle bones at Silchester were from mature animals, whereas the sheep and pig bones were from young animals, especially suckling pig. The remains suggested that there was large scale, competent butchery going on in the town. Marrow was highly prized both for its nutritional value and for its medicinal qualities. Dioscorides recommended it as a poultice for relieving weariness; it was also used for glue, soap and cosmetics. Varro said that dogs should be fed *ius ex ossibus*, usually translated as 'bone soup'. But dogs adore marrow and will gnaw bones to get it.

A large bone assemblage at excavations at Borough High Street, Southwark, suggests that the pigs killed there were mainly mature animals, unlike those at Silchester. The technique used in the towns enabled slaughterers to butcher quickly, to get the maximum amount of meat from the bones and to make the best use of the latter. At the Portchester Saxon Shore fort, the skull evidence suggested that slaughter was carried out by pole-axing, which either killed the animal outright or stunned it so that it could be hung up and bled. Cheek meat and the tongue were then boned out.

Animals are hung after slaughter, so that the muscles do not set in a contracted position, which toughens the meat. Accumulating lactic acid breaks down the walls of cell bodies which store protein-attacking enzymes. These enzymes attack cell bodies so that they degenerate into individual amino acids, which contribute to a stronger flavour for meat and a softer tissue. The process, however, takes about two or three weeks for beef and about a week for lamb. It also requires cool conditions, favouring autumn or winter for slaughter. This would also fit with the culling of herds and flocks when fodder was short in winter. Summer slaughter requires greater care because of the heat, especially for pork, which goes off very quickly.

Intensive and systematic slaughter, butchery of carcasses and processing of meat took place on a large commercial scale on the fourth-century Lincoln waterfront. The carcasses were systematically reduced to smaller joints of meat, before the fillets and the bones were chopped longitudinally and split to get at the marrow. A large proportion of whole jaws of cattle show evidence of scorching and burning, which is rarely recorded elsewhere, except in some deposits at York. This treatment might have made the bones easier to break, but more likely it was to reach the marrow and render it liquid by heating so that it could be used for lamp oil or as a base for cosmetic or medicinal products. The carcass components of the animals were sent to tanneries, horn-workers, cosmetic makers and other craftsmen in the town. They sent back their waste, which was dumped along the waterfront, building it up and stabilizing the river frontage. This suggests that fourth-century Lincoln had a highly organised system of preparing and distributing food and its associated products, and of collecting and disposing of the resultant waste.

Carcasses of animals sacrificed for religious purposes would have been disposed of quickly. The meat would have been available at any time and given away without hanging. Bulls and oxen were sacrificed to Jupiter and Mars; cows to Venus and Juno. The sacrificial scene on the distance slab at Bridgeness on the Antonine Wall shows three animals, a ram, a boar and a bull, waiting to be pole-axed before having their throats cut (**16**). This sacrifice is on a small scale and the meat could have been burnt on the altar, but the profusion of sacrifices performed in temples would have required other methods of disposal. It is unlikely, however, that Britain witnessed sacrifices on such a large scale as those which Suetonius reported took place on the accession of the Emperor Caligula in AD 37: 160,000 cattle ('victims') were sacrificed in three months. Some sacrificial meat was the perquisite of the temple priests and servants, and there are examples of kitchens attached to temples where this could have been cooked. Some would go to magistrates and town officials, but the majority of it would be sold or given to butchers or the populace.

16 Suovetaurila or sacrificial scene with ram, boar and bull. Relief on the Distance Slab erected by the Second Legion Augusta at Bridgeness on the Antonine Wall. Now in the National Museums of Scotland, Edinburgh

This might have been a problem for an ox could feed a hundred people. Possibly this was easier at country sites such as Woodeaton (Oxfordshire) and Springhead (Kent), which appear to have attracted numerous worshippers who doubtless needed feeding.

A reference in the New Testament (I Corinthians 8 and 10) seems to indicate that sacrificial meat was sold in the market place and shops to be served in private houses. Presumably the people knew exactly what type of meat they were buying. The Christians in Corinth were advised that anything bought in the Shambles (the meat butchery area) could be eaten with impunity, but if they were told that the meat came from animals slaughtered in sacrifices, they were to refuse it.

The blood alone would present a problem. Lucretius spoke of altars washed with the streaming blood of the beasts. But gushing of blood over an altar would put out a sacred flame. Some blood would have been caught in containers for ritual use. Sacrifices to Hecate or underworld deities required that the warm blood should be collected in vessels and sprinkled on the ground. Some could have gone to the butchers as a basis for blood puddings; this would have needed stirring to prevent coagulation before mixing with oats, spices and herbs. Most of it, however, had to be washed away. The temple of Claudius at Colchester was provided with huge drains, probably for this purpose.

Bones excavated from the General Accident Site at York provide evidence of systematic butchery on a large commercial scale during the late second and early third centuries, with beef cattle predominating. Young lambs and piglets were also slaughtered. There does not seem to have been any boning of the joint, as in modern butchery practice. Marks on bones indicate that, as at Silchester, meat was scraped off, perhaps even shredded. At Neatham (Hampshire) badly chopped shoulder blades show unskilled handling, unlike at Abingdon (Oxfordshire) where the bones had been carefully disjointed for stewing purposes and the butcher's cuts indicated the meat had been cut into neat joints. Evidence from Caerleon suggests an orderly approach to butchery with selection of parts of beef. Marks on scapulae found in the baths suggest that meat was cut away for stewing steak; the other bones were chopped into joints.

At York and Lincoln some of the cattle scapulae had square holes punched into them which indicated that these joints were hung up to smoke or cure the meat. It was then sold cut off the bone. Shave marks indicate that every bit of meat, including the final, stubborn, dried bits were removed. Smoking is slow preserving at a low temperature, where the surface colouration is produced by tar. The acids, alcohols and phenol compounds inhibit bacterial activity and prevent flies and maggots burying into the meat. During smoking, meat loses water, which also helps in preservation, and a combination of smoke and salt curing minimises fat oxidation. Traditionally birch wood is used, but oak and beech are acceptable; the wood used imparts its own special flavour to the meat. All three woods were available in Roman Britain. Smoking could be done at home. Cato gave instructions for curing hams and salting pork, then said they should hang in smoke for two days before being rubbed with a mixture of oil and vinegar to keep out worms.

Sheep could be kept for several years for their wool; they would be eaten when their productive capacity was exhausted or, as was suggested by the Poundbury excavators, when they died of malnutrition due to lack of winter fodder. By the third and fourth centuries, however, there seems to have been a tendency to butcher them during their second or third year, as if meat was of greater importance than wool production. At Neatham many of the sheep had been killed at the half-year stage as if to reduce the flock for winter. However, location would be all-important and some civilian sites, for example those at the Fen Edge, continued to depend on sheep and goat for meat.

Anthony King observed that there was a decisive shift by the late Roman period, changing the dietary identity of Britain. Quantification of bones from Roman sites reveals a tendency towards a predominantly beef and pork diet in preference to sheep or goat, even on the

17 A hunting dog drawn from a bronze figurine found in the healing sanctuary temple of Nodens, Lydney, Gloucestershire

Sussex Downs and in the Cotswolds, which in the Iron Age had been mainly sheep rearing territory. It was in these areas that sheep remained important for their wool, as referenced by Diocletian's price edict. This was probably due to the prosperity of the villa economy in Britain in the fourth century. The owners of those estates could choose a high status diet, which allowed them to breed flocks for wool, instead of having to eat sheep meat. In some forts, however, for example Portchester (Hampshire), the economy was decidedly based on beef. Bone evidence from Poundbury and Neatham indicates consumption of more cattle and pig. This increase in consumption of beef and pork might have resulted from an increase in demand for leather for military and civilian use. London, in particular, was served by huge tanneries and the facilities of the port would have enabled any surplus meat, if salted or smoked, to be shipped elsewhere.

Game and hunting

There were ample opportunities in Britain for hunting, both as a sport and for provisioning the larder. Strabo noted that before the Conquest, Britain had exported 'dogs specifically bred for hunting'. Arrian, in the mid-second century AD, commenting on the Celtic love of hunting with dogs, added that there were several types including one akin to the Irish wolfhound and another like a bull mastiff. This might be the one referred to by Claudian, writing in the early fifth century, which he said could break the necks of great bulls. In the third century Nemesianus indicated that the exporting of 'swift hounds' continued, and Oppian commented that the Britons bred a strong breed of hunting dog called the Agassian, 'small, squat, emaciated, shaggy, dull of eye', but armed with powerful claws and close-set venomous tearing teeth. Its skill was such that it could scent its prey in the air as well as tracking it along the ground. These dogs were not used in packs but were kept on leashes to be released on individual prey.

Symmachus, Prefect of Rome in AD 384, in a letter to a friend referred to 'swift hounds, adapted to hunting in our world'. This comment may refer to Irish hounds which, given the

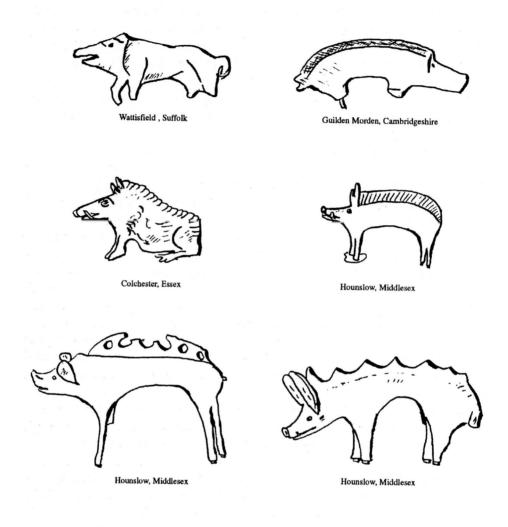

Wattisfield , Suffolk

Guilden Morden, Cambridgeshire

Colchester, Essex

Hounslow, Middlesex

Hounslow, Middlesex

Hounslow, Middlesex

18   Bronze figurines of boars

communication between the British and Irish Celts, could have been imported into Britain. One may be represented in the small bronze figurine of a hunting dog stretched out at rest, found in the temple of Nodens at Lydney (Gloucestershire) (**17**), and another, tightly curled up but with an alert eye, on the lid of a small bronze box found at the Great Witcombe villa.

Given this love of hunting it is not surprising to see decorated Castor ware pottery depicting hare, deer and hound in vigorous pursuit. Inscriptions such as the one dedicated by Julius Secundus, Centurion of the First Cohort of Thracians, stationed at Bowes, to the god, Vinotonus Silvanus, on Scargill Moor (North Yorkshire) testify to the enjoyment of the chase. At Bollihope Common, south of Stanhope (Co. Durham), Gaius Tetius Veturius Micianus, Prefect of the Sebosian Cavalry, was more specific when he dedicated an altar to Unconquerable Silvanus. He boasted of taking a 'wild boar of remarkable fineness which many of his predecessors had been unable to bag'. Small bronze figurines of boars, such as those found at Aldborough (North Yorkshire), Colchester and Wattisford (Suffolk) are probably votive offerings for the completion of a successful chase (**18**). Presumably no huntsman wished to take part in the chase of the legendary boar of Formael, 'grey, horrible, without ears, without tail, great teeth standing out long', which in a tale recounted in the Irish Fenian cycle killed 50 hounds and 50 warriors in a single day.

Birds of prey were also used by the Romans in hunting. A well at Boreham (Essex) had bones of a sparrowhawk and a thrush in it. This was suggested by the excavators to be the first evidence of this method of hunting found in Britain.

The fallow deer was introduced into Britain by the Romans, but numbers were small. Bones of roe and red deer are more common. The excavators at Poundbury suggested that deer were hunted because they were a menace to crops, but venison made a welcome addition to the diet, and antlers were useful for tools. Bones of roe and red deer found in excavations on the Borough High Street Site, Southwark, are from extremities indicating waste from meat consumption. Bones of red and fallow deer found at Vindolanda also indicate that venison was part of the troop's diet. One of the mosaics in the East Coker villa (Somerset) (**cover photograph**) shows two hunters returning home after a successful day with the deer slung on a pole beneath them. Below is their hunting dog, mouth opened wide to catch the blood dripping from the catch. One might also speculate how the elks, whose bones were found in the forts of Newstead and South Shields, met their fate.

Hares could be raised in *leporia* or hare reserves. Their bones have been found on several Roman sites and if Caesar was right that the Iron Age Britons did not eat hare, this taboo was not observed in Roman Britain. Appian, commenting on siege diet, remarks that the soldiers 'were worn out by the continuous watch, lack of sleep and the unaccustomed food of the country'. They 'fed on wheat and barley, and large quantities of meat and hare boiled without salt which upset their digestions'. Hare certainly supplemented the diet at the forts of Brancaster (Norfolk), and Vindolanda and of the civilians at Poundbury. On a relief from Bath, an unsuspecting hare is about to be caught by a hound held on a leash (**19**). A hare on a relief from Piercebridge (Co. Durham) is already in the hunter's hand, while Winter, represented on the Chedworth mosaic, stumps along, a hare being taken home for the pot dangling from his right hand (**20**). Varro comments that everyone knows that hares are prolific breeders so there would be no shortage of them in Britain. Not all suffered the fate of being eaten. A hare saved from the pot is being cradled by a small boy on a tombstone at Lincoln.

Exotic tastes

Dormice, which featured in Roman banquets, were a more exotic taste. Apicius suggests that they should be stuffed with minced pork, pine kernels and liquamen. At Trimalchio's feast, according to Petronius, they were served sprinkled with honey and poppy seeds.

19 *A man pulls back a hound from chasing a hare. Drawn from a relief found near Bath. Roman*
   Baths Museum, Bath

The taste is like that of rabbit but, like the guinea pig eaten in Peru, there is little meat on
the bones. Dormice were kept in pens and pots and fed on acorns and chestnuts to fatten
them, until lack of movement and enforced feeding made them plump. The system fooled
the dormice into believing that they were hibernating, thus encouraging growth. Varro
and Pliny give instructions for this, and Martial indicated that country visitors might bring
them as welcome gifts. The bones from the General Accident Site at York included those
of the garden dormouse, which may have been imported into Britain in the early third
century as a delicacy. Bones of this creature were found at the South Shields fort, but it
may have been accidentally imported in some grain.

Frog bones found at York and at Silchester reveal that the edible frog was another
delicacy. Disarticulated bones of dog found on some sites, as at Abingdon (Oxfordshire) and
Vindolanda, suggest the occasional consumption of dog. Cat bones are frequently found and
although cats have been eaten at certain times in history — the taste is akin to chicken — it
is more likely that the animals were kept as pets or to hunt mice.

Snails were deliberately fattened on a diet of milk until they were too fat to go back into
their shells. They were then poached or simmered, often to be eaten as an hors d'oeuvre. At
Silchester and Dorchester (Dorset) the edible snail (*helix aspersa*) was identified, while at the
Shakenoak villa the escargot (*helix pomatia*) was found. A special spoon (*cocleare*) with a pointed
end was devised to prize shellfish from their shells. Pliny noted that the end of the spoon was

20 Winter, wrapped up against the weather, portrayed on a mosaic in the Chedworth Roman Villa, carries a hare in his right hand

also used to pierce the shells of snails and eggs, in order to prevent evil spirits and witches riding in them, a superstitious practice which has survived to this day.

Poultry and wild fowl

Caesar said that the Britons reared fowls and geese, like hare, for pleasure and amusement as there was a taboo against eating them, but the frequency of bones on both Iron Age and Roman sites, with butchery marks indicating jointing and removing of feet and head, suggests otherwise. The species of fowl would be small, something like the old English gamecock and the Indian red jungle fowl. The Romans felt no qualms about eating chickens; indeed they were particularly partial to them. Apicius recorded 15 different ways of cooking chicken and gives tasty sweet and sour sauces for them. The report on the Ilchester (Somerset) excavations notes that the community may have relied on fowl for food because the amount of husbandry required is less. Chickens kept in large numbers, either roaming freely or loosely penned, would have been a common sight in any British town. Capons (castrated cocks) would have produced even more meat.

A group of wooden writing tablets found at Vindolanda, seemingly once joined together, has been identified as the accounts of the household of Flavius Cerealis,

Prefect of the Ninth Cohort of Batavians, stationed there during summer AD 104. The list contains several items relating to chickens, which were presumably served on special occasions — the discharge of a veteran from army service, the visit of a provincial governor or fellow officers on official visits. As at the present time, chicken was an easy food to serve. A reference to *pulli adempti* may be paralleled by a comment from Columella that young chickens, taken from their mother, are very expensive.

Another letter from Vindolanda mentions 20 chickens (*pullos viginti*) and 100 or 200 eggs (*ova centum aut ducenta*) in a list of foodstuffs. The recipient was perhaps Julius Verecundus, Prefect of the Cohort of Tungrians, his wife or one of their slaves. Eggs of both tame and wild birds provided a welcome addition to diet and a binding and raising ingredient in recipes. Eggs have been found in graves at Colchester and York where they were included as funerary offerings for the dead and the gods of the underworld. As a food and a symbol of regeneration in the afterlife, they represented both physical and spiritual nourishment.

Doves kept in *columbaria* were a welcome source of food, especially in winter. Their bones have been found at Waddon Hill, Silchester, Caerwent and Fishbourne. Game birds and wild fowl, however, would not have been ignored entirely. At Fishbourne were found bones of pheasant, wood pigeon, pigeon and partridge. A large quantity of pheasant bones was found at Barnsley Park villa (Gloucestershire) and the excavators drew attention to the even quality of the bones which suggested that they were hand-reared. The site also produced bones of fowl, ducks, widgeon, snipe, partridges, doves and geese, which indicates not only that tame birds were reared but also that the snaring of wild birds was part of the villa life. Colchester produced bones of mallard, teal, tufted duck, woodcock, swan and crane. The mallard or common wild duck was domesticated, and the Fishbourne report noted that the Romans had large aviaries where mallards were bred in captivity to fatten for table. Bones of the Great Northern Diver found at Fishbourne and Brancaster indicate a love of hunting for recreation rather than food.

According to Columella, geese could be bred in captivity with little trouble provided that they had plenty of water and fresh grass. By-products of this rearing would include goslings for the luxury market, together with feathers and down for bedding. Goose meat is oily and strong; it may however be tough in which case it is best diced or minced for rissoles as Apicius recommended. Pliny praised the excellence of goose liver. Columella gave detailed advice on the economic means of keeping geese; they could be bred in captivity with little trouble provided that they had plenty of water and fresh grass. The inhabitants of Silchester ate wild geese, and domesticated geese might also have been kept as an alarm system against burglars. Presumably the story of how the cackling of geese saved the Capitol at Rome from an attack by the Gauls was part of children's education in Britain as much as in Rome. They also ate duck, teal, widgeon, woodcock and plover and may have eaten swan, stork and crane. The inhabitants of Lincoln, judging by the bones found there, certainly ate crane. Apicius, who provided five recipes for cooking the bird, knew how to deal with removing the tough sinews of crane. Boil a crane with its head dangling over the side of the pot; when it is cooked, grasp the head and twist it; the head will come off drawing with it the sinews, so that only the meat and bones survive!

4 Fish, shellfish and other crustaceans

Fish

Archaeological excavations have found fish bones and scales on a number of sites, and this has given rise to such statements as 'it is reasonable to assume that fish played an important part in the Roman Londoner's diet'. Fragments of fish bones found at Doncaster are said to 'indicate that fish had a significant place in the inhabitants' diet'. Gallant, however, takes a different view. His book *A Fisherman's Tale* has as its thesis the idea that the role of fish in antiquity has been vastly overrated and that 'in dietary input fish could have played only a subordinate part'. Ovid in the first century AD implied that at one time the Romans were not overly fond of fish: 'Fish swam with no fear of being snared by people'. Nevertheless, his statement that 'oysters were safe in their shells' certainly could not apply to Roman Britain.

A problem is that, as the Romans lacked modern means of refrigeration, transferring fresh fish over long distances was difficult. It does however seem that some fish was sent from the coast to inland areas. At Silchester, for example, as well as local river fish, bones of grey mullet, herring, salmon and sea bream were found, which, as Boon remarks, 'show that there was a market for the produce of coastal fisheries far inland'. What is not clear is whether the fish were brought to Silchester as fresh fish or salted or smoked. Once fish have been gutted and decapitated, they can also be dried and, although they lose 50 per cent of their weight, they will keep for a long time.

Fish can be pickled by being packed between layers of salt in barrels, where they are pressed down with a heavy weight, allowing brine to form. The brine has to be cleared every 25-30 days on at least five occasions. To achieve the correct preservation might take up to five months but a shorter time would be considered acceptable. Fish might be put into amphorae filled with sea water and salt so that they could be taken more quickly to market, possibly 1kg (2.2lb) of salt to 2.75kg (6lb) of fish. Salt, easily prepared on the coast, would be readily available. On the handle of a globular amphora found at Alcester was written the number CXVS, indicating a weight of $115\frac{1}{2}$ Roman pounds. This is above the normal weight for an empty vessel, which had once been used for the transport of olive oil from Spain. Its re-use was indicated by the another inscription, *Flos scombri*, written on the vessel. This could be mackerel sauce or more likely best mackerel, salted and preserved.

The Romano-British diet could be monotonous and fish (especially herring, mackerel, flounder and cod), no matter how small in quantity, would add variety to a meal. Fatty, oily fish, such as herring and mackerel, are useful because they are high in unsaturated fats and the assimilation of this fat delays the onset of hunger. Less oily fish like flounder and cod make good reserve food when dried and in this form can be kept indefinitely. Even so, fish might be considered a luxury item, and both quantity and quality would change with the seasons. Recent studies in Japan, however, have revealed a strong connection between consumption of dried and salted fish and stomach cancer. This especially applies to strong fish pastes, which would apply not only to fish products, but to allec.

Sea fish

London, on the tidal Thames, housed a large community, engaged both in importing and exporting. It has produced evidence of saltwater fish, including mackerel, eel, cod, herring, smelt, plaice, flounder and dace, and river fish — perch, pike and roach. At Colchester evidence from waste and cesspits showed that cod, plaice, flounder, sole, grey mullet, mackerel and herring could be caught in estuarine and coastal waters. On the other hand, excavations at York, where large quantities of fish might have been expected and evidence for which has been found from the Anglo-Danish period, produced mainly bones of smelt, which spawns in fresh water after making its way from the sea. The implication is that the tidal range of the Humber and the Ouse was such that some sea fish could reach the town by swimming upriver in what was then relatively unpolluted water. Smelt usually spawn from March to May when they move upstream; a finely-meshed net is needed to catch them.

An unusual fish noted at Bishopstone (East Sussex) was the firm-fleshed meagre, found in late summer in the English Channel but also caught in shallow estuarine waters. Another fish, not popular today but favoured by the Romans, was wrasse. The bones of the Giant Wrasse, found at Waddon Hill fort (Dorset), a bony fish, may have been mistaken by the Romans for the Parrot Wrasse, which was highly prized. Better quality was found in red sea bream, which has a good quantity of rich, fatty meat. The bones of a large specimen were found in a fourth-century context on the temple site of Uley (Gloucestershire). As the fish was unlikely to have been caught in shallow estuarine waters, it must have been transported, probably in a preserved form, from a distance away and was probably offered as a gastronomic treat to the deity or even to the priests.

Cesspits at Dorchester (Dorset) have produced bones of sea bream, wrasse, plaice, conger eel, red and grey mullet and garfish. Sea bream and bass are the most common, both providing excellent food value. Lincoln, as might be expected in a port, in the fourth century had landed salmon, halibut, eel, turbot, conger and garfish brought up river from coastal fisheries. Bones of carp were found in a third century deposit. This fish was either eaten or brought in live for use in ornamental ponds from the Danube region, where it was apparently first kept by the Romans. Small quantities of fish bones have been excavated at some towns such as Silchester and Verulamium, and at forts on the coast, as for example Caernarfon (Gwynedd) and Maryport (Cumbria), and farther inland at Corbridge (Northumberland) and Brecon. Some villa sites like Gorhambury (Hertfordshire) received supplies of herring, mackerel and plaice; the inhabitants probably got these supplies from the nearby market in Verulamium, but trout and salmon would have been caught locally. Debris from the late third- to early fourth-century Castle Copse villa, Great Bedwyn (Wiltshire) included bones of eel, salmon, trout, flounder, herring, bass, gilthead and horse mackerel, indicating a diverse but not abundant selection of fish. The presence of gilthead and bass seem to indicate that these were specially selected fish brought to the villa as 'high status' foods.

At Skeleton Green (Hertfordshire), believed to be a trading post, bones of plaice, flounder, and Spanish mackerel, a fish local to the Bay of Biscay, were found in a well dating to the late Iron Age-early Roman period. These fish had to be transported from the coast. In the case of the Spanish mackerel, it could have been caught on one of its rare visits to Britain or be evidence of long distance trade in fish. This fish decomposes very rapidly, so it would have to be pickled in brine soon after capture. Among the salmon, eel and pike bones found at Dragonby (Lincolnshire) was a unique find, a bone fragment from a Nile catfish. So unusual an object suggests that its owner probably brought it into Britain as a talisman or curio.

At Brancaster fort (Norfolk), where the first Cohort of Aquitanians was stationed, three out of six fragments of whalebone had chop marks on them. Whalebones were also found at the fort of Valkenburg at the mouth of the Rhine, where the third cavalry cohort of Gauls was stationed in the second century. It might seem that auxiliary troops from Gaul had a fondness for whale meat. Similar chop marks were found on vertebrae dated to the Iron Age at Bishopstone settlement (East Sussex). Wahalebones were also found at Southwark and Leicester. Whales were sometimes hunted but this would be rare. Whale meat cannot be eaten safely from a dead whale washed onshore, but is excellent eating if the flesh is fresh. Both whale meat and porpoise flesh provide a significant food source because of the fat which they contain. Whale meat is important nutritionally to people who eat very little lean meat or who survive on a minimum diet. In the *Life of St Brendan* a dead whale provided meals for three days for the saint and his companions when they were on their travels. Juvenal referred to puny dolphins being beside a British whale *(balaena Britannica).*

River fish

River fish would be easier to catch than sea fish, although they were not appreciated so much. Diocletian's price edict of AD 301 indicated best-quality sea fish could be sold for 24 *denarii* a Roman pound, whereas river fish was to be sold for half that price. Bede, in the eighth century AD, commented that Britain 'produces various sea creatures' and 'abounds in springs and waters full of fish'. William of Malmesbury remarked in *De Gesta Pontificum Anglorum,* written in the twelfth century, that there was such a wealth of fish in the Fens 'as to cause astonishment to strangers'. The same was probably true in the Roman period, but evidence for the eating of fish can be summed up in brief comments such as that by Cunliffe regarding his excavations at Portchester (Hampshire): 'a few marsh birds such as mallard, may have been caught locally, as presumably were fish. A lead net weight, a netting needle and a fish-hook may be taken as reasonable evidence for this.'

There is more evidence for the eating of freshwater fish in that the bones of tench, perch, roach, chub, eel and salmon have been found on a variety of sites. At Skeleton

Green, for example, the population ate roach and chub caught in the local river, as well as eels speared or hooked as a catch. Bones of small fish such as sticklebacks probably came from the stomachs of other fish. Some bones are so small that they must have passed through the human gut. Bede mentioned that salmon and eel were found in profusion. Eels can be speared or caught in eel-bucks, basket-like traps which face upstream. They prefer clean water so eel catchers often stirred up the water to choke their breathing passages with mud. In mediaeval England osier baskets with funnel-shaped entrances were used, baited with other fish. At Roman Colchester, where large quantities of eel bones were excavated, the eels had probably been trapped in the River Colne as they migrated seawards. Eels are more easily caught in the winter months and are best eaten fresh but can be smoked.

Salmon were probably prolific. The Celts had prized the salmon as the form adopted by some Celtic gods. It was the source of Otherworld wisdom, as witnessed by the story of the Irish hero Finn who went to learn poetry from Finneces. The latter had spent seven years by the side of the Boyne watching for the salmon of Fec's Pool, for whoever ate it would have universal knowledge. When the salmon was at last caught, Finn was ordered to cook it, but on no account to eat any of it. The lad, however, burned his thumb and stuck it in his mouth, thereby tasting the flesh and gaining wisdom. Another Irish legend speaks of a salmon of wisdom in the well of Segais, the source of inspiration, into which sacred hazelnuts fell. Eating the nuts or the salmon would bring wisdom to that person.

Pliny commented that salmon were preferred to all other fish in Aquitania. These might be the Atlantic fish mentioned by Athenaeus, quoting Posidonius' views on the Celts:

> Their food consists of a small number of bread loaves together with a large amount of meat roasted either on charcoal or on spits…those Celts who live beside rivers or near the inner sea (Mediterranean) or the outer seas (Atlantic) eat fish in addition, boiled fish that is, with the addition of salt, vinegar and cumin.

The River Severn seems always to have been prolific in salmon. At Lydney (Gloucestershire) on a promontory overlooking the river, a temple site, dedicated to the god Nodens, was established in the fourth-century AD. There was also a guest house where worshippers could stay the night. On one mosaic are two dolphins, their entwined tails ended in dragon-headed eels. By the side is a smaller fish that resembles a salmon. Lydney was excavated in the early 1930s when environmental evidence was not sampled, so that it is not known whether fish formed part of the provisions of the guest house of the Romano-Celtic temple at that site.

Fishing as industry and sport

Fishing in the classical world was regarded as labour intensive and not necessarily a systematic occupation; rather, a gathering of food by men sustained by a precarious existence. The fishermen's chorus in Plautus' comedy *Rudens* gives a vivid picture of men who have never had a job or learned a trade. If they do not catch any fish, they are the ones who are 'washed and salted and go to bed hungry without any supper'. Fish can be difficult to catch. They can be caught individually with single hooks, although with hand lining many hooks can be used in open water. The scoop net is more effective. One man can use the hand-casting net with heavily weighed edges and two holding lines. A beach seine, where one man rows out, then swings round to bring the net back to shore, has to be pulled in by several men. It sweeps along the seabed but, as Plutarch remarked, fish will avoid it by hammering out a hollow on the bottom of the sea. Most fishing techniques would have to be shore-based, on a small scale, and unlikely to catch more than a few kilos of fish a day. The deep-water drift net was not used until the ninth-century AD.

These methods would be sufficient for coastal settlements and those that were on tidal rivers in Britain. Peter Marsden infers that fishing vessels worked the Thames estuary and may have ventured further afield to bring quantities of fish to London. Sprats were caught with a fine meshed net. Plaice, cod and bass could be caught in the mouth of the Thames but black sea bream, a somewhat rare fish, was fished from deeper waters. Sea fish have to be caught with a strong hook such as those found at the Richborough fort (Kent) and in London. A unique find comes from Guernsey harbour. A vessel trading in wine between Gaul and Britain caught fire when at anchor and sank. On deck there had been a hearth and an oven with a domed roof; several fishhooks were found in the wreck and possibly the fishermen had the means to cook the fish that they had caught.

Fishing could be for sport as well as an industry. Soldiers had to have the permission of their commanding officer to go either hunting or fishing; if they ignored this, they could be tried under military law. Angling was, however, regarded as recreational. Augustus took up fishing as a relaxation after the Civil War, and Martial reveals a knowledge of angling when he speaks of 'the greedy sea bream being deceived by the fly he has gorged'. The younger Pliny summed up the sporting aspect when he wrote to his friend Caninus Rufus, 'Are you reading, hunting or fishing, or doing all three? You can do all three together on Lake Como for there is plenty of fish in the lake, game in the woods and every opportunity to study in the depths of your retreat.' Fish-hooks found at the Fishbourne (West Sussex) and Keynsham (Somerset) villas, the settlement of Stockton (Wiltshire) and the forts of Wroxeter and Corbridge may indicate local anglers. Oppian, however, considered that fishing was inferior to hunting; how can drawing a writhing fish from the depths be equal to fighting deadly wild beasts in the hills? 'The hunter with his hounds hunts the bear; the angler hooks the bream' is his contemptuous comment.

Lydney has provided pictorial evidence for fishing in Britain. On a strip of bronze, two fishermen, wearing pointed caps, are depicted standing with legs braced in the river hauling on rod and line. One has caught a large fish which resembles a salmon; unfortunately the bronze is broken so it is impossible to say if the other fisherman was so lucky. This is how Oppian envisaged his angler, who sits on the rock and, with curving rod and deadly hook, catches at his ease fish of varied sheen. At Chester a broken relief provides a second example of fishing. A winged *amorino* is seated on a rock dangling a fish by its tail over what may be the top half of a lobster. A dolphin leaps over another fish to dive into the depths (**21**). *Amorini* performing a variety of roles — goldsmiths, gladiators,

21 A winged amorino *pulls out a fish. Drawn from a relief in the Grosvenor Museum, Chester*

vintners — are part of decorative arts in the Classical period. Fishing would be part of their playful activities.

Several spoons found in Britain and dated to the first and second centuries AD have a fish design on them. In London, some were found in what was once the bed of the Walbrook. One portrayal has been identified as a red mullet flanked by two salmon, both expensive fish. Tentative identifications of the others suggest carp, bream and gurnard. One design is a skeleton of a red mullet. On a mosaic found on the Aventine in Rome, designs of fish skeletons may represent the discarding of bones on the floor after the fish had been eaten and before they had been swept up by slaves. As the bowls of the spoons were so flat as to preclude their use to gather up liquid, they may have been used to consume a fish paste such as allec. On the other hand the fact that the fish is symbolic in Christian iconography cannot be dismissed.

Fish portrayed on mosaics might provide evidence of what was eaten in Britain, but most of the fish portrayed are represented conventionally and are not specifically identifiable. Unlike in the mosaics at Pompeii and in North Africa, where many of the fish represented are recognisable, shown at the bottom of a tank or strewn on the fishmonger's floor, fish in Romano-British mosaics are merely decorative. A mosaic found at the Great Witcombe villa (Gloucestershire) is in this tradition; marine animals, fish and eels play in a pool. Both this one and a mosaic at Rudston (Yorkshire) of dolphins and fish playing round the head of Neptune, whose hair is created from fish claws, were found in bathhouses and were thus appropriate for their setting.

An octagonal mosaic at the Lufton (Somerset) villa had a border of 29 fish swimming between two parallel bands of overlapping lyre patterns. It was suggested that they represented salmon, trout snapping at flies, pike chasing trout and sturgeon, but they are not obviously recognisable. Two eels, each entwined about the body of a fish, are recognisable, but it is not clear whether these are from the sea or the river. Though the fish are created from a variety of coloured tesserae and are portrayed apparently twisting

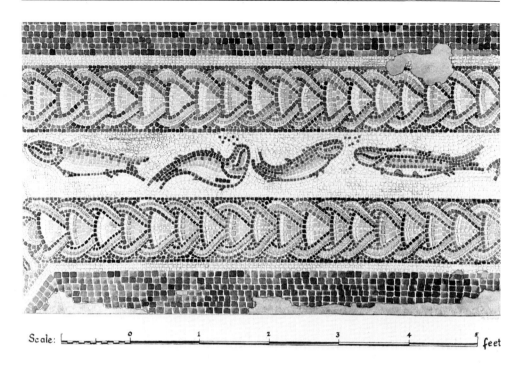

Scale: [—————] 0   1   2   3   4   5 feet

22 Part of the border of an octagonal mosaic, fourth century AD, showing a row of fishes, Lufton Villa, Somerset

and turning as if in water, there are no exact parallels; they are certainly not local river fish but some of a craftsman's stylistic repertoire (**22**). Jocelyn Toynbee suggested that they were obtained from cartoons and pattern books handed down from one generation to the next, as part of the mosaic worker's stock-in-trade. This could account for similarities of shape, style and form.

Fish breeding

The Romans farmed fish. Columella, Pliny and Varro gave instructions on keeping them in both fresh and salt water. Cereals, fruit and animal farming led to promotion of cash crops; Varro said aviaries and fishponds were other possibilities and Martial spoke of Faustinus' Baian villa where every possible commodity was exploited, including fish. Romano-Britons might have also exploited natural resources when they could, although it is to be hoped that they did not follow the repulsive habit of Vedius Pollio who, according to Seneca, fed his fish on mutinous slaves.

Excavations at two British villa sites have revealed ponds, which may have been used for fish. One was at Lynch Farm near Water Newton (Cambridgeshire), the other at Shakenoak (Oxfordshire), where the villa owner had three ponds dug in the early second century, one with a feeder stream leading into it. If all three ponds had been in use at the same time, and had lasted for about 60 years, they could have provided a fish-breeding complex with separation of spawning, young and adult fish. The Shakenoak excavators suggested that trout were kept there, but this is doubtful because trout need constant cooled water. Modern trout ponds are not less than 90cm (35in) deep, which is three times the depth of the Shakenoak ponds. They would, however, have been suitable for coarse fish, which breed quite happily in the shallow water and do not require frequent changes of water.

Diocletian's price edict indicated that the best river fish could be sold for 12 *denarii* an Italian pound (0.45kg) (equivalent to a pound of good pork in the Diocletian edict) and 8 *denarii* for the second-best quality (equivalent to a pound of beef or mutton). The Shakenoak ponds may therefore have provided a marketable commodity, enough to make fish farming economically viable. The fish could be sent to markets at the nearby settlements of Wilcote and Asthall and probably further afield to the towns of Alcester and Dorchester-on-Thames (Oxfordshire). Another area where fish farming may have taken place on an economic basis with both sea fish and shellfish was along the Essex coast, where villages and settlements could exploit their positions. The towns of Colchester, Chelmsford and Great Chesterford would provide markets for local trade.

Shellfish and other crustaceans

There appears to be only one example of crab found in Britain. Fragments of the edible crab were common in late second-century deposits at York. On the other hand, there is ample evidence for the eating of shellfish. As well as being very popular, all seafood provides an excellent source of protein. The Silchester citizens were eating mussels, cockles, periwinkles, whelks, scallops and oysters. Winkles and sea limpets were also a welcome addition to diet. Carpet shells are occasionally found on archaeological sites. But it is oyster shells which are the most prolific. The fame of British oysters was widespread, and Juvenal commented that they were a highly-regarded delicacy in Rome. Juvenal, who may have been a prefect commanding an auxiliary unit, the First Cohort of Dalmatians, at Maryport (Cumbria) about AD 90, might have developed a taste for British oysters during his time there. Pliny indicated that the British exported oysters to Rome in the first century AD. The coasts of Britain, he stated, were not yet supplying oysters when Sergius Orata made the Lucrine variety famous. As Orata's devising of a system of oyster ponds had been at Baiae before the Social Wars of 91-87 BC, this seems a sarcastic comment.

Juvenal pinpointed the source of the British oysters as Richborough (Kent). No evidence has been found there, but several timber-lined tanks at Wickford (Essex), one to 2m deep, may have been for oyster storage before transportation. The trade seems to have continued because Macrobius, in the fourth century, commented that oysters were sent from Britain to the Roman pontiff. To be enjoyed to the full, oysters should be eaten fresh, as quickly as possible; if they are traded, they need to be preserved, otherwise severe poisoning can take place. If the shells remain closed and the oysters are transported in tightly closed barrels filled with sea water, or even in the hull of a boat constantly washed with sea water, they can survive being transported for almost two weeks. Apicius stated that they can be preserved by washing them in vinegar and placing them in a receptacle treated with pitch. He probably had amphorae in mind. This might destroy harmful organisms, but would give the oysters a strong taste. Covering with brine was a better proposition and Juvenals' words indicate that Rome obtained effectively preserved oysters.

The vast quantities of oyster shells found on British sites testifies to their popularity. The excavators of the Longthorpe fort (Cambridgeshire) commented that 'it is certain that the garrison was in regular receipt of oysters'. The supply route to the settlement at Dragonby could have been from Essex along the coast to the mouth of the Humber river, then by estuary and river transport to the harbour at Winterington Haven. The excavators of the town of Caistor-on-Sea, counted 10,000 oyster shells before desisting. At Chanctonbury Ring (West Sussex), Hayling Island (West Sussex) and Stanwick (Northamptonshire), identified as religious sites, large deposits of oyster shells may either be evidence of ritual practice, such as the eating of meals, or presentations to the priest. More likely they are the detritus of snacks purchased from nearby stalls. When oyster shells are found with fish bones, in what was obviously agricultural land, they may have been part of organic manure. At Colchester seaweed was mixed with this material before being spread on the land.

Oysters provided excellent nutritional value as they are a source of animal protein and contain calcium and phosphorus. Desire for them may represent a psychological need, and they are regarded as an aphrodisiac. They may be eaten raw or cooked by placing them on a bed of coals. Shells at the Halstock villa (Dorset) were found in a corn-drying oven as if cooking had taken place there, and a hundredweight of oysters was found in a hypocaust at the Tottenhoe villa (Bedfordshire). When eaten raw, the Romans preferred them not 'au natur' but with a dressing. Apicius gave two recipes. One seems to be a kind of mayonnaise from pepper, lovage, egg yolk, vinegar, liquamen, oil and wine, with a sweetener of honey. He also provides a vinaigrette: pepper, lovage, parsley, mint, cumin, liquamen, vinegar and honey with malabrathrum and a bay leaf if required. Martial described them as 'thirsting for a noble garum' and presumably garum or liquamen would be acceptable as dressing.

Britain seems to have produced both cultivated and natural oysters. Cultivated beds could be laid down along the south and east coasts; they were not over-fished, and the oysters were gathered from unpolluted waters. Nor was their enemy, the slipper limpet, present at that time. Gustav Milne has drawn attention to two large deposits of oyster shells in Pudding Lane, London. The first, dating to the first century AD, was composed of shells of varying quality and sizes, seemingly selected from natural habitats, possibly from an oyster industry established on the Essex coast which also supplied Colchester, Chelmsford and numerous villas as well as producing a surplus for export. A high proportion of these shells had been broken as if they had been opened clumsily. This dump was infested with a small worm, *polydora ciliate*, which bore holes in the shells and is found in warm shallow waters, such as the Thames Estuary. The fact that the oysters were opened on what was then a quayside suggests either than they were sold directly by the fishermen from the boats to customers, or that some processing, possible salting or pickling, was taking place after the shells had been discarded.

The other Pudding Lane deposit, dating to the second century, contained larger shells with deep cups indicating thicker, edible meat. The inside of the shells of these oysters — pure, white, unblemished — was reminiscent of present day Whitstable oysters. The heels of the left valves were attached to cultch, a material used to entice the oyster larvae or spat to establish itself during breeding. Milne suggests that 'a deliberate attempt had been made to catch spat from an already breeding population'. The oyster shells had been opened more carefully, either because of a better knowledge of the technique or because of greater appreciation of the contents. Leicester received oysters from the Kent-North Essex coasts as those found there were noted to have been infested with the worm *polydurs hoplura* which causes blisters on the inner part of the shell and is common to that coastal area. It would seem that oyster cultivation introduced to Britain by the Romans was now an important industry satisfying both home consumption — shells found on many villa sites are of the Colchester 'native' variety — and an export trade.

Roman writers wrote appreciatively of the oysters' supposed medicinal properties. Celsus considered them to be a laxative and an easily digestible food. Pliny extolled them as settling the stomach, restoring lost appetite, cleansing an ulcerated bladder and alleviating colds. Crushed shells stopped itching, cured sores, smoothed rough skin, soothed burns and, if mixed with vinegar, acted as a dentifrice. Chopped raw oysters were recommended for curing chilblains, a problem in the cold northern provinces. It is therefore not surprising that they were consumed in a shop in the forum at Caerwent and at Verulamium and by soldiers relaxing in the fortress baths at Caerleon, who also enjoyed mussels, cockles and whelks.

Oysters were sent as presents. The Apicius who lived in the second century sent fresh oysters to the Emperor Trajan on his Parthian campaign, in packing especially devised by himself. A writing tablet from Vindolanda in a list of supplies acknowledges a gift of oysters from Cordonovi. This could be Cordanum, an island at the mouth of the River Gironde in Gaul or Cordonovia, possibly situated in the Thames estuary. Either place indicated the ease with which oysters could be transported. Oyters may have been transported by coastal shipping and kept fresh with seawater before being carried by land to the northern forts. This might have been the case at Verulamium where mussel, winkle and oyster shells were found, but if so, after the shellfish had been eaten the shells were used for making lime or mortar, especially as skeletons of bryozoan colonies inside some oyster shells indicate that they were dead on arrival.

A bonus was that pearls could be obtained. Tacitus, in the first century, said that they could be collected as they were thrown up on the shore. Caesar hoped to find them during his invasion of Britain and succeeded so well that he could dedicate a breastplate covered with small British pearls to Venus Genetrix in her temple at Rome. The shells themselves may have been used as ornaments. On some sites, such as Stonea (Cambridgeshire), small holes have been deliberately drilled in them so that they could be threaded together as a necklace or worn as an ornament. Oysters were seemingly a valued marine product used for food and decoration; if they could be eaten for their medical or aphrodisiac reputation, their consumption was all the more enjoyable.

5 Dairy products

Milk

Dairy products would be a necessary part of diet, but, not surprisingly, given the ephemeral nature of these products, Romano-British evidence relating to both quantity and quality is lacking. Given the importance of these products in the Empire as a whole, however, some suggestions might be made regarding Britain. Roman writers had much to say on the subject. Pliny implied that cows' milk, though important nutritionally to the Romans, was more productive in cheese-making. His reason may be that milk quickly goes sour in a hot country. In Britain, given the cooler climate, both milk and cheese could have been equally important.

Milk is produced by cows, sheep and goats. All these animals were important both to the Romans and to barbarian tribes. Strabo commented that the Belgae had large quantities of food including milk and all kinds of meat. Columella says that for nomadic tribes that have no corn, sheep provide their diet; hence the Gaetae are called 'milk-drinkers'. For the Romans, sheep and goats' milk was more highly regarded than cows' milk. Virgil esteemed goats for their abundant and nutritious yield of milk. Goats give a milk yield five times as much in proportion to their body weight as cattle and four times as much as sheep; in modern France a goat yields about 700 litres (155 galls) a year, an average yield of 2-2.5 litres (0.44–0.55 galls) a day. It might be more economic to allow the milk from these animals to be given to kids, which could have a higher monetary value.

Milk was thought to have some medicinal value. With bread it was commended as a treatment for dysentery. Pliny gave a list of problems which it could cure, some bizarre, but others not out of place today, such as its efficacy for stomach ulcers. He recommended it for those persons who were convalescing or suffering from consumption and in a poor state of health. He also praised goats' milk for being the sweetest form of milk and more suited to the stomach than cows' milk, which may imply that the Romans had some knowledge of bovine lactic intolerance. Milk does, however, have to be kept fresh. Tainted milk can transmit tuberculosis and undulant fever, which can attack bones causing an abscess to form. Examples of this were found in skeletons excavated in the Poundbury (Dorset) and the East London cemeteries.

There were also milk drinks. Celsus mentions *lactantia* in a list of foods which move the bowels: this could be a form of invalid food. Apicius mentioned *melca*, a form of curdled milk, probably like a thin yogurt. This is similar to Pliny's *oxygala,* an astringent, coagulated milk, made by adding sour milk to fresh, which has also been suggested to be buttermilk. Martial gave a present of beastings, the first milk drawn from the mother; this is also highly praised by Varro. These are rich in nourishment and are part of the diet of nomadic communities as in present-day Mongolia. In that country milk drawn from mares is put into a bag made from leather or sheepskin and stirred with a stick by whoever passes it, often being stirred 2,000 times (**colour plate 7**). The result is a fermented drink (*airag*). If a similar method were to be used in the Romano-British countryside, it would have left no trace.

Butter

Pliny commented that the barbarians have lived on milk for centuries, but that they do not know the blessing of cheese. Among the barbarians he presumably included the Celts, and the evidence belies Pliny's words. An Irish poem written in the twelfth century A D, but believed to be part of an earlier tradition, describes a fort in culinary terms as being surrounded by a sea of new milk, and having thick breastworks of custard, fresh butter for a drawbridge, walls of curd cheese and pillars of ripe cheese.

Wooden casks containing a fatty substance given the name 'bog butter', some containing as much as 18.2kg (40lb), have been found in Irish and Scottish peat bogs. Although this is suggested to be adipocere, a waxy material formed from animal fat, some is conceivably butter, and the cask was put into the bog to preserve it. The earliest dated find is from the fifth century AD, but other finds are suspected to be earlier, and the custom was known to have existed in the Highlands of Scotland until the nineteenth century. The butter is salted, which helps preservation and prevents it from going rancid.

The Celtic diet was distinguished from the Roman one by its emphasis on animal fats, rather than olive oil. The latter was more easily obtained in, and exported from, Mediterranean regions and imparted a completely different cultural food experience. The Romans regarded butter more as a base for an ointment. Columella recommends treating animal injuries with an ointment which included butter ('goat's fat'), akin to the remedy still sometimes used of putting butter on burns. There is one possible reference to butter in the Vindolanda writing tablets. In the same list is lovage, which was an ingredient in an eye salve, so the list might have been concerned with items intended for medical use.

Pliny maintained that the barbarians considered butter their choicest food, the differing quantities of which distinguished the wealthy from the lower orders. Cows' milk was most commonly used, but sheep's milk gave richer butter. He recommended a traditional method of putting warmed milk in a tall container with a hole pierced close to the stopped mouth. As the milk curdles it is scooped off and salted. There might have been other ways of making butter that have left no literary or archaeological evidence. In Tibet, for example, warmed milk is put into a yak-skin bag, which is swung from a tree branch until butter is formed. Two other methods are to let children kick the bag about or to stir the contents violently with a stick with a club end; in both cases the milk solidifies to butter.

Cheese

Cheese is a nutritious food with a high energy and protein value. 100g (3.5oz) of cheese can contain 700mg (.025oz) of calcium and 400 calories. It is also high in saturated fat but, like milk, does not agree with people who are lactose intolerant. This fact was known to Hippocrates, who said that some people could eat as much as they liked without any problem, whereas others suffered acutely if they ate even the smallest amount. Celsus and Pliny emphasised that hard cheese causes flatulence and constipation.

Barbarian tribes ate it with great enjoyment. Tacitus wrote in the *Germania* that the Germans eat plain food — wild fruit, fresh game and curdled milk. The term he uses, *lac concretum*, can be identified as the solid milk formed when the milk is left to go sour. This type of milk-cheese, naturally formed by lactic acid, has been a staple product throughout Europe for centuries. Harder cheese is made by putting curds into a container to drain off whey, which has always been a natural drink for humans and is often fed to pigs as part of a fattening diet.

Both sheep's and goat's milk have a greater concentration of short-chain fatty acids in their fat content and cheese made from their milk is easier to digest because of its smaller milk particles. Sheep's milk has almost twice the fat content of cow's milk — 7.5 per cent against 4 per cent, but the animal is harder to milk. Goats' milk curdles in about half the time of cow's milk; though mild when fresh it develops its full flavour in several stages over four to five weeks. This gives the cheese a stronger taste, which some people find unpleasant.

Cheese-making often took place in rural areas where it might be inconvenient to take milk in pails to market. Columella directed the shepherd to make cheese in the best possible manner, warning that, if cheese is made in a thin consistency, it should be sold as soon as possible while it is still fresh. One difficulty might be in obtaining a continuous production of a supply of sheep's milk, because the highest yield comes at lambing time, when ewes produce more milk than is needed for their young.

The Roman appreciation of cheese can be noted from the fact that writers give details of cheese-making and discuss the differences between hard (or dry, salty) cheese and soft cheese, which was akin to the modern Italian ricotta cheese. Varro in particular favoured soft cheeses for being more nutritious and less constipating. Pliny named several cheeses, even pinpointing the locality of two villages near to Nîmes in southern Gaul famous for their cheeses. In particular demand were cheeses from the Apennines, from Sarcina in Umbria and a Luni variety from the borders of Etruria and Liguria, which weighed up to 453kg (1000lb). Martial said it would provide lunches for a thousand slaves. Making a cheese of this weight would be feasible, if somewhat impractical. Modern weights of cheeses are not so great: Parmesan rounds weigh 40.8kg (110lb) and Emmenthal 108.8kg (242lb).

Athenaeus made the actor Philemon say that while Sicily produces fine goats' cheese, a Tromilic cheese from the city of Acheia admits no comparison with any other. A Vestinian cheese made in an area close to Rome is the only named cheese in the recipes of Apicius. Martial gave its shape as a *massa* (a lump). In another verse he mentions a *quadra* (square) from Tolosa (Toulouse) in Gallia Narbonensis. This may imply that the

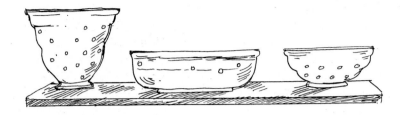

23 *Three different forms of cheese presses, reconstructed from pottery sherds, Longthorpe Fort, Cambridgeshire*

cheese was a hard one, which could be cut into blocks. He refers to the Sarcina cheese as cone-shaped and later compares it to a rounded breast. In modern France the cone-shape and pyramid-shape are often chosen because these cheeses mature more quickly than round or log-shaped ones.

Cheese-making

Cheese-making in modern times can still be the concern of local producers. This would have been even more so in the Ancient World, although mention of cheese from different localities implies an export trade from some areas, especially to Rome. Cheese presses or squeezers found in Britain at Camulodunum (Essex), Lower Halstow (Kent), Silchester and Leicester, including flat ones with large holes acting as strainers, imply local industries. Others, found at the forts of Bainbridge (Yorkshire), Usk (Monmouthshire), Holt (Flintshire) and Corbridge, suggest that cheese was one of the easiest products made by soldiers. Cheese was included in iron rations carried by soldiers as part of their regular diet. The Emperor Hadrian made a point of following the life of an ordinary soldier when with his army, and in camp ate bacon and cheese, and drank sour wine. Rustius Barbarus, in a letter written on ostraca (pottery sherds) found at the fort of Wâdi Fawâkhir near Thebes in Egypt, tells his friend, Pompeius, he has received bunches of cabbage and one cheese.

A bowl-shaped vessel from the Templeborough fort (Yorkshire) with small holes in the base could have strained either curds or honey from a honeycomb. Twin-handled jars with holes in the bottom from Colchester and Silchester were strainers. Wicker baskets could also be used to let the whey run off. Curd residue, which resembled the modern Italian ricotta cheese, was shaped into cakes or put into a press. Three different types of cheese presses were found at the Longthorpe (Cambridgeshire) fort. A disc-shaped cheese could be produced from a Nene Valley ware flat pot and there were two presses for bowl-shaped cheeses (**23**). Conical presses, found at the Eccles (Kent) villa, suggest that the occupants were preparing cheese for marketing. The residue of milk products found in the bases of pots at Poundbury may be the residue of home products or those bought in the market place. A round pottery strainer in London had concentric rings on the bottom inner part to hold the cheese while the whey drained through the holes (**24**).

The best vessels for making cheese would be the heavy, rounded, flat mortaria, common on Roman sites, which often have grit fired into the base of the interior (**25**). After the curds had been scraped out, some bacteria would remain on the gritted pieces, thus acting as a starter for the next cheese-making session and avoiding the need for adding fresh rennet. A wide spout on the rim allows easy pouring of the whey. Modern milk bowls in Northern France and the Savoy almost exactly reproduce the shape of mortaria and use the same technique. Milk left overnight also acts as a starter, but

24 *Round cheese press showing concentric rings in the base on which the cheese rested while the whey drained off. Lower Halstow, Kent*

Columella stressed milk must not be left to stand for a long time because it can turn sour.

The process of natural souring is aided by the addition of rennet, the digestive juices secreted in the stomach of certain animals; this contains an enzyme which helps the milk to clot. Columella regarded lamb's rennet as being the best — a small piece the size of a silver *denarius* was all that was needed. Varro favoured that of hare or kid, utilising a piece the size of an olive. The juice from some plants can also be used, in particular wild thistle, nettles and fig. Palladius recommended a small piece of skin from a chicken's stomach; presumably the bacteria would instigate curdling, though it might also be a source of disease. Once rennet is added to the milk, it can be left in a warm place to thicken, such as on a shelf in a warm outhouse or even near the fire kindled on the hearth.

To make hard cheese the curds are placed in wicker baskets or a *ficus* (a flexible leather bag pierced for straining) to drain the whey, then pressed with weights in a mould for further drainage. Columella said the cheese should be taken out of the mould, sprinkled with salt, and put into a cool, shady place to drain off further liquid and harden. It was pressed again for nine days, then washed with fresh water and set in a cool room to dry. This method must be followed, otherwise the cheese becomes full of holes, a result of not being pressed sufficiently, and is too salty and dry.

If a cheese is to be eaten soon, then it is merely drained, dipped in salt and dried in the sun, which would seemingly produce a creamy cheese with a stiff rind, somewhat like a Camembert. Columella also mentioned a cheese that could be hardened in brine; the test was that cheese would float in it. Pliny directed that a cheese should be steeped in vinegar to preserve it. Prepared brine was placed in pitch-lined vessels and 'held covered in the sun, for the action of the sun takes away all mustiness and causes a pleasant odour'. The recommended ratio was two parts vinegar to one part brine. This would help to retard the mould. Columella suggested that cheese should be sliced, put into a vessel treated with

25 *Pottery, second-fourth century, from the Lullingstone Villa, Kent. Left to right: Nene Valley ware jug, Rhenish black metallic coated beaker, late samian pot, indented beaker. At rear are mortaria*

pitch and filled with *must* (grape juice or thickened wine), then covered for twenty days. He was not too sure about the taste as he added that although seasoning may be added the product is not too unpleasant by itself.

Cheese can be flavoured with crushed pine kernels, thyme and other herbs; in fact Columella said that adding any chosen seasoning can give cheese any flavour. Smoked cheese was produced commercially in Rome. One street in Rome, the Velabran, on the west side of the Palatine, was famous for producing this; Trebula, in the country of the Sabines, had cheeses which, according to Martial, 'were tamed by a moderate fire'. Smoking imparts its own special flavour according to the type of fuel used and Pliny said that it increases the flavour of goats' cheese. Some woods and charcoal give an aromatic flavour; Columella suggested the use of applewood. Smoking was well within the capability of cheesemakers in Britain, the cheese being produced in outhouses attached to villas and sold in nearby towns. Cheeses might also be hung in baskets on the rafters of rural round houses being left to mature in the smoke from the central fire.

Varro pointed out that the pasturage on which cows are fed affects their milk, a fact known to Pliny who commented that in Bythynia cows which eat on salty pasture produce a salty cheese. This is well known to modern dairy farmers in Cheshire because the salty pastures round the Northwich and Middlewich areas produce some of the best Cheshire cheese. It is tempting to think that the salt producers and the soldiers in the auxiliary fort at Middlewich ate a cheese similar to that produced in Cheshire today.

6 Vegetables, fruits and nuts

Vegetables

Tacitus' remarks on Britain included the comment that 'except for olives, vines and other products of warmer countries, the soil will produce good crops. They are slow to ripen, although they shoot up quickly, both facts being due to the same cause, the excessive moisture of the soil and atmosphere.' The Romans, however, soon found that both soil and climate were suitable for the practice of horticulture on a large scale. In discussing conditions on a farm, Varro stated that it is profitable near a city to have a garden on a large scale so as to grow produce suitable for sale in the local market. Vegetables, according to Columella, would grow well with sewage used as manure. In nineteenth-century France the most valuable fertiliser was a kilogram of urine which was said to be equal to a kilogram of wheat. Urine could have been collected in the broken amphorae which served as urinals in kitchens or were strategically placed at street corners in Roman towns.

New plants introduced in Britain would be ideal cash crops, as would improved indigenous crops. It is possible that, given the wide variety of vegetables available, some of the settlements may have specialised in growing a certain crop; the inhabitants of Owslebury (Hampshire), for example, seem to have had a preference for beans. All vegetables would be eaten in season, although some might be dried as preservation for winter foods.

Crops introduced by the Romans included parsnips, radishes, beets, endive, lettuce, broad beans, turnips, cabbage and a better type of carrot (**26**). These plants were probably tougher and more fibrous than those grown today; wild carrots, white and tough, can be very woody. One way of making them edible was to pulverise them using a pestle and mortar or rub them by hand in large mortaria. Both the roots and leaves of turnips were eaten, and the roots could be left in the ground for winter produce. Pliny said that the parsnip prospered in cold localities and that the Emperor Tiberius obtained an annual supply from Germany. The roots of parsnips are improved by exposure to frost because this increases the sugar content. A cold British winter would be excellent for this crop.

Carrots, radishes, parsnips and turnips are known to have been eaten and probably grown at Silchester. Cucumber seeds have been found in London; cucumber was usually cooked, for it had a reputation even then of being indigestible. The Romans also preferred to eat lettuce cooked. Celery, found in environmental evidence at York, Silchester and Bearsden, was a small plant. It was usually eaten green and not in its blanched form. The Romans, in fact, preferred to eat the leaves, which were used to flavour soups and stews; Apicius commended the condiment use of celery seed, leaf stems and roots. Seeds and leaves could be used as a seasoning for wine if it tasted watery. Hippocrates recommended

26 *Reconstructed scene created in the Verulamium Museum utilizing Roman pottery, kitchen equipment and food which would have been available in Roman Britain. The gridiron has been reconstructed from an original. The black pudding hanging on the wall would have been stuffed into a long skin and not curled. The sausages would have been made from meat stuffed in the lining of the intestine of a calf creating a long sausage. An inn at the corner of the Via di Mercurio at Pompeii has a painting showing men dining at a table. Above them is a rack from which hang strings of onions, cheeses and a long sausage. The first mention of a string of sausages occurs in the Byzantine* Life of St Simeone Salos *by Leontius of Naples. Leontius comments on the saint having a string of sausages round his neck and dipping each one into mustard held in his left hand before eating it.*

celery for eliminating bodily fluids; recently scientists have isolated nutrients (phthalides) which are probably responsible for this diuretic effect. Wild radish seeds were found in York, London and Caerleon. Many grain deposits contained evidence of this product, so it would seem that in its wild state it was a common field weed.

Beds outside the Balkerne gate at Colchester were said to have a resemblance to asparagus beds. There was a native form of wild cabbage but the Romans introduced at least one cultivated variety, an example of which was found in a pit in Southwark, together with peas and lentils. Cabbages, of which the Romans were particulary fond, were grown at Fishbourne. Columella described 15 varieties grown in Rome, while Cato extolled its medicinal properties and exclaimed that it was 'the cabbage which surpasses all other vegetables; it promotes digestion marvellously and is an excellent laxative'. He advised eating raw cabbage seasoned with vinegar before and after a dinner, which will enable people to drink as much as they want during the meal. Martial recommended that soda should be added to the water to retain the green colour, a fact emphasised in modern cookery. It was a variety akin to kale which most readily adapted to Britain.

Peas, found in London and Silchester, were a welcome addition, as they could be added to a pottage, which would be improved by their sugar content. These were probably dwarf field peas as garden peas are less hardy. The vegetation is used for feeding stock. Pliny considered both peas and beans to be amongst the earliest foods eaten by the Romans antedating the discovery of bread-making; both could be ground and added to bread flour. Beans and peas could be eaten in the pod, which would provide fibre, and were welcomed in all households. Beans could also be dried to preserve them; some were found in a drier at the Odell villa (Bedfordshire). One of Martial's epigrams comments that 'if pale beans bubble for you in the red earthenware pot, you may decline the dinners of rich hosts.' Pliny, however, said that beans clouded a person's vision and recent medical discoveries have shown that the bean can produce favism, an haemolytic disorder, common amongst Mediterranean peoples, which may be caused by eating broad beans. Examples of lentils have been found in London, Southwark, Caerleon and on other sites (**colour plate 8**); a jar full of lentils was found in the north wing at Fishbourne. The eating of lentils, Pliny remarked, was considered by authorities to promote an even temperament and modern nutritionists recommend them as a high-fibre, high-protein food. This pulse must have been imported as it is doubtful if the climate could support its cultivation. Some of the finds, however, could be the result of contamination of imported grain.

Certain types of fungi were native to Britain. Puffballs were part of the vegetation at Vindolanda in the first century AD. These could have been used as a haemostatic, similar to those used by surgeons in the nineteenth century, but are also suitable for eating. In addition to vegetables, the Romans ate the bulbs of certain plants such as gladiolus, usually pounded or cut up and added to stews. They could, as Pliny suggested, be baked in ashes and eaten with oil and salt; this might have been done in time of shortage when food was scarce.

A vegetable repertoire can also include plants that are referred to as weeds, which are hardy and have a food value equal to that of vegetables. Nettles, according to Apicius, could be taken as a cure against illness, and Pliny particularly recommends them. Their frequency in Britain would provide an excellent addition to food supplies, especially in spring, for they are rich in vitamins and minerals and can be used as a vegetable or in a salad. The Britons probably collected the leaves of wild plants such as mallow, plantain, docks, black bindweed, dandelion and Good King Henry. Later these would be cultivated by the Romans, who also introduced some of their own varieties. The dandelion can be a particularly useful crop; its baked root can be ground into flour, the flower heads may be steeped to make a drink, and the leaves, rich in vitamins A and C, provide a welcome vegetable throughout the year.

The native Britons had cultivated certain crops such as the Celtic bean, a smaller version of the broad bean, vetch, used for both animal and human consumption, and fat hen, whose ground-up seeds can be used in bread-making. This plant, grown since the Neolithic period, tastes like spinach when cooked. Both this and the Celtic bean were also useful in replacing nitrogen in the soil, although one problem was that bean plants were very susceptible to weevil and aphid attack. It was probably inevitable that weed seeds would be eaten as part of a grain crop.

Fruits

Fruits and nuts, the produce of forest and wilderness, supplemented cultivated crops, as a natural resource. Stones of sloes indicate a means of flavouring a drink. Fruits indigenous to Britain include raspberries, bilberries, blackberries, elderberries, wood strawberries and crab apples. These would provide a welcome natural sweet addition to a diet, both in pre-Roman and Roman times. The range of wild fruits found on the Dragonby (Lincolnshire) site included sloes, blackberries, crab apples and elder flower.

The Romans imported new fruits into Britain including the domesticated plum and the damson, which soon became established as cultivated crops. Pliny remarks that Lucullus brought cherry trees from Pontus, south of the Black Sea, about 65 BC and that in the first century AD they were planted as far away as Britain. Kent would provide a favourable area, but stones found at the port of London suggest that some fruit could have been imported. Cherry stones found in a well at the Chew Park (Gloucestershire) villa are better evidence of local cultivation. Together with pears, plums and apples, evidence for which was also found in the well, they would have formed a useful cash crop.

Medlar and elderberry seeds were found at Silchester; in fact seeds of elderberry were so common that the excavators suggested the berries were eaten frequently. Flowers of the fruit will flavour drinks, and Pliny commented on its medicinal properties. The medlars were probably grown in Silchester gardens as they are too frail to be imported. Their sharp taste is an acquired one but adds variety to a diet. The citizens of Silchester also enjoyed bullaces, damsons and plums. Bullaces are a sharp-tasting fruit often left on the tree until late autumn when their acidity may be softened by a hard frost. Plum stones have also been found at Doncaster and Colchester.

Soft fruits such as mulberries are considered too fragile to travel long distances; thus their presence on sites in Dorset and Devon must mean that they were a local crop. They must be picked when fully ripe, being then very juicy and easily squashed. The variety of fruit eaten in London is indicated by the contents of a pit found in a second-century building in Southwark, which included apple and grape pips, mulberry, blackberry, raspberry, elderberry and fig seeds and cherry, damson and plum stones. One peach stone has been found in London in the second-century level at New Fresh Wharf. A mortaria of second-century date found at Silchester had the remains of pulped fruit, stones and pips in it. The inhabitants of Silchester, as well as soldiers in the Bearsden and Lancaster forts, also enjoyed strawberries, raspberries and blackberries, either gathered from the wild or cultivated. The citizens and soldiers at York continued to enjoy these fruits well into the third century, as the faecal remains in one of the main sewers have revealed. A rare find is the pomegranate seeds found in the excavation at Poultry, London. This fruit, used both medicinally and for conserves, was probably imported to satisfy sophisticated tastes in a cosmopolitan city.

Fig seeds were found in York, Silchester, Verulamium and on many other sites. At Verulamium, carbonised figs were found in the remains of a building burned in the Boudiccan rebellion of AD 60-1. The Emperor Julian (AD 360-3) commented that figs could be grown in Gaul as far north as Paris; in winter they were protected by covering the trees with straw, but there was a problem as far as Britain was concerned. Figs would have to be imported as dried fruit because figs need a pollinating agent, the caprificatory wasp, which was not present in Roman Britain.

Dates were also imported; carbonised dates were found at Colchester in the Boudiccan debris. Although Pliny was scathing about figs, regarding them as food for slaves, their laxative property was appreciated, as was that of dates. These have a high sugar content and are a valuable source of energy. The Colchester dates were reported to be individual not compressed, as if they had been imported in a firm container. Evidence of importation comes from a sherd of amphora found in the annexe ditch of the first fort at Carlisle, established about AD 72. Painted on it was the Greek word *KOYK* (Latin *cuci*). This has been interpreted as the fruit of the doum palm, a tree limited to the Nile valley in antiquity. The tough, sugary fruit, tasting somewhat like gingerbread, has to be soaked before it can be eaten. Another inscription *PRUNA* on an amphora sherd at the fort of Brough-on-Noe (Derbyshire) seems to indicate a container for plums.

The crab apple is indigenous to Britain but the Romans soon imported other varieties. Cato, Pliny, Varro and Columella all provided information on apple growing which included grafting, and this could have been done onto the native crab apple tree. Seeds of *malus sylvestris*, as found at York, suggest apples could be grown commercially; the word 'mal' on an amphora sherd may indicate apples were imported to the city. London received an amphora containing dried sorb apples. A richly-flavoured desert apple *Court Perdu Plat* has been suggested to have been grown in Kent with its less heavy rainfall. A pit at Frenchfield, Doncaster, contained 1400 apple pips, which would derive from a quantity of 150-300 apples, and suggested the making of a fermented apple drink.

Nuts

The Romans introduced the sweet or Spanish chestnut and the walnut. Chestnuts can be fed to livestock, eaten whole, ground into flour and used in soups and pottage. To produce a good crop the tree requires very hot weather, which might not be possible in Britain. In Italy the flour (*farina dolce*) was used for bread making. Pliny noted that walnut shells could be used in dyeing wool. He suggested, more from hope than experience, that if the nuts were eaten before a meal they would lesson the effects of poisoned food, a property more useful perhaps in Rome than in Britain. Walnuts have been found at Scole (Norfolk), Winchester, Rotherley (Wiltshire) and in London at New Fresh Wharf, evidence perhaps for their importation. At the Bar Hill fort on the Antonine Wall and at Vindolanda, the troops had enjoyed both these nuts and hazelnuts, which are indigenous to Britain. The troops in the forts of Newstead, Holt (Flintshire), Castleshaw (Lancashire) and Slack (West Yorkshire) had also eaten hazelnuts, and fragments were found in a drain in the bathhouse at Bearsden, presumably having been eaten by soldiers relaxing off duty. Charred hazelnuts were found amongst burnt Boudiccan debris at Colchester. Waterlogged pine cones and carbonised pine nuts from Winchester may indicate cultivation of pine nuts in Britain, but the almond stones found in the Wiggonholt villa (West Sussex) bathhouse and in London on the pyre of a woman burned in a London cenetery were almost certainly part of an imported crop.

7 Herbs, spices, salt and honey

Herbs

Herbs were a necessity, being cultivated both as a flavouring and for their medicinal purposes. Those native to Britain could either be left in their wild state, where it was believed they would have more potency, or transplanted to the kitchen garden where they could be bred to produce stronger plants and ensure a continuous supply. Pliny considered that this should be the case with plants used for herbal remedies. Many herbs native to the Mediterranean were brought to Britain; soldiers in particular brought their culinary tastes with them. The popularity of herbs as a flavouring in the Roman world must have been helped by the fact that most of those used were freshly picked rather than dried, for the latter have a duller aroma, because a considerable proportion of the volatile material is lost in the drying process. Nevertheless dried herbs made a piquant addition to a winter meal.

Some recipes in Apicius use a bouquet of herbs, but usually herbs and spices were crushed or ground in a *pila*, a small mortar similar to that used by most cooks today, or they were rubbed, pulverised and pounded in a mortarium. Columella instructed 'put into a mortar savory, mint, rue, coriander, parsley, chives, rocket leaves, green thyme or catmint, pennyroyal and salted cheese. Pound altogether and mix a little peppered vinegar with them. When you have put the mixture into a small earthenware vessel pour a little oil on top of it'. This recipe produces something akin to a pesto sauce. Excavations have produced a number of rounded vessels and stones to which the term pestle and mortar can be applied. L-shaped rubbers were used with mortaria, where the gritty interior surface was excellent for pulverising herbs.

Wild chives were native to Britain and widespread, although they were probably not cultivated until the mediaeval period. Herbs introduced included dill, fennel, marjoram, mint, sage, rosemary, rue and thyme. Dill, common in the classical world, was found at Caerwent, Silchester and the Caernarfon fort. Both it and fennel were discovered at New Fresh Wharf, London; excavations on the site of Billingsgate market produced evidence of mint and dill. Fennel, dried and powdered, makes an excellent eyewash and can be used as an anti-flatulent. Environmental evidence from York included dill, rue and savory. Rue was used sparingly because of its pungent musky flavour. Martial said eggs were wrapped in rue leaves. Pliny commented on its properties as an antidote to poisoning from mushrooms or snakebite. Presumably this was because it can induce vomiting when taken in large quantities. His recommendation of its use in improving eyesight must mean infusing the leaves to bathe tired eyes. Borage has been found in Roman contexts on the South Downs. This has a high content of calcium and potassium and, as well as being eaten, the leaves can be used as a poultice to soothe inflammation and bruises. Pollen grains of mallow were recovered from the latrine debris at the Bearsden fort; Pliny recorded many medicinal uses for this plant. The leaves can be boiled and used as a vegetable and the roots made into an ointment and a soothing cough syrup.

Parsley is said to have not been introduced into Britain until the sixteenth century, but it is such a common herb and so useful to the Romans in cooking that it would be surprising if they had not grown it in Britain. It is difficult to grow as its seeds take between 70 and 90 days to germinate in an alkaline soil in a sunny area, so that this may have precluded extensive growth except in southern Britain. The introduced mint was of the spearmint type; the round-leaved mint is native to Britain. The marigold, native to Southern Europe, has petals which may be used as a substitute for saffron, giving a slight aromatic bitterness to food. Other plants included those valued for their medicinal qualities, such as henbane used for nervous complaints, hemlock used as a sedative and for epilepsy and St John's Wort used for a variety of purposes, including the healing of burns.

Spices

Flavour has been described as 'the simultaneous appreciation of the sense of taste on the tongue and linings of the mouth as well as the less defined attributes such as temperature and pungency' (Tropical Products Institute 1973). If the Romans made the fullest use of produce such as herbs to enhance these sensations, they made even more use of spices. Herbs and spices prevented food from appearing insipid, helped to stimulate the gastric juices and prepared the digestive system. Spices disguise a tainted taste; they would certainly add zest to a meal in an era when it was difficult to keep food fresh. Pliny quoted Varro as saying that pounded coriander, cumin and vinegar rubbed into meat will keep it fresh in the summer heat. It is therefore ironic that modern treatises on spices warn that they may be extremely suspect from a hygienic point of view as they can become contaminated with bacteria and mould spores, as well as dirt derived from their handling and storage.

Cellulose forms the bulk of spices; it encapsulates the essential oils that confer the aroma and flavour. These oils are released by pounding and grinding, hence the use of the pestle and mortar, and provide a 'bite' and flavour, which is released slowly as cooking temperatures rise. That the Romans could over-spice their food is noted by Plautus who, in *Pseudolus,* warns against cooks, who 'when they season their dinners, they season that fodder with more fodder. They serve them sorrel, cabbage, beets, spinach flavoured with coriander, fennel, garlic, parsley, pour in a pound of assafoetida, grate in murderous mustard which makes the grater's eyes ooze out before they have it grated. When these chaps season the dinners, they use for seasoning no seasoning but screech owls which eat out the intestines of their guests alive'. He finishes rather cynically that 'men will eat herbs which the cows will leave alone'.

People may however get used to a certain flavour and want more of it; this particularly applies to spiced food. Recent research at CSIRO, the Australian National Research Organisation, suggests that people who constantly eat hot spicy food experience a sense of pleasure and well-being and thus may become addicted to it; the food also stimulates the endorphins, the body's natural painkillers. The report was commenting on curry, but the effect could equally arise from any highly spiced food. The more the flavouring of the food was boosted by spices, the greater the reaction of the taste buds and the sense of well-being. These feelings would help to explain the love of spices and the search for new and ever more exotic tastes in the Roman Empire.

The spice trade was one of the oldest known to the ancient world and, long before the Roman era, the routes were already established. The Queen of Sheba came 'to Jerusalem with a very great train with camels that bare many spices and very much gold and precious stones' (1 Kings 10.2). When she left she gave King Solomon 'an hundred and twenty talents of gold and of spices very great store; there came no more such abundance of spices as these which the Queen of Sheba gave to King Solomon' (1 Kings 10.10). The coupling of spices with gold and precious stones indicates the value given to this commodity.

Once the Romans conquered Egypt, they had access to a vast emporium of spices but had to rely on Arabian merchants who controlled the trade from Asia. Pliny complained that, by the time pepper reached Rome, it was a hundred times its original price. In AD 24 the Emperor Augustus tried to break the trading monopoly by ordering Aelius Gallus, prefect of Egypt, to use troops stationed in Egypt to try to gain access to the overland trading routes hitherto kept secret from Rome. Gallus mismanaged the expedition. He refused to make contact with the merchants who knew the routes and took his troops along the unhealthy coastal area, rather than seek out the more healthy inland parts. Strabo noted that sickness, fatigue and hunger defeated the troops rather than the enemy. Later, however, as Suetonius reported, emissaries from India came to Rome having heard of the fame of Augustus, so that trade with India began to increase, including that of the precious pepper.

During the reign of the emperor Claudius, the wind system of the monsoon was elucidated by a Greek merchant, Hippalus, who sailed from the Red Sea to the Indian Ocean. As the south-west monsoon prevailed from April to October and the north-east from October to April, it became possible to sail from the Egyptian port of Berenice on the Red Sea to Calicut in India in 70 days and to make the return voyage within a year. This reduced Roman dependency on the Arabian overland routes so that direct trade between Rome and India expanded. After AD 90 when an unknown writer produced the *Periplus of the Erythraean Sea,* detailing the harbours, sea conditions and safest routes of the trade between the Mediterranean and the East, it was clear that the Arabian monopoly had been broken. New products in ever increasing quantities appeared in the markets of Rome; her curiosity and interest in the spice trade was insatiable. Soon spices would be distributed throughout the Empire and imported into Britain.

Oriental spices, especially pepper, played a great part in Roman cuisine. Pliny mentions both black and white pepper and a special long pepper. Apicius added pepper to most of his dishes, even those of a sweet confection such as custard made of milk, eggs and honey. Someone at Vindolanda had ordered and bought pepper worth two *denarii*, which seems an expensive purchase. It could be that this was not to be used as a condiment but as the basis for another commodity. Other spices known to the Romans include ginger, cassia, cinnamon and saffron but there is no direct evidence for their use in

Britain. A claim has been made for saffron, but the legend is that this plant was smuggled into Britain in the fourteenth century, either by a crusader or a pilgrim from the Holy Land, who carried a corm back in the hollow of his staff. By the sixteenth century it was commonly cultivated in Essex, giving its name to the town Saffron Walden. The value of saffron to the Romans is indicated by the fact that saffron from Arabia was priced at 2000 *denarii* a Roman pound in Diocletian's Edict of AD 301, and even that from Africa cost 600 *denarii*. That compared with a pound of black pepper at four *denarii* and white pepper at seven *denarii*.

Black and white mustard seeds, used as a spice or a condiment, have been found at Silchester and London. Apicius mixed crushed mustard with honey, oil and vinegar to form a dressing. Coriander was known in Britain in the Late Bronze Age. It is not a native plant, but it could grow in Britain and produce ripe seeds in the British climate, so that some of the finds may be from local plants. The Romans used it a great deal to flavour food; its seeds have been found at York, Silchester, London, Caerwent, Godmanchester (Cambridgeshire) and Colchester. In herbal medicine it is used to aid digestion and relieve colic as well as being a narcotic. The Colchester shop, burnt in the Boudiccan destruction, also provided evidence of dill and poppy seeds.

The evidence from the second-century fort of Bearsden on the Antonine Wall, mentioned previously, provided faecal remains of coriander and opium poppy seeds. Those coriander fragments paralleled those crushed by pestle and mortar, a method which releases the aromatic substances. Pliny gave an example of mixing barley with coriander and salt and mentioned that poppy seeds were sprinkled on top of the crusts of country loaves, first brushed with egg to make them stick. Cato mentioned *globi*, a kind of cheese bread, spread with honey and sprinkled with poppy seeds. Similar faecal material has been found at the Lancaster fort and at military sites in Germany, especially the forts of Neuss and Welzheim. Poppy seeds have also been found at civilian sites in Britain.

Salt

If spices were regarded as essential for flavourings in Roman cookery, salt was a necessity in culinary preparation and was the most efficient preservative known at that time. It also ensured that the proper flavour-producing organisms developed in bacon, ham, cheese and fish products. These were also accentuated by the use of spices. Salt is a natural drying agent, which draws water out of a product by osmosis. Food could be rubbed with it, placed in strong brine or put in casks between layers of salt and pressed with stones so that the natural juices flowed out. Only good meat and good salt would ensure a decent result, because poor quality salt will not penetrate meat quickly enough and the inner part will deteriorate before the salt or brine reaches the centre. Salt and brine can also be used to preserve fish. Pliny said that the best salt must be sharp and dry and added that salt was indispensable to all civilised life, but rather surprisingly saw it as an agreeable condiment rather than a necessary food.

The Romans kept salt production under imperial control organised by a Procurator, although extraction and distribution could be leased out to private contractors as may have happened in Cheshire. The distribution of salt was carefully regulated, and it might have been difficult to obtain a regular supply in some places without access to official sources. Evidence of imperial control in one area of Britain is suggested by an increase of population in the Fenland region after AD 120, when the forms of settlement seem to have been laid out at the behest of a central administration. Salt production may have been exploited by order of the Emperor Hadrian during his visit to Britain. The natural watercourses would provide an ideal means of transporting a heavy cargo of salt.

Evidence of Imperial salt works elsewhere comes from a human story in the 49th book of Justinian's *Digest of Roman Law,* where Sextus Pomponius, a second-century jurist, quotes a case from Britain. A slave belonging to the centurion, Marcus Cocceius Firmus, whose service in the Second Augustan Legion is recorded on an inscription at Auchendavy (Strathclyde), had committed some crime which meant she was condemned to hard labour in the salt works. Later she was captured by bandits and sold as a trading commodity to slave traders. Cocceius eventually bought her back, but after litigation the money was returned to him by the Imperial Treasury. Presumably it was held that the owners of the salt works should have been more diligent, while she was under their control, and they were responsible for her safe return to the centurion, when she had finished her sentence. The mines, and this may mean salt works, would have been within reach of Auchendavy, perhaps on the Fife coast.

Sodium chloride is one of the minerals essential to human and animal life. Part of a man's pay could be made in salt, hence the term *salarium* or salt money. The buying of salt at times became part of the taxation system. In Rome the salt box was kept under careful guard and Horace implies that it was an ancestral heirloom. Apicius declared that aromatic salts prevented all diseases and relieved colds; they aided the digestion and moved the bowels. In this case he might be referring to sodium chloride containing magnesium sulphate (Epsom Salts). Diocletian's edict in AD 301 gave a price of 100 *denarii* for a *castrensis modius* (about 8 pints), the amount which Cato suggested should serve one person for a year.

In Britain salt was obtained both in the Iron Age and Roman periods from evaporation methods along the coast and from inland brine springs. The former method would provide sea salt, which included the trace element iodine. Coastal areas of salt production extending from Lincolnshire round the coast to Dorset can be identified by saltern sites, where broken pottery, clay supports and baked clay pans or hollows have been excavated. These were normally associated with settlement sites where workers were housed. The majority of the Lincolnshire ones seem to have been most active during the first two centuries AD.

Saltern sites, called 'Red Hills', are prolific in Essex. Over 150 have been found formed of debris from salt production. Seawater was run into flat clay-lined tanks and allowed to evaporate into a more concentrated brine, which was then placed in iron pans. These were placed on fire-bars over beds of glowing charcoal and kept simmering to crystallise the salt, which was scooped out periodically. Packing into containers provided cakes of salt. At one site there had been an extractive industry of 150 boiling hearths. Amphorae of wine, brought to the works to slake the thirst of the salt workers or their masters, were later used as containers for the crystalline salt. Salt was also transported in pots sealed with pitch or clay, in barrels or in leather sacks.

On the north Kent marshes the presence of lead in the salt indicates that a lead container was used for heating the brine, a somewhat dangerous procedure, for this added lead to a diet. Excavation of the saltern sites on the Lincolnshire fen edge indicated that kiln-type structures were built of tiers of evaporating dishes supported on briquetage stands. At Denver (Norfolk) feeder channels led into ditches where the water was naturally evaporated to become a concentrated brine; this could be heated on surface hearths. Slow heating produces crystals; fast heating, followed by rapid cooling, produces fine grains. In the mediaeval period egg-white was added to brine to produce a thick scum, which allowed impurities to be skimmed off easily. Investigation of some of the Roman briquetage at East Huntshill (Somerset) revealed traces of protein, as if a similar method had been used.

This method of producing salt is a seasonal activity, which is best carried out between March and August or the shorter period April to June, when high tides are followed by the highest sea and air temperatures, the most hours of sunshine and the least rainfall. It can be a hazardous industry if salt gets into cuts and wounds. Usually it was combined with another industry, such as pottery making or cattle ranching, so that tanning of leather could be carried out on the spot.

Many of the extensive salt-producing sites on the south and south-east coasts, especially in Hampshire and Sussex, were abandoned in the late second century. It has been suggested that those round Essex may have been suppressed by landowners unwilling to allow industrial production to continue near their handsome new villas. But this period coincides with an increase in the exploitation of the brine springs in the midland area. It is also possible that trade transferred to other areas including Cornwall, the marshes of the Fenlands and the Somerset levels, all of which show evidence of increased production at this time.

Inland, salt was produced at Droitwich (West Midlands) and at Middlewich (Cheshire), which are both called *Salinae* in the *Ravenna Cosmography*. At Droitwich a large curving ditch was found to contain many cow and sheep skulls, perhaps the skeletal remains of a by-product industry, the pickling of beef and mutton in brine. The skins would be used in a leather industry. Barrels found nearby may have held the brine or been containers prepared for the transport of salt. This industry, however, also seems to have faltered in the second century, and it was in Cheshire that greater activity took place.

A salt industry was established at Middlewich in the late Iron Age and the Romans quickly took advantage of this. During the late first and early second century, an early earth and timber fort was built, occupied by an auxiliary regiment, *Ala Classiana Civium Romanorum*, to guard the industry and control the native salt exploitation of the industry. Recent excavation has revealed that different types of kilns and hearths were in use from AD 80 until the fourth century. Experimental archaeology has revealed that some of the kilns could reach temperatures of 800-1000 degrees centigrade, well above the 150 degrees needed to produce clear crystals. One salt workshop, dating from AD 100-60, seems to have had brine pits, kilns for salt evaporation and a supply of amphorae (**27**). These could have been used as packaging, but one amphora had the graffito *AMURCO* scrawled on it — 'waste from brine', which the excavators suggested referred to the storage of brine or the liquid left over from the salt-boiling process. The jar had originally contained wine imported from southern Spain.

27 *Salt pans showing a method probably used in Roman Britain. Shallow evaporation pans were filled with brine. A fire was lit underneath to evaporate the water and crystallise the salt. After crystallization, the salt was scraped from the pans and packed into jars or bags ready for transportation*

Salt pans have also been found at Nantwich and Northwich. At Nantwich a plank-built tank or box, sunk into a pit, was either a brine container or a crib for supporting lead pans. Two such pans, also found at Nantwich, could be supported over the tank on a stretcher or by ropes. Another suggestion was that the box might have been a well-head for the brine springs, which rise locally and contain deposits of rock salt dissolved in spring water from the topmost layers of the salt bed.

Fragments of a salt pan found at Shavington (Cheshire) measured 100cm (39in) by 96cm (38in) by 14cm (5.5in) when restored and weighed about 118kg (260lb). Marks on it indicate attempts to remove pan-scale, deposits of calcium and magnesium sulphate. Failure to remove this would lead to 'furring up' of the pans and over-heating. The salt industry was well organised and seems to have spread into the surrounding river valleys. From Middlewich, salt-ways probably crossed the Pennines, going north and east, part of a series of trackways known to have been used by packhorses bearing salt until the nineteenth century.

Honey

Honey had been collected in prehistoric Britain where one of its chief uses was as the basis of mead. In the Roman world Columella, Varro and Virgil were eager to give advice on bee-keeping. In Britain possibly the most common form of hives were those made of baskets, wood and withies, which would leave no trace and could easily be moved. Thus heather honey, for example, could be obtained in summer from the upland regions. So-called pottery hives, previously identified at the Iron Age site of Casterley Camp (Wiltshire) and the Roman villa of Rockbourne (Isle of Wight), are now thought to be storage jars. In not having such hives, British beekeepers might be thought to be following the advice of Columella that earthenware hives were the worst possible because they are 'burnt by the heat of the summers and frozen by the winter's cold'. This was proved at the experimental Iron Age site of Little Butser, where bees kept in these hives did not survive cold winters.

Honey was used as sugar would be used today, either as a sweetener or to correct a sharp or sour taste; it would also supply a source of instant energy as it contains liquid glucose, an effective digestible form of sugar. It could be spread over meat or fish during the cooking process, as it removes an oily taste. Smeared over meat honey acts as a preservative and Apicius advised that honey and defructum will also preserve quinces and other fruit. The Romans used it to sweeten wine; Virgil used the phrase 'to soften the wine's harsh flavour' and this would be particularly appropriate with young or rough wine. Apicius recommended spiced honey wine 'which keeps for ever' for people going on a journey. A traveller could take such a wine in a leather bag if a pottery jar was inconvenient. Honey was added to beer in large quantities to produce mead.

Honey was prized by Pliny and Celsus for its antibacterial properties. Modern research has proved its effectiveness to treat *salmonella* and *staphylococcus* bacteria. Its antibiotic property is said to be due to hydrogen peroxide, one of the products of a glucose-oxidising enzyme secreted by the pharyngeal glands of the bee. The fact that it is hypertonic, meaning that it draws water from bacterial cells causing them to die, has ensured that the use of honey to treat wounds continued until the twentieth century. Its use as a decongestant is well-known. One of the Vindolanda writing tablets recorded the purchase of a modius (8.6 litres, 1.9 galls.) of honey. This was suggested to have been bought for its medicinal purposes, very appropriate if it was intended for the hospital. Graffiti on a storage jar at Southwark recorded 24 *librae* of honey equivalent to 8.6 litres presumably the standard weight for a container of this commodity.

Two-handled pots with holes in the bottom, found at Silchester and Templeborough, may be containers for the combs, allowing honey to drop through into a collecting dish placed below. Honey can also be strained through a bag of loosely woven withies; these, of course, would leave no trace.

8 Olive oil and liquamen

Olive oil

Posidonius, as reported in Athenaeus' *Deipnosophistae*, stated that the Celts did not use olive oil because of its scarcity and because its taste appeared unpleasant to them. However, amphorae sherds of the type of container used for olive oil have been found on a large number of Iron Age sites dating to the last decades of the first century BC. These sites include Owslebury (Hampshire), Prae Wood (Hertfordshire), Hengistbury Head (Dorset), and Poundbury, and some of the amphorae in the Welwyn-style burials may have been of this type. Six amphorae from Spain were present in the Mont Bures grave (Essex) and two in one of the Stanfordbury (Bedfordshire) graves.

Its use may indicate a change of dietary habits and its versatility was quickly realised for it could be used for lighting, sealing wood and lubrication. In the army, according to Livy, it was rubbed on the limbs in the belief that it made them supple and gave protection against the cold. Frontinus indicated that it could be used to ease the metal joints on armour. Pliny said that a 'happy life was one that used wine inside and olive oil outside' and advised that it should be used within a year.

Olive oil, in distinctive globular amphorae from southern Spain, was being sent to the Wessex and Hertfordshire regions in the late Iron Age. It came exclusively from the Guadalquivir Valley in Baetica, and this area continued to dominate the British import trade until the third century AD. Early imports of this type of olive oil were sent to Sheepen, Verulamium, London and Skeleton Green (Hertfordshire). The Spanish Baetican trade, supplemented by imports from Tarraconensis, reached its peak in the second century AD, although it was to continue for another century. Spanish oil seems to have been one of the requisitioned goods supplied to the army by the state, hence its frequency on military sites. It had reached the Nantstallon fort (Cornwall) by AD 55. Spanish amphorae have been found at Silchester, many bearing stamps of the pottery makers or shippers on the handles. Some bear the names of owners of the estates where the oil was produced: L Junius Melissus (who may also have shipped wine) and G Antonius Quietus were two of the suppliers of olive oil in the second century AD.

Spanish supplies declined in the third century because of the barbarian invasion of the Iberian peninsular. They were overtaken by the North African trade, which had begun to export to Britain in the first century AD and later received encouragement from the Emperor Septimius Severus (193-211) who came from North Africa. The African amphorae were recognisable by being trimmed with a knife and could hold up to 76 litres (17 galls). Canterbury and Chester were some of the many sites receiving oil from this source. London, which had received oil from Spain, moved almost entirely to the North

*28 Amphora from Tarraconensis, Spain, found in the Thames. This contained 6000 olives.
National Maritime Museum, Greenwich, London*

African supplies by the third century and also sent them to its hinterland; Holborough (Kent) received oil from the Algerian region. Some oil also came from the eastern Mediterranean.

The top of a mid-first-century amphora found in London bore an inscription which indicated that it had contained green olives transported by Gaius A.... L.... under the control of Avernus. The figures CCL 250 may represent its capacity in *cyathi*. As one *cyathus* equalled 0.0456 litres (0.01 galls), the amphora would have held the equivalent of 11.4 litres (2½ galls). A multi-perforated jar at Poundbury may have been used to strain olives. Olive oil stones have been found at York, Colchester, Caerleon and London, but a Tarraconensis amphora recovered intact from Pan Sand in the Thames Estuary contained 6,000 olive stones which indicates the large quantity of olives that an amphora could hold (**28 & colour plate 9**). It was suggested that the original total had been at least 6,500, and that the amphora had contained at least two varieties of olives, one of which, the Posian, a large fleshy fruit, was especially commended for its eating qualities by Columella. Unfortunately the fisherman who found the amphora had drilled a hole through the neck and poured away the fluid. Sugar detected in the remains could have been part of the fermentation process or a means of preservation, possibly *defrutum*, into which the olives had been placed. The olives would take up the flavour of the medium into which they had been put.

In spite of North African imports there was a major decline in the trade in the third century, possibly because the needs of the army had lessened. By that time more troops were serving from the northern parts of the empire, so the desire for a Mediterranean type of food may have lessened. Olive oil had become more of a luxury than a necessity, and traders were discouraged by the disruption of trade because of the troubles of the Gallic Empire and the usurpation of Britain by Carausius (AD 260-73).

Liquamen, garum and allec

Salted fish products were introduced into Britain by the Romans. Parts of fish normally considered as refuse were made into fish sauce of which there were four kinds — liquamen, garum, muria and allec. Liquamen was made by placing whole fish in troughs or pits and mixing them with salt. The mixture was left to ferment for anything up to six months. As the process, which is enzymic proteolysis or the reaction which takes place when the guts of fish react with salt to produce brine, often took place in the open, the sun would hasten the process. The liquid (liquamen) would be drained off and put into amphorae. Allec or hallec can be the most precisely identified as being the thick sediment left when most liquid is drawn off. Pliny labelled it as being the sediment of garum. Liquamen and garum, according to Crocock and Grainger, were distinct products, garum being the most expensive, a blackish blood sauce made mainly from mackerel. Muria was the term for a pale fish brine.. Martial considered it as an inferior product made of the entrails of fish other than mackerel, mostly of tunny.

Curtis, in his intensive study of these products had proposed that garum was a clear liquid, liquamen was weaker in salinity and colour and muria was the solution drawn off after salting the fish; allec was the mushy substance containing bone and other parts which did not rot. Some Romans were very particular as to the product; Pliny reported that Apicius made his from the livers of red mullet. Pliny stated that garum can be made from any fish, but mackerel (*scomber*) was the most popular. Other writers suggest tunny and anchovies, even sea urchins, oysters and other shellfish. Liquamen can be considered akin to the fish sauces used today in the Far East: Filipino *patis*, Vietnamese *nuoc-mam* and Thai *nahm-pla,* though *nahm-pla* tastes more of salt than fish. Allec is akin to the fish paste *blachan* used in South-East Asia.

Both liquamen and garum could be made in any quantities provided that a precise ratio of salt to fish was observed and that the produce was allowed to mature for the required time. The ratio could be between 5:1 and 1:1. (Thai *nahm-pla* has a 1:1 ratio). Each production area would have its own distinct taste, which could be due to a variety of factors. The obvious ones are the addition of wine, added at a ratio of 2:1, herbs and spices. The freshness of the fish, the length of preparation time, the quality and quantity of the salt and the temperature could all produce different results.

Liquamen once had an undeserved reputation amongst some modern writers. One wrote 'the Romans drenched their subtly conceived dishes with garum, alec and other sauces, which were so strong that it would have been hardly possible to distinguish a fresh fish from a putrefied cat — except by the bones'. This seems harsh. The Romans used it far more subtly in every kind of dish, savoury or sweet. Serving both as a food and a medicinal product, it may have provided some salt needed for a healthy diet. Apicius has a recipe for patina of pears — pears pounded with pepper, honey, cumin, liquamen and a little oil, then combined with eggs to make a kind of custard. When baked it has a sharp aromatic taste. The frequent mention of liquamen in Apicius's cookery book indicates that it was an acceptable part of Roman culinary taste, being used to enhance a flavour, increase the salt content or possibly to disguise a tainted taste. In a fish recipe liquamen served the purpose of a fish stock; in the case of other ingredients, the aim was to act as a blend for the disparate flavours. Worcestershire sauce, which has a basis of anchovy and vinegar, uses an ingredient idential to one used by a liquamen derivative, *oxyporum*, which helps to promote easy digestion of food.

André suggests that liquamen was the term used at the beginning of the empire and later superseded by garum. A medieval Greek farming manual, *The Geoponica,* gives a number of recipes detailing liquamen as being a liquid made from the salted entrails of small fish, such as sprats, red mullet and anchovies. In Bythynia anchovies were impregnated with salt, then placed in an open vessel and stirred at intervals for two to three months. If mixed with sufficient salt, placed in the sun and allowed to marinate for a few months, the mixture of fish, their innards and blood did not putrefy. Instead fermentation produced the bacteria which allowed the fish to dissolve.

If hallec or allec was the residue of liquamen, then it might also have contained small fish which otherwise would have been wasted. Sometimes oysters and sea urchins were included. According to Pliny, allec was used for a variety of purposes, including cures for burns, ulcers or pains in the mouth or ears, as well as alleviating dog and crocodile bites. It could also be mixed with *mulsum* until it was sweet enough to drink. Horace spoke of it as an hors d'oeuvre to stimulate the appetite.

Such an important ingredient in Roman cookery was not to be excluded from the province of Britain. Its presence is detected in the remains of amphorae and in the inscriptions painted on their sides (**29**). Soon after the Conquest, Colchester imported amphorae containing it, together with high-salt marine foodstuffs. One inscription on an amphora identified the contents as the product of Proculus and Urbicus, who were known by similar amphorae inscriptions to be supplying fish sauce to Pompeii before AD 79. York imported the fish sauce of Postumus; Chester favoured a sauce from Baetica made from mackerel fish tails. Merchants and traders imported it into London, storing their amphorae on the waterfront. In the first half of the second century, Gloucester received Spanish garum amphorae amounting to 30 per cent of the total amphorae importation. A painted inscription on the neck of an amphora reads *G III C,* which may be taken to read *G(ari) IIII C(ongii),* four *congii* of garum, that is 13.13 litres (2.9 galls).

Even more detailed information was given on an inscription on an amphora from the Poultry excavations in London. This contained '80 measures of fermented fish sauce matured two years from tunny of best quality, the product of Gaius Asicius Probus'. The name Asicius is known in Cadiz, which was well situated to take advantage of the seasonal migration of tunny through the Straits of Gibraltar. Diocletian's price edict of AD 301 gives two qualities of liquamen; the second quality sold for 12 *denarii* an Italian pint and the first or best quality sold for 16 *denarii* (for comparative wages at that time, stone masons, blacksmiths and bakers each earned 50 *denarii* a day). Another amphora from Southwark was inscribed *LIQUAM/ANTIPOL/EXC/I TETTE AFRI/CANI* followed by, in cursive script, *AFRI,* which indicated that it contained Lucius Tettius Africanus' finest fish sauce from Antinopolis (Antibes) in Gaul. Both the London finds suggest one supply route was from the Mediterranean along the Rhone, through Gaul and across the Channel, following the route taken by the wine trade. Another was along the Atlantic coasts of Spain and Gaul.

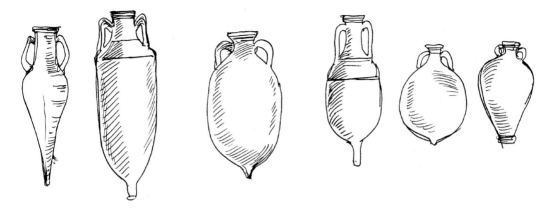

29 Different forms of amphorae found in Britain. Left to right: Rhodian, North African, Spanish, Gaulish, Spanish, Gaulish

Army supply lines ensured that one of the necessary foods of the Romans reached the troops at forts throughout Britain. At Vindolanda, muria was named on a writing tablet as one of the supplies disbursed to the commanding officer's household in June, sometime between AD 97–103, possibly for a religious festival. On another tablet, a slave of Julius Verecundus, Prefect of the First Cohort of Tungrians, is said to have received together with his other supplies eight *sextarii* (2 litres) of fish sauce.

At Kingsnorth on the Isle of Grain (Kent), a pottery works making Upchurch ware also made amphorae. This site seems to have been a transhipment site for garum, which was put into the amphorae and taken elsewhere. At Canterbury, however, importation ceased in the mid-second century and in London somewhat later. The product was replaced for a while by African products, but this does not seem to have been adequate. By then the taste had been acquired to such an extent Britain had to produce its own variety to satisfy demand. Excavations on the Roman waterfront in London have uncovered a mid-third-century re-used fish sauce amphora of a type associated with herring and sprat indigenous to northern waters. There were also remains in a wooden trough, in use from the early to the mid-third century, forming a 80mm (3in) layer of between 3500-6000 herring and 800-1500 sprats, together with bass, flounder and sand eels. This site was suggested to be that of a local garum industry. Another may have been situated at York where a late Roman deposit of fish debris, about 8mm (3in) deep, containing 35 per cent herring and 25 per cent sprats, again implies an enterprise producing fish sauce for the local market.

Excavations on the fourth-century Lincoln waterfront revealed a large deposit of sand eels. This could be fishmongers' waste from the gutting of marine predators such as cod and haddock — quite possible as the River Witham is navigable this far. But the deposit may have been raw material for allec. Pliny noted that allec was produced from very small fish otherwise economically useless. On the other hand the remains might be the result of disposing of spoilt garum. If the waterfront was indeed the site of processing industries it must have been dominated by a strong putrid smell, which in a late Byzantine text is linked to that of very ripe cheese. Seneca was even more derogatory; liquamen imported into Rome from the provinces, he says, 'burns up the stomach with salted putrefaction'.

Fragments of amphorae containing fish sauces have been found mainly on military and urban sites; very few have been found in a rural context. This might mean that the condiment was not popular with the inhabitants of villas and settlements. The rural population, however, could have bought smaller quantities from local markets. Whether this was confined to Roman administrators and those members of the British elite who wished to emulate what they considered to be sophisticated tastes or whether the Romano-British population had acquired a taste for this condiment is unknown.

9 Wine, beer and water

Wine

Wine was popular both for drinking and as an ingredient in cooking. Wine had been imported in the Iron Age, when traders established a limited market amongst certain tribes in Southern Britain. Wine was consumed heartily in Gaul. Roman writers commented on the quantity drunk by the Celts and of the violence which could occur because the Celts preferred to drink their wine without water. Diodorus said disapprovingly: 'They are exceedingly fond of wine and sate themselves with the unmixed wine imported by merchants; their desire makes them drink greedily. When they became drunk they fall into a stupor or into a maniacal disposition'. He adds that as they drink their fulsome moustaches 'act as it were a kind of strainer'.

The Celts drank their wine neat, while the Romans preferred to dilute it with water because this would delay the onset of drunkenness. Pliny declared sourly that 'nothing is more detrimental to our pleasure if moderation be lacking'. In a paean of praise, however, he describes wine as 'a tonic to the stomach and a sharpener of the appetite'. It checked vomiting, expelled urine and dulled sorrow and anxiety. Diodorus records that 'many Italian merchants with their usual love of lucre look on the Gallic love of wine as their treasure trove … [they] receive in return for it an incredibly large price; for one jar of wine they receive in return a slave, a servant in exchange for a drink.' This may not be as dear as it sounds; captured tribesmen were easily enslaved and a slave would not be an excessive price for an amphora of wine.

Excavations at the Iron Age fort of Hengistbury Head (Dorset) have produced 40 vessels which could have contained imported wine. The quantity was small, being the equivalent of only 720 litres (158 galls) over some 50 years but it provided a privileged existence for the recipients. The Welwyn-style tombs (Hertfordshire) contain amphorae indicating quite clearly that the Celtic aristocracy intended to drink wine in the next world (**colour plate 10**). The Lexden tumulus (Essex) contained 17 amphorae, with some once containing wine imported from Pompeii. One amphora held 22 litres (4.8 galls). The Mount Bures, Snailwell (Cambridgeshire) and Stanfordbury graves contain Spanish amphorae. These not only indicate the liking for wine but also the importance of the emerging Spanish wine trade in pre-Roman Britain.

Amphorae fragments from different countries found at the pre-Conquest Roman fort site at Sheepen, Colchester, indicate that large quantities of wine were entering Britain by AD 5 and that after the Conquest the site was supplied from at least 19 different sources. These included Italy (Latium and the fine Falerian wine of Campania), the Iberian province, Rhodes and southern Gaul. Wines from Pompeii were imported before the

30 Large pottery jars packed in straw and carried on a cart in Italy, early twentieth century. A similar method could have been used to transport amphorae through Roman Britain

supply was abruptly terminated by the volcanic eruption in AD 79. Canterbury also seems to have been importing wine from Italy towards the end of the first century BC.

Different areas produced different shapes of amphorae and these shapes altered throughout the centuries so that it is reasonably easy for archaeologists to discover the origin and date of amphorae. The amphora was the most convenient form of container, ungainly to look at, but useful for stacking and easily portable horizontally or vertically in

31 Man carrying an amphora over his shoulder. Mosaic in Square of the Corporations, Ostia

wicker or straw packing (**30**). The jars could be sealed with pottery bungs such as the two found at Sheepen or by cork bungs secured by mortar; one such bung, found at Silchester, had a gash on it where a tool had prized it out. On the underside of it there is still a speck of resin. Two men could carry an amphora slung from a pole with ropes through the handles, as seen on a relief from Augst, or one man could carry it on his shoulder, as portrayed on a mosaic in the Square of the Corporations at Ostia (**31**).

Amphorae could be heavy, up to a capacity of 80 litres (17.6 galls). The usual capacity was between 25-30 litres (5.5-6.6 galls), which would give a weight of 25-30kg (55-66lb). The spike on the base was an aid to lifting (**32**), and it enabled a wine merchant to place the container upright in a hole in the ground. A shipload of amphorae might weigh up to 350 tons, and the unloading would require hard labour and skill, especially if the ships were moored against a quayside on a rising or falling tide.

Wine was of varying quality not only because of where it was produced but because the grapes went through a series of pressings. The Romans took viticulture and the making of wine very seriously. Columella discussed the economics of wine-making in great detail and Pliny gave information on the taste and appearance of wine when the grapes undergo four pressings. The fourth pressing produced a vinegary wine (*posca*), which was mixed with water as a beverage for soldiers and slaves. This was probably the type of wine which the soldier offered in a sponge to Christ at his crucifixion. This has been regarded as a gesture of contempt because it was handed up on a sponge, almost certainly a toilet sponge

32 Amphorae in the Römisch-Germanisches Zentralmuseum, Mainz

cleaned for the purpose. But it was none the less the most practical way of conveying wine to a thirsty, dying man on a cross.

Some wines were softened with gypsum or lime, or had fruit juice, herbs, spices or honey added to them. One drink, *conditum* — wine and hot water with the addition of honey, pepper and spices — was a popular wine in Roman bars (*popinae*). In several bars at Ostia, the port of Rome, were found pestles and mortars used for grinding the spices. Aristotle recommended wine heated with spices as a remedy for intemperance, while Pliny and Cato advocated oil of black myrtle in wine. A hangover is basically an upset stomach and dehydration, so spiced wine could have served as a pick-me-up, a hair-of-the-dog cure. Wormwood was a favourite addition, usually prescribed on medical grounds as it was by the Greek physician, Dioscorides, in his *De Materia Medica* (*c.*AD 78). Wormwood produces a bitter taste creating a wine somewhat like modern vermouth. Other wines would gain a distinctive flavour from the interior coatings of bitumen, wood pitch or resin in the amphorae. Pitch was used to make the amphorae impervious. Pliny recounted a method of coating the interior with pitch where the pottery was heated to a high temperature, the resin poured in and the amphora rolled on its side until the entire interior surface had been coated. To cleanse a vessel, it was washed out with seawater; ashes or potter's earth were sprinkled inside and the interior was rubbed with myrrh. This mixture probably did little for the wine. Silchester received wares of this quality, as many amphorae fragments were found coated with pitch.

Wines were not intended to be laid down for long periods and were probably drunk within two or three years. As well as wine from the different regions, there were both acidic and sweeter wines. Wine could also be reduced to form *defrutum*. Varro and Columella said that this was made by reducing it to one-third of its volume, Pliny to one-half. Palladius said that *defrutum* is ready when the wine is reduced to a thick consistency; when it has lost one-third of its volume he defines it as *caraenum* and *sapa* when it has lost two-thirds. *Mulsum* was the name given to wine mixed with honey, and *must* to *defrutum* boiled down to thick consistency. As this was often done in lead pans, some degree of lead poisoning was inevitable. It was added to poor or bitter wine to improve the quality.

Amphorae sherds from London prove that by AD 50 wine was being brought up the Thames to what was an increasingly important port. At first wine came from Italy, including the Pompeian and Campanian wines, and later from Southern Gaul, Rhodes and Spain. Rhodian wines included a dessert wine, and the Spanish Baetican and Tarraconensian wines were highly regarded. A named vintage was marked on an amphora from Italy: Falernian wine from the vineyard of Lollius had arrived from the Campania region. Canterbury seems to have received wine continuously from the late first century BC onwards, mainly from Italy and Spain, but with a little from Eastern Mediterranean and the Dodecanese. By the late third century, however, North Africa had become the main source of supply, replacing the Spanish wine trade.

In London one amphora had the date *V(KAL A)PRILIS* (5 April) scratched on it; on another was recorded the quantity *VIIS VIMI* (7½ measures). The taste for life's luxuries continued in London even as the Roman Empire crumbled in the fifth century. A piece of amphora found in a large house in Lower Thames Street was certainly from the eastern Mediterranean and possibly from Gaza. Wine was still being imported from these places to satisfy customers as supplies nearer to Britain had been disrupted by barbarian invasions in Gaul, Spain and Italy.

Sometimes the name of the shipper or the estate owner appears on the amphora. A piece of an amphora found at Silchester has the name Lucius Junius Melissus painted on it; he is known to have exported wine from Spain. To Colchester in the first century AD came Falerian wine of good quality from the Campanian Region; this had been bottled by Lollius, according to the painted inscription. Some wine from Rhodes was less good, a kind of *vin ordinaire*. Pliny reports that it could be mixed with seawater and be left up to seven years in barrels. It is no wonder that he warns that this wine could be injurious to health.

Wine was sent to the forts as a matter of course. Kingsholm, an early fort founded about AD 47 and later replaced by Gloucester, received wine almost exclusively from Rhodes, until it was abandoned in the mid AD 60s. This might have been the result of a revolt in Rhodes in the Emperor Claudius' reign (AD 41-54). The citizens were punished by being incorporated into the Roman province of Asia in AD 44 and having their supplies confiscated. Some of the wine surpluses were probably distributed to military garrisons in the provinces, as the *vin ordinaire* was deemed suitable for the troops. Some of this wine seems to have been distributed at Colchester, but one amphora coated with resin and inscribed on its neck *Leg II Aug* had contained raisin wine, the sweeter wine. The best raisin wine, according to Pliny, came from Crete, but Martial called it the poor man's *mulsum*. Rhodian wine could also contain figs or honey. The Colchester wine, however,

33 Roman barrel found at Silchester. It was reused in the lining of a well

may have been a raisin wine of the first pressing and thus suitable for export. Wine from southern Spain reached the troops at Carlisle and Catterick. Two amphorae inscribed Borus and Rufus may have been marked by soldiers anxious to secure their property.

At Carpow the Sixth Legion seems to have been supplied with a medicated wine. One amphora had written on it part of the Greek word *prasion* (horehound), a noted remedy for the cough complaints no doubt endemic in the colder northern region. Horehound comes from marrubiin, a bitter oil contained in the stem and leaves of the plant. It acts as an expectorant and was recommended by Pliny and Celsus as a cure for coughs and chest complaints. A piece of an amphora from Caerleon was marked *AMINE*. This would have contained Aminean wine, one of the best quality wines in Italy. It was, however, recommended as a cure for diarrhoea and as relief from a cold. No doubt it was appreciated by the garrison.

Wine was also contained in barrels. Pliny gave examples of their use in the Alps and Strabo referred to their use in the northern Italian wine trade in the reign of Augustus. London received wine in barrels of silver fir, cedar and larch, evidence of long-distance trade, which reached its peak in the early second century. Many had a secondary purpose, being reused as linings for wells. One large barrel with 18 staves made of silver fir found in the German alpine region had held 550 litres (120 galls). On one stave were the letters *CEGRC,* probably the name of the shipper. Other barrels had a capacity of 1000 litres (220 galls). Silchester imported barrels from Aquitainia (**33**), and barrels also came from the Rhineland. A stave of silver fir from a wine barrel made in southern Gaul was found at Carlisle, marked 'property of Novixius', and another at York had been fitted into part of a bucket.

Some staves had numbers on them. At Silchester the staves of one barrel were numbered from I to XVIII and the name *VERCTISSAE* (of Vertissa) stamped on seven of them. Another had the name Sulinus on it, either the name of the cooper or a shipper of wine. The capacity of two of the Silchester barrels has been estimated at 880 litres (194 galls) and 930 litres (205 galls). These would probably have been transferred by water from London to a landing stage near to Silchester.

Staves of barrels found at Vindolanda had branded inscriptions and graffiti on them, indicating that the majority of the containers originated in Gaul or the Rhineland. One has

34 Roman bireme with ram and 22 oars on each side carrying a cargo of wine barrels on its fighting deck. Tombstone from Neumagen in the Rheinisches Landesmuseum, Trier. The deceased was indicating that he had supplied wine to the troops, because the labour needed to row such a vessel would have been too expensive in relation to the cost of the cargo

the graffito *DOLVLI*. This seems to be *DOLIOLI* or little cask, which merely described the barrel. These barrels were probably reused by brewers of Celtic beer situated at Vindolanda.

It is possible that wine produced in one region and transported in amphorae was decanted into barrels to be exported to or moved within the British province in larger containers. A passage in Caesar's *Gallic Wars* indicates that barrels were used in Gaul in the first century BC. If this method was part of the Gallic export trade it is therefore by no means certain that all the wine came from one source. Blended wines were a distinct possibility and a Trade Descriptions Act was not part of the legal system.

Wine was also transported in bottles of various forms. Cylindrical bottles could hold as much as 5 litres (1.1 galls), but the more common square ones held much less. Some bottles found at Silchester bear the letters *CCA* meaning *Colonia Claudian Agrippinensis*, the official name of Cologne. Wine from the Rhineland was exported from that region, being shipped down the Rhine, across the Channel and landed at the port of London. These bottles, possibly holding superior wine, would have been packed in wicker or wooden cases, surrounded by straw. Some of the square bottles, however, are badly rubbed as if they had been packed in crates without packing.

Graphic evidence of transportation methods comes from Trier where sculptures depict huge barrels being transported in vessels with prows ahead and astern; one has a fine dragon's head prow (**34**). One boat is steered by a sailor who has only too obviously broached one of the casks. Epigraphic evidence from Bordeaux provides the name of L Solimarius Secundinus. He was a Treveran from the Moselle valley, who plied his trade between Britain and Bordeaux in the first century AD. It is tempting to think that a man connected with two wine producing regions was supplying wine to Britain. L. Viducius Placidius, referred to as *negotiator* on an inscription dated to AD 221 in York, came from the territory of the Veliocasses (now Rouen) in Gaul. He paid for the erection of an arch and a temple and seems to be the same man who erected an altar to the Goddess, Nehalennia, at Domburg on the Dutch coast, where goods were brought from the Rhineland. Possibly money for the buildings in York came from profits made in the Rhenish wine trade.

An altar erected at Bordeaux by M. Aurelius Lunaris, a *Servir Augustalis* of the coloniae of York and Lincoln (**35**), suggests that the wine trade was being carried on between northern Britain and Bordeaux two centuries later. Soldiers and veterans at the two coloniae who appreciated such imports would pass on their liking for wine to their colleagues. Wine had ceased to be a drink confined to native aristocracy and upper class Romans; it had become essential drinking for the majority of Romano-British citizens. Many would have agreed with Pliny's remark, *Vino aluntur vires, sanguis colosque hominum* (By wine are improved men's strength, blood and complexion) (**36**). The joy of wine drinking is expressed by a small bronze figure of Bacchus found in London who dances along carrying a bunch of grapes in his right hand and balancing a basket of grapes on his shoulder. The despair of deprivation is best expressed at Wroxeter on the tombstone of Titus Flaminius, who, having died aged 45 after serving 22 years with Legion XIV Gemina, bemoans, 'The gods prohibit you from the wine grape and water when you enter Tartarus'.

Although most wine in Britain was imported, there were attempts to grow vines. At North Thoresby (Lincolnshire) an arrangement of trenches may indicate a vineyard prepared in response to the removal by the Emperor Probus in AD 277 of restrictions imposed by Domitian in AD 92 on the planting of new vineyards in Gaul, Spain and Britain. These had been meant to prevent competition with those in Italy, as well as to prevent a glut of wine and encourage the growing of corn. If this was the case — and another opinion is that the trenches were for fruit trees — the climate seems to have been against it, for by AD 285 it had been abandoned. Evidence for viticulture was reported on a sheltered slope at the Boxmoor villa (Hertfordshire). At Brockley Hill (Middlesex), however, local potters, including one named Dares, made a type of amphora in the late first century which could have been used to bottle a local wine, perhaps produced in small sheltered vineyards in the Verulamium region. If so it was resin flavoured, as indicated by the residue on some of the amphorae sherds. This wine may have been drunk at Colchester and London, where Brockley Hill amphorae sherds have been found. The amphorae seem to have been between 91.4-106.7cm (36-42in) high with carinated shoulders. Production ceased in AD 92, probably as a result of Domitian's edict.

Pollen in soil samples from trench cultivation near Wollaston (Nottinghamshire) included those of grapevine. The trenches also produced evidence for postholes, probably for vine supports and the root bulbs of individual plants. This is akin to the system described in detail in Columella's system of cultivation by *postinatio*. Vines were planted at

35 Altar set up at Bordeaux by M. Au(relius) Lunaris, Sevir Augustalis of York and Lincoln, The altar was exhibited in the Yorkshire Museum, York, in 1971

1.5m (5ft) intervals in rows of flat bottomed trenches, 1m (3ft 3in) wide and 5m (16ft 3in) apart. Vine pollen was also recovered from widely spaced trenches at Irchester (Somerset).

Elsewhere the evidence is more tentative. The winemaking scenes on barbotine jars from Colchester merely indicate that people prefer to drink out of interesting beakers, while grape pips found at Silchester, London (Bermondsey and Cannon Street), York, Doncaster, and the Winterton Villa (Lincolnshire) and many other places could be the remains of imported raisins or grapes preserved in *must*. Grape skins and pips in a pit at Gloucester once suggested to be Roman are now believed to belong to the mediaeval period. It has also been suggested that some cultivation of vines took place in late third-century allotments outside Colchester, and the Colchester jars were held to reinforce this theory. However, if there was a large-scale production of wine in that region there ought to be some evidence from the surrounding villas, perhaps in the form of winepresses, and this is absent.

36 Cupids and panthers play amongst loaded vines. Detail from a Roman sarcophagus

Vineyards are labour-intensive and in Britain production must have been regarded as accompanied by commercial risk. With the easy importation of wine, this risk might not have been worth taking. If a villa owner planted vines in a sheltered place, the resulting wine may have been purely for home consumption. On the other hand, the decline in wine imports from AD 300, which has been attributed to the disruption of trade due to barbarian invasions into Spain, may mean that Britain was producing almost enough wine to be self sufficient. If, however, the wine trade were shrinking, then possibly wine would have been replaced by beer on the British table.

The quantity of wine might seem to be considerable but it should be set against quantification of wines elsewhere. Pliny records that the general and administrator, Lucullus, distributed 100,000 amphorae of wine on his return from Asia and the orator, Hortensius, left 10,000 amphorae to his heir. Admittedly both these men have become associated with a luxurious life, but there is also the evidence of cargoes of shipwrecks. Wine may have been imported to Britain on the scale of that calculated in a cargo of amphorae in the Madrague de Giens ship, which sank off the coast of Gaul. There were 6000 amphorae, each holding 24 litres (5.2 galls) of wine, a possible total of 144,000 litres (31,680 galls). If each ship entering Roman London carried this cargo, then the British wine drinkers would have been assured of ample supplies.

Beer

The drink native to prehistoric Britain was probably mead. Honey, if diluted with water and left for a long time, will ferment so that an alcoholic drink is produced which can be flavoured with herbs and fruit. Wheat, rye and oats will also ferment, but barley was the most useful grain. If barley is allowed to germinate and produce shoots, it develops an enzyme, diastase, which converts grain starch into fermentable sugars. To encourage this to happen, the grain is spread out and dried to convert it to malt. This malting process can be stopped by roasting, after which the crushed malt can be steeped in water to produce a sweet brown liquid known as wort.

To increase the taste, the wort can be boiled with honey, wormwood or herbs. One such could be costmary, a hardy perennial brought to Britain by the Romans. Its other name is alecost, as its main use is in flavouring ale. The beer produced in Iron Age and Roman Britain was more like barley wine or ale than beer. Ale, lacking hops as it does, deteriorates quickly so that it needs to be brewed frequently. Beer, with its bitter tang, requires hops which were not introduced into Britain until Flemish traders brought them in the fifteenth century. The mildly-intoxicating, barley-created drink is thus referred to by archaeologists as beer.

In Britain corn-drying ovens may not have been used entirely for drying large quantities of grain, but also for drying small quantities of barley in order to convert it into malt. Charred grain found in excavations in Culver Street, Colchester, had been deliberately germinated to make malt for brewing here. The mixture was 90 per cent wheat and 10 per cent barley, which might have been for a specific or specialised brand of beer. Carbonised barley grains, found in the flue of a T-shaped oven at Barton Court,

Abingdon (Oxfordshire), could have been the remains of a similar operation. The making of beer on small villas and farms would provide a yearly income, which would avoid cash-flow problems. Boon has suggested that several of the so-called 'round furnaces' in one of the buildings at Silchester were the bases of brewing vats which would have supplied beer to the town on a commercial scale. Kilns at the Halstock, Hambledon and Whitton villas also contain tanks, which would be suitable for brewing purposes.

In the Iron Age beer was well-known. Athenaeus indicated that the Celtic 'lower classes drink wheaten beer prepared with honey, though most people drink it plain. It is called corma. They use a common cup, drinking a little at a time; not more than a mouthful, but they do it rather frequently'. Strabo said that the Celts drank a barley beer called zythos and that 'they also drink the water with which they cleanse the honeycombs'. Dioscorides, in his first-century treatise *De Materia Medica* commented that 'there is a drink called curmi prepared from barley which is often drunk instead of wine but it causes bad humours, headaches and is harmful to the nerves'. Tacitus in the *Germania* said that the Germans 'extract a juice from barley or grain which is fermented to make something not unlike wine'.

Shepherd Frere pointed out that the ears of barley on the coins of Cunobelin, the Belgic King hostile to Rome, portrayed British beer as opposed to the imports of wine suggested by the vine leaf on the coins of Verica, who sought Rome's support. Beer thus became part of political propaganda. It had other uses than thirst-quenching, for Pliny records that the froth of beer was used as a cosmetic. Certainly the habit of washing hair in beer has continued to the present day. Diocletian's price edict in AD 301 costed British beer at four *denarii* an Italian pint, twice as much as Egyptian beer, but less than ordinary wine priced at eight *denarii*. Frere suggests that beer kept its popularity because the drinking vessels made by British potters in the third and fourth century would hold a quart or more; this seems too great a quantity for wine. A large bronze tankard found at Shapwick Heath (Dorset), and tankard handles from Trawsfynydd (Gwynedd) and Waddon Hill (Dorset) also suggest functional vessels for beer.

That beer was appreciated is indicated by the altar found in Derbyshire dedicated to *Mars Braciaca* (Mars, the god of malted beer). A letter from Vindolanda records the receipt of goods including a cask of beer (*cervesae metretam*). A *metreta* was a container holding about 40 litres (8.8 galls). As the cask was received in November, it could have been for some festival, perhaps the December Saturnalia.

Cider

A type of alcoholic cider may have been made at the Frenchgate site at Doncaster. A pit contained 1,400 apple pips presumably derived from 150-300 apples, crushed to produce a fermented apple drink. Cider has an alcoholic content of three to seven per cent. There is some evidence for the cultivation of pears in Britain, although they are not indigenous, so a perry drink might have been available.

Water supply

The Romans were aware of the need for a clean water supply. Varro stated that stagnant water bred certain minute creatures, which cannot be seen by the eyes; these float in the air and enter the body through the mouth and noise, causing serious disorders. Athenaeus indicated that running water is better than static water and when aerated becomes better still. Mountain water is healthier to drink than water from the plains, because it is mixed with less solid matter, and water which cooks vegetables slowly — such as that with soda and salt — is poor. Thus Athenaeus had noted the hardening of vegetables by the formation of calcium pectate through heating them in water containing calcium ions. Hippocrates agreed that waters with 'a very solvent nature' were preferable for cooking in order to stimulate digestion, and that boiled vegetables should not be 'hardened' by water.

In providing a good water supply, the Romans improved lifestyles, and they enhanced the amenities of civilised life by the provision of cisterns and fountains. Adequate water was necessary to supply the public baths and, if possible, private houses. Army and civilian engineers ensured that almost every town, large or small, had a fresh supply brought to it, often by means of an open leat, as at Godmanchester. At Lincoln water was conveyed for over 3.2km (2 miles). Where it crossed valleys the pipes were sheathed in concrete for support and for the last part the water was pumped uphill to a distribution tank just inside the town walls; from here one pipeline supplied the baths and another seems to have supplied water for other public use.

Wroxeter was supplied with 9 million litres (2 million gallons) a day by a leat leading from a reservoir created one mile east of the town, which led to a distribution point near the baths. From here certainly the baths and possibly private houses were supplied. The cost of providing a water supply had to be borne by the townspeople, which may account for the modest provision of private amenities. Vitruvius remarks that water has first to be piped to supply fountains, cisterns and baths. Private customers came last and had to pay for the privilege; some households at Catterick and shops at Verulamium and Wroxeter were prepared to do this, as excavation has revealed pipes going into houses to carry drinking water and possibly to flush latrines. Dorchester (Dorset) could arrange to bring in 59 million litres (13 million galls) of water daily from a source 14.5km (9 miles) distance by an open and unlined channel. The contours allowed a fall of 7.6m (25ft) over its length.

Water pipes were buried to protect them. At York the lead water main was buried 0.91m (3ft) below the surface and encased in a mass of concrete for protection, which seems a little extreme. Normally wooden pipes were lain in narrow trenches just under the surface. London, as was only to be expected, had a series of water pipes by the second century, consisting of wooden sections joined by iron collars laid in the streets, presumably to supply water to public and private buildings. At Canterbury there was a substantial conduit, a U-shaped channel with a crude barrel vault roof, on a concrete base, probably bringing water from the hills east of the town. The pipes at Bath were laid in a narrow channel and soldered with a continuous seam along the top. Soldering was easy in Britain where there were substantial tin deposits.

Wooden water pipes were found in Cirencester, but lead deposits in skeletons found

37 Fountain at crossroads in the Via della'Abbondanza, Pompeii

in the cemetery may indicate that lead pipes may instead have been used to convey water. This could be regarded as a source of poisoning, though a furring of calcium carbonate in the pipes would mitigate it. Vitruvius declared that water flowing through earthenware pipes was more practical and safer: 'For the water seems to be made injurious by lead, because white lead is produced by it and this is said to be injurious to the human body'. Hodges, however, states that the calcium carbonate deposits forming inside the pipes and aqueduct channels meant the water did not touch the lead. Also, as water ran constantly through the pipes because the Romans did not have taps, it did nor remain long enough in those pipes to become contaminated.

The public water supply fed channels and pipes, the bath establishments and the *mansiones.* It also flowed into collecting points, because water could lose its freshness when brought along the open leat; aerating the water in some way, most likely by cascading it from one tank to another, could restore this. If water was delivered on the constant flow principle, then much could be wasted, especially at night; this may have been calculated, which accounts for the large capacity of certain leats. At Pompeii and Herculanium almost every street corner has a cistern from which fresh water was supplied (**37 & colour plate 11**). A timber-lined drinking fountain was found in Wroxeter adjacent to the north portico of the baths. In addition to those towns mentioned above, others in Britain where traces of a water supply have been found include Caerwent, Caistor by Norwich, Leicester, Silchester, Exeter and Winchester, and it could be assumed that almost every town would have had some system.

1   Grain gathered ready for
    winnowing, Nepal, in 2000

2   Woman winnowing corn through a
    wooden riddle, Nepal

3 The 'Modius Claytonensis' or
   corn measure found at Carvoran,
   Hadrian's Wall. Museum of
   Antiquaries, Newcastle on Tyne

4 A man pounding grain in a
   mortar with a large pestle near
   Peshawar, Pakistan, in 1995

5 A bakery in the Via di Stabia,
Pompeii. The oven is on the
left. To the right are four mills.
A counter was at the front of the
shop

6 The baker and his wife. Fresco
from Pompeii in the Museo
Nazionale, Naples

7   *Leather bag hung by the door of a herdsman's ger, Juulchin, Mongolia, in 1999. Every person going in or out must stir the milk with the stick until fermented milk or butter is produced*

8   *Coarse ware pottery from Newstead Fort, Scotland, containing vegetables and pulses similar to those which could have been eaten by the Roman soldiers. The carrots would have been small and white as red carrots were a product of Dutch agriculture in the seventeenth century. This also applies to the display of food in plate 25. On the right is a mortarium stamped with the maker's name, BRUSC(IUS). National Museums of Scotland, Edinburgh*

9   *Tarraconensis amphora found in the Thames which contained 6,000 olives. National Maritime Museum, Greenwich, London*

10 *Late first-century BC Iron Age grave found at Welwyn Garden City, reconstructed in the British Museum. Around the body of the man, probably a chieftain, were placed his important goods, including five wine amphorae*

11 Fountain at crossroads, Herculaneum

12 Experimental Roman domed oven built by re-enactment Group, Cohors V Gallorum, to bake bread

13 Table in reconstructed kitchen, Museum of London, showing coarse ware pottery, mortaria and food

14 Trader using a steelyard in the market place, Gyantse, Tibet, in 1993

15 *Reconstruction of the Roman Villa site at Castle Hill, Ipswich, showing a couch, table and cupboard of authentic Roman design. The floor mosaic has been reconstructed from the original*

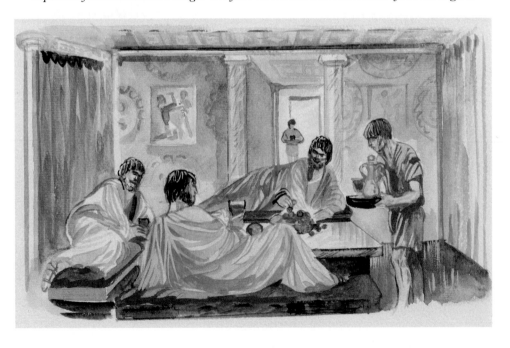

16 *An intimate dinner party*

DMCIVLMATERNVS
VETEXLEGIMVIVSSIBI
TMARIE MARCELLINAE
COllVGI DVLCISSIME
CASTISSIME OBITAE F

17 *Tombstone of Gaius Julius Maternus, veteran of Legion I Minervia. He reclines on his couch
with his pet dog at his feet. Before him is a table covered with an elaborately decorated cloth.
His wife sits in a basket chair holding a bowl of fruit. More fruit lies on the table. With one
hand he raises a cup, in the other he holds a serviette. Servants stand on either side. Römisch-
Germanisches Museum, Cologne*

18 *Reconstruction of a living room as it might have appeared in Roman London, Museum of London*

19 Samian ware from Newstead, containing fruit. National Museums of Scotland, Edinburgh

20 Samian bowl decorated with gladiatorial scene. Verulamium Museum

21 Pottery displayed on a table and stored in a cupboard for safe keeping, Museum of London

22 Roman glass, first to third centuries, from Ospringe, Kent

23 Butcher's shop drawn from
a relief in the Staatliche
Kunstsammlungen,
Dresden

24 Shops at Herculanium
showing shuttering
carbonised as a result of
eruption of Vesuvius in
AD 79

25 The interior of a baker's shop as reconstructed in the exhibition, High Street Londinium, organised by the Museum of London, 2000-1. The information for the display was obtained from excavations at Poultry, London

26 *A Roman legionary prepares a meal in the barrack block for his contubernium*

27 *Soldiers of re-enactment Group, Cohors V Gallorum, relaxing after baking North African style bread*

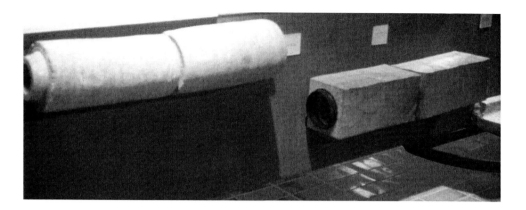

38 Water pipes at the Fishbourne Villa

Some villas made their own arrangements. The owners of Fishbourne laid down an elaborate arrangement of ceramic pipes (**38**), while those at the Chedworth (Gloucestershire) villa collected the spring water in a cistern, presumably a nymphaeum dedicated to the those minor deities who presided over refreshing waters. Smaller communities probably did not spend much on elaborate water arrangements, partly because of cost and partly because, as the water level was higher than today, wells would supply most needs. Even large towns were dependent on wells. London had a vast number to augment the piped supply. One problem was that because there was no concept of water-borne disease, a well could be partly used as a cesspit or dug next to one, so that seepage occurred. Pliny warned that water should issue from the bottom not the side of wells; the practice of lining wells with stone, timber or basket work indicates that this concept was accepted. Often, as at Silchester and London, wells were lined with the staves of wine barrels; silver fir was excellent for this purpose. In the country, matters might be arranged a little better, so that at farms and villas wells were dug near a convenient water supply, often at the spring line. The collection of rainwater would augment the supply.

Forts would have their own water supply. At Housesteads there were a large number of open cisterns with joints caulked with lead to make them waterproof. Rain can be channelled from roofs into the cisterns. Other tanks were set into the rampart, near to bake-ovens, so that water would be available for baking. The tanks would be a handy source of water to put out a fire. Two water tanks in the north-east corner held 2,562 litres (563 galls) and 2,340 litres (515 galls) respectively. These, when full, would be sufficient for the men billeted in two centurial barracks. In times of shortage, one of the duties of the soldiers would be the filling of these cisterns with water from the Knag Burn.

Water pipes, discovered running alongside the walls of Caerleon, supplied the fort. It is possible that the basins found in the centurion's quarters could be either the impluvium of an atrium or the bases for a water supply. Similar structures were found at Chesters, but there was no direct supply of water. They would have to be manually filled, but ample manpower was available. J.C. Bruce noted in his account of Hadrian's Wall, written in 1857, that he saw water flowing in a stone-lined water course 274m (300yd) from a

39 The Corbridge Lion. A lion crouches over a deer. The sculpture was originally part of a funerary monument, but was later adapted as a fountain decoration reconditioned to hold a lead water pipe in its mouth

spring to the west side of Birdoswald. This led to a cistern near the centre of the fort. At Corbridge, a statue of a crouching lion (**39**) had an iron pipe in its mouth from which water would have poured into a tank, a decorative as well as a practical feature. Great Chesters was supplied by water two-and-a-half miles from Haltwhistle Burn in a channel 1m deep (3ft 3in) for 4km (2½ miles) cut into the side of several hills. This took such a circuitous route that the actual distance was 9.65km (6 miles).

10 The kitchen

The kitchen

The more sophisticated cuisine of the Romans meant that cooking arrangements would be very different from those utilised in Celtic Britain. That is not to say that every part of Britain would have adapted to the new household arrangements. In some areas there would have been little change. The central hearth round which the family gathered in one room would remain. Even in the town, the former ways of life would continue, as the evidence from the Poultry site in London revealed. In a room of what was believed to be a carpenter's shop, where the whole family lived, ate and slept, the hearth had cooking pots amongst the ashes, and a waste pit by the side where food debris could be dumped.

Elsewhere, however, more demanding culinary requirements would have led to what was, in a Romanised context, a modernised kitchen. Often this resulted in a separate room or one placed at the end of a wing of a town house or villa; separate kitchens, like one at Verulamium which had a brick hearth, were more practical because of the danger of fire. Fires had to be banked up overnight to save rekindling the next morning. Pliny pointed out the problems of rekindling and the inconvenience of going round to a neighbour for hot coals or flint and tinder. Fire was an ever-present danger. The Emperor Augustus had created a corps of *vigiles* or fire-fighting watchmen who policed Rome and this scheme was intended to be adopted throughout the provinces. Every ward in a town had to have such a patrol which would carry out a fire watch and if necessary order houses to be pulled down to stop fires spreading. That towns were divided into wards is evidenced by inscriptions from Lincoln, one referring to the ward of the Guild of Mercury and another to the ward of the Guild of Apollo.

Horace said that when he was dining, at an inn at Beneventuum, on thrushes which were being spit roasted, a spark set the kitchen ceiling alight, leading to panic amongst guests and slaves, some rescuing the dinner, others trying to put out the flames. Something similar happened in the *vicus* of the fort at Greta Bridge (Co. Durham) where a late second-early third-century two-winged timber house, with a kitchen in the centre block, may have belonged to a veteran. This had a free-standing cooking range in the middle of the room, possibly a safety measure as it was not set against the wall. Post-holes in a corner may have held a device for swinging heavy pots onto the stove. In the cobbled courtyard was a bread oven, set against the wall of a room in the south-west wing, with a shovel nearby, used for taking out the hot bread. Inside that room the grain was stored, together with querns made from Pennine stone. In spite of all precautions an accumulation of pyrophoric carbon from the kitchen range, collected in the roof timbering and thatch, seems to have led to a flash fire ignited by sparks from the stove, thereby destroying the south-west wing.

40 Reconstruction of a Roman kitchen. On the left is the stove with a gridiron and pottery. A cauldron chain hangs on the wall

A Roman kitchen usually had a raised hearth set against a wall and edged with a curb to hold in the hot charcoal (**40**). This would reach waist height, so that cooking could be done while standing. A gridiron, such as those found at Icklingham (Suffolk) and Silchester (**41**), supported pans. That at Silchester measured 45 by 45cm (18 by 18in) and was 10cm (4in) high. It has all its bars riveted in place, a feat described as a tour-de-force in smithing. An iron tripod, trivet or semi-circular gridiron, such as that found at Colchester, would serve the same purpose. The top of a hearth in the House of the Vetii in Pompeii had charcoal spread all along it, providing glowing coals to heat pots in which a meal was cooking, before the owners ran away as the ashes of Vesuvius rained down on them. A square or semi-circular hole in the front of the large oblong stove was used to store wood.

Some ovens, especially those for bakers, would have been constructed like the one portrayed on the tomb of the Roman baker, Eurysaces. These were semi-circular in shape and set on a raised hearth (**colour plate 12**). A fire was lit in the interior and allowed to burn until the chamber was hot. Then the ashes were raked out, the dough put in, the door sealed and the bread allowed to cook in the dry heat. A more sophisticated oven can be seen at Pompeii. A beehive-shaped mound was constructed inside a square chamber to increase heat efficiency as the open space retained the heat. Vents allowed the smoke to escape and the entrance to the opening was at waist height. An iron door closed the domed entrance.

41 Top: trivet from Great Chesterford
Below: Gridiron from Silchester

Experiments were made with a reconstructed oven at Kingscote (Gloucestershire). A squared base was raised to 90cm (3ft) high to form a combustion chamber, with a large stone slab to form the base of an oven. This was surmounted by a dome with a chimney at the back to provide a draught. The higher the chimney, the more effective the cooking function of the oven. Food placed in this type of oven baked satisfactorily on the hot surface of the stone, without the need for a fire to be lit and raked out.

Some houses such as the fourth-century house at Clementhorpe, York, had a domed oven, which would cook food by the dry heat method. Food could also be placed in pans; sometimes meat and fish were placed in wetted leaves. An oval structure found at Bourton-on-the-Water (Gloucestershire) with a narrow opening and a burnt clay floor probably served as a hearth. Other tiled hearths, such as one found at Clementhorpe, York, showed evidence of burning. Fire would heat the hearth allowing the surface to act as a griddle; it would also support a gridiron. At Verulamium a similar hearth was placed,

42 A Roman kitchen. Servants are washing up after a meal, scouring out a bowl and tipping the contents of a jar into a bowl set on the stove. Drawn from a relief on the Igels Column, Moselle Valley, Germany

rather riskily, next to a wooden wall. The villa at Lechlade (Gloucestershire) had a huge rectangular room serving as a kitchen, which had reconstructed hearths and ovens over a period of many years.

Tiled hearths were found at the Newport (Isle of Wight) and Folkestone (Kent) villas; the cook at the latter place did not bother to clear up, for food remains were found scattered round the fire. This villa had a second kitchen with a stone corner-hearth. Close by was a large stone platform. A fire on the platform would heat water in a tank supported by two upright stone posts. Some households might possibly have followed the prehistoric method of using potboilers. Stones were heated, then placed in a trough of water gradually bringing it to the boil. Experiments at Ballyvourney (Co. Cork, Ireland) utilising a stone-lined pit proved that 454.6 litres (100 galls) of water could be brought to the boil in 35 minutes. A leg of mutton, wrapped in straw to prevent it getting dirty, was cooked to perfection, allowing 20 minutes to the pound plus 20 minutes more.

Wealthy households or those of administrators might have a male cook, a Greek or someone trained in Rome. These would know their own worth and if they were freedmen would earn a wage. Even so, the cook must not be too independent, nor make extravagant demands. Martial grumbled that he would not have the palate of a slave — a cook ought to possess the taste of his master. Both he and Livy, writing many years previously, implied that cooks were becoming pretentious and that cookery had taken on art forms, but Cicero labelled it as one of the vulgar arts. A glance at some of the more elaborate recipes in Apicius will show what he meant. Cooks waited in the marketplace to be hired for special occasions, and a household then took its chance on what he could do. Other households managed with a male or female slave who was under legal obligation to the family. It was hard work (**42**), and some help would have been necessary for the heavier tasks, such as lifting heavy amphorae to get at the contents. Someone, perhaps the kitchen hand, would take on the daily task of grinding

43 Little Butser Demonstration Iron Age Farmstead, Queen Elizabeth Country Park, Hampshire

corn for bread. In the Trentholme Drive Cemetery at York several female skeletons showed evidence of squatting facets on the leg bones, a feature linked with those who had spent much of their lives in that position. These could have been caused by squatting down to cook by a fire or by crouching over a rotary quern. In rural peasant communities cooking would be a shared task, with the bulk of the work falling to the women.

Kitchens in Roman Britain were not necessarily clean places. The neatly arranged theoretical reconstructions in museums such as at London and Cirencester can mislead (**colour plate 13**). Kitchens might have been warm and comfortable in winter, smelling of herbs and spices, but there would be a lingering smell of stale, cooked food; in summer they might be uncomfortably hot. In the absence of chimneys, smoke was a problem. Martial mentioned a steamy, sooty kitchen; Horace moaned about smoke making his eyes water; Virgil mentioned a good fire blazing in the hearth and doorposts blackened by soot. Ovid recounted the story of Jupiter, Neptune and Mercury taking shelter with an old man, Hyrieus, in 'his house begrimed with black smoke. Two pipkins stood by the fire; the lesser contained beans, the other kitchen herbs'. Smoke drifting through the house would gradually flavour a joint. Juvenal spoke of feast days in the good old times when a side of dried pork hung from a *carnarium,* a rack composed of wicker strips and pieces of wood suspended from the roof and usually placed over a hearth. Simulus cut pieces of hard cheese from a round, which hung near the hearth in his kitchen by a string going through a hole in the middle.

This had been the practice of pre-Roman Britain. Celtic round houses had rafters from which hams and bacon could hang with the object of curing them in the smoke which swirled up from the fire. At Little Butser (**43**), a round house has been constructed based on archaeological evidence from an Iron Age site at Pimperne

44 Round House, Little Butser, recreated from postholes of a Round House excavated at Pimperne, Dorset

(Dorset). The house is intended to simulate living conditions in Iron Age and rural Roman Britain (**44**). There is a central hearth with firedogs to hold spits on which joints of meat can be cooked. By the side is a dome-shaped oven. On a still day the house reeks of the smoke which filters up to the rafters; on a windy, rainy day, when the doors are shut, the smoke swirls through the house. These conditions would be replicated in a pre-Roman round house or a Romano-British kitchen.

In some houses at Silchester, in rooms assumed to be kitchens, pots were sunk into the ground to act as storage containers. One careful owner had sunk a large earthenware vessel into which were put ashes raked from the fire. Other pots contained food debris including lamb and chicken bones and the complete scales from a carp. At Poundbury, analysis of residue in pots was suggested to be milk products, olive oil, wine, fish sauce, honey and fruit extracts. The cleaning out of these pots must have been a tedious and revolting job for the household slaves. Some houses and villas, such as those at Hartlip, Burham and Chalk in Kent and Park Street (Hertfordshire) had cellars in which to store goods. These would include amphorae and *dolia*, large storage vessels sometimes having a capacity of 900 litres (200 galls), but normally of 90-295 litres (20-65 galls) (**45**). They were cleaned by slaves, who thrust burning iron torches into them, before scraping pitch up the hot inner sides. In Pompeii and Ostia these large pots were set into the ground up to their rims (**46**).

Separate kitchens or even the Roman-style cooking hearth do not seem to have lasted, but food has to be cooked regardless of place in troubled times. Towards the end of the Roman period, burnt patches on the floors of villas seem to indicate that more sophisticated Roman

45 *Boscoreale Villa, Italy, Model in the Museo della Civiltà, Rome. The villa carried out commercial operations in wine and oil production.* Dolia *were placed in the courtyard*

46 Dolia *in situ in courtyard of house at Ostia*

ways had given place to primitive habits, and that the inhabitants cooked where they could rather than conventionally in a kitchen. By the fourth century such patches could indicate abandonment and occupation by hostile groups. In the Piddington villa (Northamptonshire), food had been cooked on a fire lit on the tessellated floor, with mounds of animal bones tossed against the walls. If food carefully cooked on a Roman-type stove indicates living a cultured and civilised existence, then this lifestyle had been abandoned by those who now occupied the villa.

Cauldrons

The main cooking implements both in Iron Age and Roman Britain were cauldrons. In the Iron Age they had a symbolic purpose for they indicated a plentiful life. The Dagda, one of the greatest Celtic Irish gods, had a huge cauldron which he cleaned out with one sweep of his fist. Warriors killed in battle were placed in the cauldron to be restored to life. An Irish poem details a list of implements which should be standard equipment in the house of a great chieftain; foremost amongst them are a cauldron and spits. An Iron Age chieftain in a grave at Hochdorf (Germany) was buried with a highly decorated cauldron that had held 350 litres (77 galls) of mead for his drinking session in the next world. The cauldron for the Celts was symbolic of the social gathering: the ideal of eating together to form a social bond. It was central to the gregarious gathering where loyalty to the tribe and the clan were paramount; hence the cauldron had the central placement on the hearth in a Celtic house.

Although it has been suggested that many cauldrons continued to have ritual purposes, those in Roman Britain also served a more prosaic purpose. They would be used over the open hearth or, more practically, placed in the open over a wood fire. Great Chesterford (Essex), Appleford (Berkshire) and Silchester are amongst many sites that have produced cauldron chains. The Great Chesterford example was a long chain of double-looped links, which divided near the bottom into two, with strong hooks at the end (**47**). A cauldron found at Prestwick Carr (Northumberland) had been patched continually as if the cook could not bear to throw away a favourite cooking implement. In the end, and possibly somewhat reluctantly, this was deposited in boggy land where it would be under the protection of a water deity. Cauldrons would be necessary to take such large items as suckling pig, if the animal was not to be roasted on a spit. One of Apicius' recipes states that the pig should be hung in a basket in a boiling cauldron. This is depicted on a relief from Bonn (Germany). A slave or servant carries a pig on his back ready to cast it into the cauldron, which is hanging by iron chains apparently fixed to the ceiling by an iron peg.

Frying pans

Many Roman cooking implements are similar to modern ones because they had a similar function. Utensils included the *sartago* or frying pan, which sometimes had a

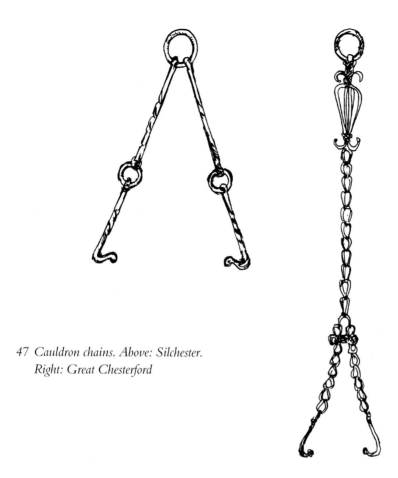

47 *Cauldron chains. Above: Silchester.*
  Right: Great Chesterford

folding handle (**48**). This pan was used for cooking most meat and fish and for heating oil, an important ingredient for cooking. Several frying pans have been found in Britain, including a copper alloy one at Great Lea, Binfield (Berkshire) and iron ones at the Stanwick villa (Northamptonshire), Icklingham (Suffolk) and Rushall Down (Wiltshire). One with a decorated handle was found in London. At one end of the pan is a pointed projection (**49**). The sides of this are turned up and holes cut into them. The handle at the point nearest the pan ends in a scroll made by turning up the metal. This was placed between two upright parts and an iron peg passed through them to fold the handle in place. An iron bracelet passed underneath kept the handle in place when it was extended. This, though primarily functional, was also decorated by being twisted, although this was not a common form. The fact that the handle could fold neatly over the pan (**50**) means that it was portable and might form a useful part of military equipment. Similar equipment made of aluminium was used by American soldiers in the First World War, serving a dual purpose of cooking utensil and plate. Another square pan with a handle, found at Pompeii, had round indentations in it, resembling the modern tins in which small sponge cakes and tarts are cooked.

48 Roman frying
pan from Egypt

49 Details of bracket supporting handle of
frying pan

50 Frying pan
from Egypt with
handle folded

51 Handle of patera
with decorated
bird's head from
Wroxeter. Rowley's
House Museum,
Shrewsbury

52 *Baking pan from Pompeii*

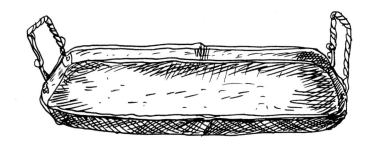

53 *A heating apparatus from Pompeii. A square base resting on four decorative legs supports a barrel-shaped lidded urn. The mask beneath the lid acts as a safety valve for steam. Another valve is on the side of the semi-circular water box. The three birds on the rim act as a stand for a vessel. The open box could have held water or charcoal*

54   Ladle combined with flesh-hook, Great Chesterford

Other utensils

Other utensils were *paterae* (hemispherical-shaped pans) (**51**), *patellae* (round shallow pans) and *patinae* (deeper pans). Apicius directed that *patinae* were to be placed amongst the coals as if in a fire or 'in the ashes', which could mean the oven before the ashes were removed. The recipe mentions *impones in thermospodio*. This is for a dish which includes brains, eggs, wine and liquamen; it obviously needs to be cooked gently or it will curdle. A hoard from the Newstead fort contained seven bronze, globular-shaped cooking vessels of various sizes, together with the gridiron on which they were placed. The globular shape recalls a statement by Celsus that food is more digestible when boiled than when fried. Three of the vessels still retain their handles; all show traces of hard use, some having patches soldered onto them.

Most cooks would have a favourite pan; the Prestwick one has already been mentioned. Oconea visited Bath especially to have a curse tablet made and cast it into the waters, condemning the thief who stole her pan and invoking the divine intervention of Sulis Minerva to try to get it back. Exsuperius also sought help with a curse tablet for the theft of a pan, possibly an iron frying pan. Lead pans are also known, but these could lead to problems because lead is toxic and accumulates in bones. Skeletons containing lead were found in the Cirencester and Poundbury cemeteries. Iron pans will add traces of iron to the food cooked in them but this is a useful trace element because it can combat anaemia. Recent research in Indian *balti* cookery has shown that a curry cooked in a traditional iron pan provided five times the normal dietary intake of iron. This is even more than occurs in liver, one of the richest sources of iron. The Amish community in Lancaster County, Pennsylvania, USA cooks in iron pans and sells them in its stores for those persons who want to add iron to the diet. As the human body is efficient in getting rid of excess iron, there is no danger of having excess. The Romans also knew the use of the *bain-marie* and the *operculum* (covered pan) (**52**); a tinned bronze vessel with a flat surface from Silchester, may be the inside of a *bain-marie*. Water heaters have been found in Pompeii although none are known in Britain (**53**).

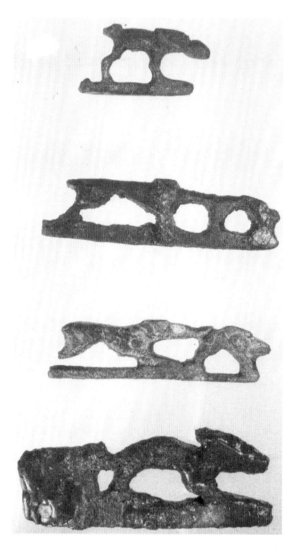

55   Knife handles, Silchester, in Reading Museum

Ladles, cleavers, knives

Other implements used in the kitchen were wood, bronze or iron ladles, cleavers, flesh hooks and knives of all kinds. One ladle from Great Chesterford (Essex) was combined with a flesh hook (**54**); another, found in London, and carved from a single piece of wood, had a wide shallow bowl and an cleverly angled terminal, which meant it could be balanced on the rim of a vessel when not in use. Knives were used continually in the kitchen; those found in London vary from a few inches long to over a foot. Plautus made Congrio say that there is no more fitting implement for a cook. The cook in Petronius' *Satyricon* welds with dexterity a sharp knife to slit open a pig, from which

56 Roman balance reconstructed from beam and scale pans found in London

pour carefully prepared sausages and blood puddings. Knives, often with decorated or bone handles (**55**), were used to cut up food which was then eaten with fingers. A favourite design was a crouching lion or a dog chasing a hare; a rare design from Wroxeter is of a hunched tiger. Spoons and spatulas made of wood have been recovered from damp deposits.

Balances and steelyard weights

Weighing was done by the balance (*libra*) (**56**) or the steelyard (*statera*) (**57**). Balances, such as those found at Icklingham (Suffolk), and Dorn Farm, near Moreton in Marsh (Gloucestershire), have two scale pans, each dangling from a chain held on hooks on either side of a rod. One amusing scene on a Roman lamp from Pozzuoli in Italy shows a stork weighing an elephant against a mouse — the mouse weighs heavier. Bronze scale pans found at Sea Mills (Somerset) and Hacheston (Suffolk) have the inscription *BANNA F(ecit)* on them; other scale pans from this maker have been found in Gaul and along the Rhine.

The steelyard remains in common use today in many countries, especially being used in markets and by travelling salesmen (**colour plate 14**). The principle of the steelyard is that it is an asymmetrical balance, in which a weight placed at a distance from a fulcrum will balance a greater weight placed closer to the fulcrum on the opposite side. The load to be weighed is either hung from a hook or placed in a pan and the weight moved along until in equilibrium with the load. One steelyard of first-second-century date, found preserved intact with its weight in the Walbrook in London, had retained the numerical gradations on the main. On two hooks hanging from the right side it could weigh up to 8 Roman pounds. On reversing the suspension, and hanging items from another hook, the beam could weigh up to 30 Roman pounds.

Weights could be in the form of a head, often representative of a deity (**58**); a splendid head of Bacchus was found at Silchester (**59**). Roman weights were in the

57   Bronze steelyard found at Silchester with graduated beam

58 Steelyard weight in form of a Celtic head found at Old Carlisle, in Tullie House Museum, Carlisle

59 Steelyard weight in form of the head of Bacchus, found at Silchester, in Reading Museum

form of *librae* (pounds), *unciae* (ounces) and *scripuli* (scruples), but few of the objects described as weights correspond to known Roman measures. At Colchester, however, one possible weight had five raised dots on it, corresponding to five unciae. A set of four lead weights found at Charterhouse-on-Mendip had from one to four dots on each respective one and these seem to conform to the weights of the unciae. A weight from Duntocher has *s(emis)* on it, corresponding to half a libra or six *unciae*. A Roman pound weighed approximately 340g (12oz) so that a lead weight from London, marked *VIIII*, weighs approximately 8.5 Roman pounds (2.9kg). It is rare, however, that weights are given in Apicius' cookery book; the Roman cook, like all good cooks, relied on taste, smell and his own version of a measurement.

60 Black burnished cooking ware: jug, flanged bowls and pie dish

Pottery

Earthenware or terracotta jars were used for cooking, the most common being an *olla*, an earthenware cooking pot, in which food of all kinds could be cooked. Apuleius wrote of a pretty kitchen maid who prepared *mellitum pulmentum* in a little *olla*, a direct ancestor of a vessel used in Italian houses today for cooking lentils. The *olla* was pushed into the embers of a fire. Some pots were found coated with lime inside, as if they had been used for boiling water. Pots which were left unglazed and had become soured with use could be cleaned by rubbing them with sand, but it was usually easier to throw them away. Masses of broken pottery found on Roman sites shows how often this was done. Some pottery was used as salt containers: hand-made shell-tempered storage jars found in London had pitch on the rims and shoulders, indicating that they had contained food prepared with salt.

The most prolific cooking ware was black burnished ware. This made excellent cooking pots, either being placed over a fire or in the oven (**60**). There were two classes of fabric. The Iron Age tribe of the Durotriges in Dorset had developed a black gritty handmade ware (BB1). This form was imitated in the mid-first century AD in south-east Britain, especially Kent, by potters who produced a silky, more regular surface (BB2). Contracts with the army enabled potters to supply forts as far north as Hadrian's Wall by AD 120 and by AD 140 that pottery was supplying forts on the Antonine Wall. Both types of black burnished ware continued to supply the army and civilians to AD 250 and BB1 then continued to the mid-fourth century. Some pots

61 Severn Valley ware: Glevum bowls and honey jar. Savernake ware: tankard

62 Kitchenware found at Verulamium. Colander, jug and mortarium

were squat with short necks and upward rims, others were more elongated in the neck. Most were distinguished by a lattice pattern.

Local industries developed other forms of cooking ware. Dales ware was a shell-gritted, handmade ware, which was widely used over the north of Britain. Potters in Lincolnshire copied it with wheel-thrown, sandy-grey fabrics. Some Derbyshire ware pots had dished rims to hold a lid in place. The Trent Valley potters produced a tall cooking pot in a dark grey fabric. Savernake ware, first developed in the mid-first century to supply the army stationed in the Gloucestershire region was a light grey, flint-gritted ware (**61**). Alice Holt (Hampshire) pots were grey with a combed texture.

63 Glass vessel, first century AD, found at Caerleon. After being used as a storage vessel, it was deposited in a cemetery as a container for ashes

Not all the wares were manufactured throughout the whole of the period; certain wares dominated the market at different times.

With their necks cut off and the point dug into the floor, amphorae could be used for storage. One at Silchester had the word *AVEN(A)* (oats) written on the side. Placed in a corner of the kitchen they also acted as urinals. Pottery jars could be sealed by a wooden stopper or covered with an inverted jar placed over the neck. Clay sealants would keep out moisture or air. There were pottery colanders (**62**), but more delicate straining could be accomplished by linen, fine cloths and wickerwork baskets. Chilled wine was obtained by pouring it over ice placed in finely decorated bronze strainers.

Pestles and mortars were used for pounding spices and herbs. Spices were not usually sold powdered in the ancient world, but powdered spices gain flavour as well as losing any tough or undesirable texture. Mortaria were classical Roman vessels which did not exist in Britain before the Conquest. The Romans introduced them through the agency of the army, as they were a staple military vessel. Their heavy rims made them easy to grip and the grit on the interior base provided the rough surface for pulverising food, especially fibrous vegetables. A mortaria of the second-century AD, found at Silchester, had the remains of pulped fruit, stones and pips in it as if the flesh had been rubbed away.

The army first imported mortaria from Gaul in the first century AD, including those manufactured by the potter, Q. Valerius Veranius, whose name is found impressed on the rim of many of these vessels. Local potters in the south-east gained contracts to supply the army further north. Brockley Hill, Radlett (Hertfordshire) and Colchester were the main suppliers in the first century AD. Their mortaria were a creamy-buff fabric with large hooked rims, well-made spouts and tiny flint gritting in the interior. By the second century the Mancetter and Hartshill potteries had been developed, which were to dominate production until the fourth century. Other local workshops included the Oxford and Nene Valley potters and the so-called *Raetian* mortaria, made in orange fabric with a glossy red-brown slip, was manufactured near Wroxeter and at Wildespoon. In a heap of late second and early third-century broken ware, used as part of hard core material for the timber quay at the St Magnus House site at London, were many lion-headed spouted mortaria, useful for decanting liquids or ground powders. These were handsome enough to grace any upper-class kitchen.

In the early third century pottery kilns at York were producing pottery imitating shapes made in North Africa. In AD 208 the Emperor Septimus Severus was in York and possibly these vessels were made for his retinue and for the soldiers brought from North Africa who expected to be able to cook food in the vessels to which they were accustomed. One type of pottery was a bowl designed to be used as a brazier which allowed food to be cooked in a drier form preferable to this ethnic group.

Glassware

Huge glass square, hexagonal or globular shaped bottles, with one or two handles, were used for storage. Scratches on the side and bottom show that they were kept in wooden crates for safety and that they had been frequently pushed in and out. Stoppers were of wood and cork. Many of these bottles, after their domestic purpose had been served, were used as containers for cremated ashes and placed in cemeteries (**63**). In the fourth century, round, barrel shapes made their appearance, many having the names of the maker on them; one from Faversham had the words *Felix fecit* (Felix made me). The Romans were aware of the advantage of glass over pottery for preserving herbs and spices. Apicius, having put the rare and costly spice, silphium, into a glass container, added pine kernels. He then used only the kernels, which absorbed the flavour.

11 The dining room

Celtic customs

In the Celtic round or long houses, diners sat cross-legged on the floor round the fire eating from plates or wooden platters passed round the guests. Diodorus had noted that 'when dining the Celts sit not upon the ground but on the earth, strewing beneath them the skins of wild animals'. This is confirmed by Posidonius: 'They also scatter hay on the ground when they serve their meals, which they take on wooden tables raised only slightly above the ground.' Diodorus continued 'beside them are hearths blazing with fire, with cauldrons and spits containing large pieces of meat'.

This is spelt out in such Irish tales as *The Intoxication of the Ulstermen* and *Bricriu's Feast*. In the latter, allowing for the exaggeration of the storyteller, Bricrui served to the seated warriors a cauldron full of drink, a seven-year-old boar fed on 'fresh milk and fine meal in springtime, curds and sweet milk in summer, the kernel of nuts and wheat in autumn and beef and broth in winter', a seven-year-old calf, and five-score wheaten cakes cooked in honey. This was to be consumed by the champions of Ulster. Classical writers give more prosaic descriptions. Posidonius says of the Celts that 'their food consists of a small number of loaves of bread, together with a large amount of meat, either boiled or roasted on charcoal or on spits ... those who live beside rivers or near the Mediterranean or the Atlantic eat fish in addition, baked fish, that is, with the addition of salt, vinegar and cumin.'

Roman dining habits

Lack of evidence makes it difficult to say how far Roman dining habits were adopted. Celtic dining habits would have continued, especially in rural areas where round houses and long houses were being built and in the less wealthy parts of the towns. There is no evidence that the inhabitants of Silchester, Cirencester or even London and those living in villas such as Woodchester (Gloucestershire) and Winterton (Lincolnshire) copied the Mediterranean custom of lolling on couches. They might have done so if they had adapted to a Roman lifestyle or had come as administrators from Rome or Gaul. Although it is possible that a certain room in a town house or villa may have been a dining room (*triclinium*), proof of its use is lacking.

Yet, although Celtic ways probably endured, especially in the less civilised parts of Britain and amongst those persons hostile to Rome, the design of Roman town houses and villas dictated a change of lifestyle (**colour plate 15**). It was easier to sit or squat on an earth floor in a round hut than on a mosaic or tiled floor. The design of a mosaic

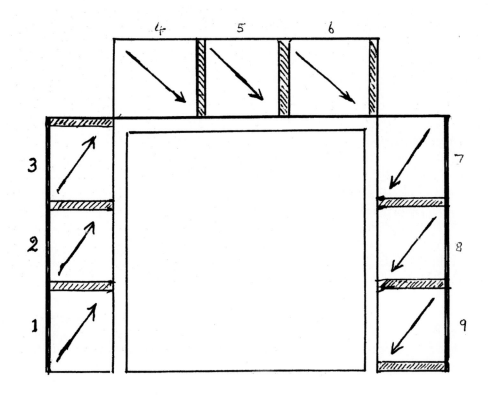

64 *The arrangement of the triclinium. The table is surrounded by three couches on which people reclined in the direction indicated by the arrows. The left arm rested on cushions, the right hand was used for eating. The middle table was for the most important guests, place 5 being reserved for the guest of honour. The next important guest sat in place 7. If a consul or an important official was present, he sat in place 4 so that he could easily receive any urgent messages. The host sat next to him in place 3 ready to issue order to the servants. The hatched areas indicate where rolled cushions could be placed for supporting the body*

dictated where couches should be placed. Its position, which was laid so that diners could face inwards to admire the pattern and the compilation, indicates that the custom existed. It is possible that Roman dining habits were part of the education that Agricola ordered should be part of the education of the sons of British chieftains. Tacitus noted that during Agricola's governorship (AD 77-83) the British were gradually introduced to the amenities that make vice agreeable — arcades, baths and sumptuous banquets. Even allowing for Tacitus' contemptuous words, the Britons would not be permitted to sit on the ground if they were to be trained in Roman ways.

The Romans had devised their own method of eating (**64**). Some Romans copied Greek habits, taking meals reclining on three couches, placed round a table. Originally only men did this, although during the early empire women began to copy them.

65 *Some of the contents of the so-called 'child's grave', Colchester. These included four reclining figures and five standing figures reading from scrolls. Also present were a child's bust, a figure of Hercules, a triple-horned bull, several animal vessels, Gaulish lead-glazed ware and a feeding bottle. The contents are now in the Castle Museum, Colchester*

Reclining meant total relaxation of the body. Sitting — a posture halfway between lying and standing — is only semi-relaxing. Cato, to show his stoicism, sat at a table and reclined only to sleep. Squatting or crouching was to assume the posture of a barbarian or a slave. Lucian was positive that the ability to imbibe while reclining distinguished man from beast and gentleman from slave. Reclining was also a sign that a boy had reached the age of manhood (**colour plate 16**). Food was cut into small portions so that people ate with their fingers. Sauces were scooped up with a spoon or bread was soaked in them, which necessitated washing of hands during and after every course. It was a slave's task to go round the diners holding bowls of water in which hands were dipped, and to have a napkin ready for drying them. Some diners had their own napkins. Trimalchio carried one with a broad purple stripe, an ostentatious gesture recalling the purple stripe on the toga worn only by senators.

Four terracotta figures from a set of nine, found in the first-century so-called 'child's grave' at Colchester, caricature this reclining position (**65**). They rest correctly on the left elbow, leaving the right hand free for eating. Other terracotta figurines mock the diners and the reciters who provided entertainment at the meals. The depiction of these figures, however, implies a degree of sophistication, for only those who understood completely the characters' attitudes would appreciate their satirical content. In other words, such a banquet would be a well-known feature in Colchester and was probably introduced to the civilian inhabitants of the *colonia* by the veteran soldiers settled there.

The custom of reclining on couches while dining can be seen on the stereotyped funerary banquet tombstones such as that at Chester (**66**). A couch with head and footrest is seen on the tombstone of Julia Velva (**67**) and one with a high back on that of Aelia Aeliana, both of whom died at York. Greek couches had only a head and footrest, the addition of a back is attributed to the Romans. Julia's couch has a thick mattress or cushion probably placed on a latticework of cords or leather strips. Similar couches may also have served as beds. It is this item of furniture to which Martial refers when he lists the contents of a poor man's house in Rome, though he acidly refers to the bed as bug-ridden, which was possibly also the case in Britain. Couches were made of many kinds of wood, with oak probably predominating in Britain, and were polished with wax or cedar oil.

Tombstones in the Rhineland show people eating at gate-legged tables (**68 & colour plate 17**), which implies that this was a custom in the more northerly Roman provinces. One relief from Neumagen shows two members of the family standing behind such a table, which was covered with a fringed cloth (**69**). Another sits in a round-backed wooden chair and a woman sits in a basket chair. These appear to have been common in Britain (**colour plate 18**). Julia Velva's daughter sits in one, as does an unknown woman on a tombstone from Murrell Hill (Cumbria). Diners could also sit on stools. A folding stool was found in a grave at Bartlow (Essex) and another at Holborough (Kent). Tables were usually of wood, but Britain produced fine ones of shale, a black clay rock akin to slate mined at Kimmeridge Bay, near Purbeck (Dorset). Fragments of the legs of shale tables, found at Dorchester and the Preston villa, near Weymouth (Dorset), show they could be carved with animal's heads at the top and paws at the bottom. This type of table, however, was more likely to be a small three-legged table, similar to that shown on the York tombstones.

Meals

Roman eating habits on the whole were sensible and abstemious. Most people ate frugally during the day; they needed to keep their wits about them for hard or official work. Poorer people could not afford to eat large quantities of food. For them it would be a case of bread and gruel or pottage. As the only implements were knives and spoons, most of the food was in the form of a stew or porridge. Slivers of meat could be cut from bones with a knife, but the state of people's teeth might dictate what they could eat and in what form. Many of Apicius recipes' deal with pates, minced meat and omelette-type dishes. Seneca remarked scathingly, 'I expect dishes will soon be put on the table ready chewed for us, for there is very little difference between so doing and what the cook does now.'

In theory and probably in practice most Romans ate three meals each day. Most people distinguished clearly between eating to live and socially dining. During the day, food prepared the body for hard work by satisfying hunger and providing energy without slackening effort; in the evening food had a social and relaxing purpose. It was a time for leisure (*otium*), for forgetting the worries and hardship of the day. Breakfast

66 *Tombstone of Curatia Di(o)nysia. The deceased lady raises a goblet and reclines on a*
high-backed couch with mattress, cushion and baluster legs. In front is a three-legged table with
food on it. Grosvenor Museum, Chester

67 *Tombstone of Julia Velva, who 'lived most dutifully for 50 years'.*
She reclines on a thick mattress placed on a couch. Her heir, Aurelius
Mercurialis, who had the tombstone erected, is apparently the bearded
man on the right. The two smaller figures may be her family or her slaves.
Drinking vessels are set on the three-legged table in front of the couch.
Yorkshire Museum, York

68 *The family meal. From left to right: servants take down jugs to be filled with wine; the family sits round a table, the women in basket chairs, the men reclining on couches; one servant places a dish on the dresser, another wipes the plates. Drawn from a relief on the Igels Column, Moselle Valley, Germany*

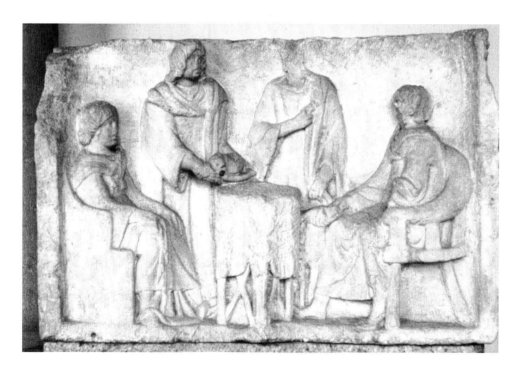

69 *Funerary relief from Neumagen showing a family sitting round a table covered by a fringed cloth. The woman on the left sits in a basket chair. Rheinisches Landesmuseum, Trier*

(*ientaculum*), the breaking of the nightly fast, might be little more than some fruit and a piece of bread washed down with water or wine. Lunch (*prandium*), which was taken any time between 10am and 2pm, according to when breakfast had been eaten, was a snack meal — vegetables, fruit, bread and a drink. The idea was that these two meals were restorative, but not too heavy.

The evening meal (*cena*), was the social meal, a time of relaxation when friends could be invited and entertainment provided for the guests. Martial invited his guest to 'crush the piled couch' at the ninth hour, 5pm, but the meal could be eaten any time between 4pm and 7pm. It might be a formal banquet (*epulae* or *cena rectae*), a small private dinner (*convivia*) or a meal taken with the family. This meal comprised three courses. The first (*gustatio*), consisting of prepared vegetables, shellfish and eggs, was a taster. The main course (*primae mensae*) included roast, boiled or braised meats, poultry, sausages, rissoles and vegetables, often sharply flavoured with herbs and liquamen. The last course (*secundae mensae*) was for desserts — small cakes, fruit, pastries sweetened with honey, egg custards or puddings made with pulses. It was also for savoury dishes that did not require hard eating — shellfish, oysters and snails. Soft dishes or those which would not keep a long time were regarded as the height of luxury at a meals. Oysters were opened with a short-bladed, sharp knife and often picked out with the special spoon (*cocleare*) or served on a shell-shaped dish (*conchiclar*)

Wine or beer could accompany all the courses, but the more abstemious kept to the Roman custom of taking it only with the second course or after the meals. Although the Romans professed themselves to be shocked by Celtic drinking habits, they were more concerned with drinking beer or wine undiluted than with the quantity consumed. Martial was caustic about Sextilianus who drank twice the allowance of wine allowed and did not dilute it with water. Roman writers disapproved of women drinking too much because heavy drinking might lead to immorality. Cato said men kissed women on the cheeks when they met to ascertain if they had been drinking. Roman attitudes to wine, as today, were ambiguous. Romans were fond of wine but disposed towards an austere lifestyle, which made them feel guilty if they over-indulged. Drinking wine was pleasurable, but heavy drinking implied lack of control. Heavy drinking can lead to health problems. Cases of gout noted in cemeteries at Cirencester, Pondbury and East London might be the result of immoderate drinking habits.

Entertainment had to be provided after the meal. One caricature figure from Colchester is a reciter, and poems were an acceptable diversion. Musicians and singers celebrated the host, his dinner, his likes and dislikes. Trimalchio's feast had elaborate entertainment. A loutish man held a ladder while a young boy climbed to the top and danced to a sung accompaniment. He then jumped through burning hoops and picked up a jar with his teeth. To the horror of the guests —'everyone screamed' — the boy fell on Trimalchio, bruising his arm. The unease of the guests as to what would happen to the boy increased as a slave was beaten for using a white instead of a purple bandage on their host's arm. But Trimalchio set the boy free on the grounds that no one should say that a great figure had been injured by a slave.

Evidence for entertainment is lacking in Britain, but the reciter amongst the Colchester figurines indicates that it was appreciated. Athletic performances after

70 *A dancing girl entertains the guests after a banquet. She wears bikini trunks similar to one found in a well in Roman London*

banquets might have been seen in London. A bronze figure of an athlete, casually adjusting his hair, was found in the Thames near London Bridge. A torn bikini, tossed casually into a well, may have been the sole, or one of two garments covering a dancing girl athlete who entertained well-fed diners (**70**). After-dinner entertainment was conspicuous consumption. It emphasised the wealth and generosity of the host and placed the guests in his debt. In that sense, it mirrored the relationship between the Celtic chieftain and his warriors and therefore would be acceptable to those Britons who, in the contemptuous words of Tacitus, 'were led on to those amenities which made life agreeable' and 'spoke of such novelties when they were only a feature of enslavement'.

71 Cologne beaker, with hunting scene. Verulamium Museum

Tableware

A dining table has to look attractive to guests as well as having pottery useful to the diner. The use of fine tableware was essentially a Roman introduction to dining with style (**colour plate 19**). Before the Conquest, only a small number of communities, mainly in Kent and Essex, were importing or using good quality, wheel-thrown pottery. Elsewhere, pottery was hand-made and used locally. After the Conquest the spread of Romanised habits by the army and administrators, together with importation of goods, meant that huge quantities of tableware became available to the native population. Merchants who wished to have contracts to supply the army began to locate suitable workshops and to develop local potteries. They also imported pottery, especially the distinctive samian ware — cups, platters, bowls — from southern Gaul (**colour plate 20**). These were impressed with stamps of animals, birds and scenes from mythology. The samian tradition spread so that by about AD 120 central Gaulish samian, mainly from Lézoux, had begun to take over the market. From the late second century, the Gaulish potters of north-east France and Germany exported to Britain. It was understandable that British workshops should want to share the success of these wares. Workshops in London and elsewhere produced imitations of the forms in both fine orange and fine grey fabrics (**colour plate 21**).

Most pottery was imported for army use, but would obviously be copied for civilian markets. Forms included the flagon, a narrow-mouthed globular vessel, and carinated bowls

72 Rhenish ware (Moselkeramix) drinking beakers. Verulamium Museum

with flat-grooved rims. Beakers were imported from central Gaul in the mid-first century. In the second century they were imported from Cologne and the Moselle (**71**) and these wares were soon copied by the Nene Valley potters. By the mid-second century, civilians were used to buying fine tableware. This led to a flourishing production of local ware in Britain — fine, sometimes elaborate, colour-coated wares, which were to continue until the third century. Many of these, such as those made by the Colchester and Nene Valley potteries, had first been produced to supply the army.

The Nene Valley potters produced Castor ware, a fine white fabric. This copied the hunting beakers with lively scenes of running animals. Colchester potters also copied the hunting scenes, but added other motifs, some religious, with Celtic mythological scenes. Some potteries, such as those in Oxfordshire, continued to copy samian ware, using a brown-red slip. This pottery was mainly sold in the southern area, as was that of the New Forest colour-coated ware. It was Cranbeck ware which dominated the northern area. This was a late-developed pottery, manufactured near to Malton (North Yorkshire). The potteries began about AD 270 and production increased until, by the mid-fourth century, the fine tableware had flooded the whole of north Britain. The vessels included yellow-ware, parchment ware bowls with red painted stripes and cream flagons with horizontal red stripes.

Some of the more lavish tableware were beakers imported from the Moselle decorated in barbotine or white paint, with instructive phases: *Bibi* (Drink), *Frui me* (Enjoy me). Phrases such as *Vinum vires* (Wine gives strength) and *Parce aquam* (Spare

129

the water) could be countered with *Vinco te* (I overcome you) (**72**). Accompanying a burial in a cremation cemetery at Welwyn was a beaker with specially chosen words for the deceased on the journey to the underworld: *Feliciter* (be happy).

Glassware

Glassware would be bought by the better-off (**73**), partly because fine glass flasks and jars were status symbols but more practically because their fragility meant they had to be kept in a safe place. Cupboards were essential and required the space that only a villa or town house could provide. Some people would cherish a prized piece. Britain was swift to adapt to ways which were more practical, hygienic and which, no doubt, enabled individuals to indulge their personal preferences. It is difficult to decide whether glass vessels were intended for kitchen or dining table. Bowls, flasks or jars could be used for storing or serving food and small flasks for medicinal use. It might be assumed, however, that the finest pieces would be reserved for the dining room.

Some fine pieces, imported into Britain before the Conquest, accompanied their owners into their graves, like the ground-ribbed bowl at Hertford Heath (Hertfordshire) about 50-20 BC. Imports, especially of coloured glass, continued, but a British glass-making industry grew up at Mancetter and Wildespoon (Cheshire). A glassmaker who worked near the amphitheatre in the mid-second century was one of at least 16 known to have been active in London

In the first two centuries strong colours were preferred — dark blue, yellow brown, green and orange-red (**colour plate 22**). A splendid blue-and-white moulded vessel was buried with its owner in a late first-century grave at Radnage (Buckinghamshire), but one of the finest pieces, imported in the first century, came from a grave at Colchester (**74**). It was an elaborately moulded piece divided into three bands. Round the bottom one, a

73 *Glass vessels AD 70-170. These vessels, usually made of blue-green glass, were blown into moulds*

74 *Glass vessel from Colchester showing scenes of a stadium and a chariot race. Castle Museum, Colchester*

chariot race was taking place — four horses harnessed to chariots dash round the circuit. On the second band are displayed the spina, shrines and other stadium features. Round the top are the names of the contestants; *Crescens Ave* (the winner), *Hierax vale, Olympae vale, Antiloce vale.*

By the second century glass becomes less colourful, probably following fashion, and for the next two centuries this was used for good tableware. Pliny said that the most highly prized glass is colourless and transparent, almost resembling rock crystal. Both cast and moulded pieces include attractive flagons and bowls. In the third and fourth centuries, splendid drinking vessels featured mythological and hunting scenes. A complete bowl found at Wint Hill (Somerset) shows the hunter riding with cloak billowing behind him, accompanied by two hounds which are chasing a hare into a net; cross hatched engraving

75 *Base of a figured bowl from Wint Hill, Banwell, Somerset showing a lively hunting scene. Ashmolean Museum, Oxford*

76 *Bronze strainer, probably manufactured in a Capuan factory about AD 250. Ice would have been put into it and wine strained through to cool it*

is used to create shadows (**75**). Only a few fragments remain of some of the finest glass, which was imported from Trier. The outer part of the thick glass has been pared away to leave a net of glass as an outer frame. Complete vessels in the Trier and Cologne museums show what a magnificent display they would have made. Their presence in Britain indicates that there were some householders wealthy enough to afford such decorative tableware.

Metalware

Decorative bronze and silver jugs, skillets for sieving or cooling wine (**76, 77**) and silver, and bronze bowls would be in use. Such silverware as the Mildenhall Treasure (if it was intended for household purposes and not for religious use) was too valuable to be used at meals and was probably placed on a side table to provide an attractive and valuable decoration (**78**). Stone side tables have been assumed to exist in villas in south-west Britain, abutting into a wall. An example can be seen on the sarcophagus from Simpleveld (Holland) (**79**), which displays a room where there are also cupboards and shelves for storage. Square bottles are placed side by side on a small chest.

One metal, particularly popular in Britain in the third and fourth centuries, was pewter. Several hoards of these vessels were buried in pits, probably because of the disturbed conditions in part of the fourth century. One table service, found in a well at Appleshaw (Hampshire), had been deposited by its owner in a forlorn attempt to save it for future use. Moulds found at Lansdown near Bath and at sites in south-west Norfolk suggest local manufacturing areas.

An inventory on one of the Vindolanda writing tablets may have been some of the contents of the praetorium, the commandant's house. The list included *scutulae*

77 *An elaborate skillet handle, late second-early third century, from Capheaton, Northumberland. At the top is the goddess, Diana, in her role as guardian of the countryside. Below is Mercury, giver of wealth and protector of traders. On the base are Bacchus and Ariadne (or a Maenad). The two reclining figures are a water nymph, with water gushing from an overturned urn, and a river god, with a dolphin beneath his elbow. The recurring theme of well-being and prosperity may suggest that the skillet, rather than being used in a domestic household, was part of ritual table ware. British Museum*

78 *Bacchic platter from the Mildenhall Treasure. On the left is a dancing Pan, on the right a dancing Maenad. At the top of the platter, a water nymph reclines on an urn which gushes forth water. Below are a fawn and a serpent. British Museum*

(dishes or plates), *paropsides* (side plates), *acetabula* (vinegar bowls), *ovaria* (egg cups), *calices* (cups), *trullae* (bowls) and *panaria* (bread baskets). All these had been kept in a chest. Add to these a collection of glassware and bronze vessels and jugs, and a picture emerges of a comfortably furnished home boasting a well-prepared table.

79 In the third century AD, a wealthy lady had been buried in an elaborately-carved coffin which depicted her wordly possessions. These included a basket chair, a low chest on which rest bottles, shelves containing toilet articles and a handsome three-legged table. There are two jugs, seemingly of bronze, with hinged lids probably used for heating water. Above are cups or beakers, all part of a wine drinking set. She even wished her bath-house to be included. Found at Simpleveld, Holland

12 Shops and markets

Shops

The Romans brought a money-based market economy to Britain. Cheap manufactured goods and a surplus of food products could be bought in shops based in towns, large villages and the *vici*. The importance of the money was increased by the taxes imposed by the Romans during the first and second centuries AD. If people were not in receipt of a salary, they had to raise money by commercial transactions. Taxes might be paid in kind; for example, in requisitions demanded by the army, but the preferred way was to sell goods to raise money. Even allowing for the large number of slaves, this led to an increase in the number of artisans and hired agricultural workers. None the less, many people in the empire and in the province of Britain remained part of a subsistence economy. Surplus food might be sold in the market, but, if there were problems with money supply, it could be bartered.

Shopping habits are revealed by the reliefs of the wine shop at Dijon, the patisserie at Metz, the butcher's shop at Dresden and the frescoes of Pompeii. At Dijon, the customer appears to be holding up his own container, into which the wine will be poured, a sensible method of collection (**80**). On the Dresden relief the butcher is chopping what appears to be a breast of lamb on a three-legged chopping block (**colour plate 23**). At the back of the shop is a rack from which hangs a similar joint, together with a leg of lamb, pigs head and other items including what appears to be liver and sows' udders. A bowl to collect the offal lies in front of the butcher and to the left, seated in a rounded basket chair, is his wife, totting up the accounts. Behind him is the steelyard on which he will weigh his products. A fresco at Pompeii reveals bread, stacked up on the counter ready for sale; the actual bread, carbonised by the effect of the eruption of AD 79, is in the Naples Museum (**81**).

No such evidence has been found in Britain (**82, 83**) and the difficulty of identifying shops illustrates the problems facing excavators. Classical literature gives some idea of what might have been the situation. Every town had a large number of ambulant vendors, such as pancake, confectionery and sausage sellers, whose cries, according to Seneca, disturbed honest people in their homes. People could buy fast food from them or from shops and bars. A *taberna* referred both to a shop selling general goods and to a wine shop (**84**). In Ostia these tended to be placed on street corners so as to attract trade; no doubt this practice was followed elsewhere throughout the empire. A *caupone* at one time referred to a hotel (**85**), but became a place which sold only drink, while a *thermopolia* was a bar where snacks and hot drinks were served (**86**). A *popina*, which according to Martial had stools, sold food but more specifically was a drinking and eating establishment, with a sometimes dubious reputation as the haunt of thieves, drunks, prostitutes and murderers.

80 *Two reliefs on a funerary tomb. On the left a customer is buying a flagon of wine from a wineshop. The scene on the right would have displayed a butcher's shop as hanging up are breasts of lamb, pig's heads and large joints. Musée Archéologique, Dijon*

81 *A baker's shop drawn from a fresco at Pompeii*

82 Counter of a baker's shop, Pompeii

83 Rear of a counter of a wine shop at Herculaneum, showing how it was constructed round dolia

84 A shop counter, Herculanium. The glass covers are modern

The excavators of one building in the Housesteads fort *vicus*, thought to have been a *popina*, found two bodies under the floor, which raises the possibility of foul play. Juvenal sneers at the consul, Lateranus, for frequenting all-night taverns, where a shameless barmaid lies in wait, when he should be preparing to defend the borders of the empire on the Rhine or the Danube. Horace speaks of an *uncta popina* (what we might call 'a greasy spoon') and of *immundae popinae* (foul pubs), which probably refers to the smoke of a brazier, used for heating as well as cooking, as well as the smell of stale food. At Pompeii, many *popinae* were next to the baths so that customers could get snacks and return to their social activities without wasting time.

Some shops specialised whilst others sold general goods. A writing tablet found in London has on it the words *ex taberna sua* which suggests that somebody was buying something from a shop. Commercial properties excavated in London and Verulamium were in the form of strip premises, with doorways in the side-walls opening into alleyways. The Verulamium ones were rebuilt several times between AD 61, when Boudicca destroyed the city, and AD 155, when they were destroyed in another fire. They were timber-framed buildings, with wooden sill beams that probably rotted and needed replacement. At Poultry in London there was a parade of shops, timber-framed with mud bricks and straw infill, where goods would be displayed in the open shop front on the street and secured by shutters at night. A similar arrangement can be seen at Herculanium, which was overwhelmed by lava in the Vesuvian eruption; the remains of the charred wooden shutters still survive (**colour plate 24**). Possibly the London shops were not owned by one family but let to a series of tenants. Tiled brick hearths in the centre of a

85 Drawing made from a relief and inscription found at Aesernia (modern Iscernia), Italy. The inscription relates a dialogue between an innkeeper and a departing guest. Musée du Louvre. (An as was a small copper coin; 16 asses equalled one silver denarius)

'Let us calculate the bill'

'You have had a sextarius of wine . For the bread one as, for that which went with the bread, two asses'

'Correct'

'A girl. Eight asses'

'Correct on that as well'

'Hay for the mule'. Two asses

'That mule will give me to the bailiffs'

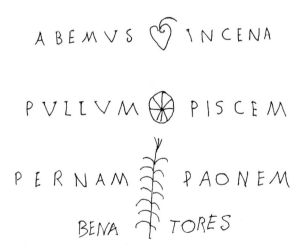

86   A bill of fare outside an inn at Pompeii. The graffiti read:

We go into dinner

Chicken Fish

Ham Peacock

The Hunters

87 A wine shop, Herculaneum

room or set against a wall provided cooking and heating facilities. One building, which seems to have been a wine shop, had remains of amphorae fragments from Spain, Italy and southern Gaul. A group of brick ovens found on the western side of the forum area may be a baker's shop. Lamb skull fragments in a ditch at Southwark and cattle-bones in a pit in London may be debris from butchers' shops.

One shop at Verulamium contained so many broken amphorae that it seems wine was sold there; by the shop was a cellar and scratches on its walls were probably marks caused by the pointed ends of amphorae being rolled along. At Herculanium (**87**), one wine shop had the long amphorae stacked horizontally in wooden racks on the walls. A shop at Verulamium was suggested to be a butcher's although here, according to the bones found, the principal meat seems to have been horseflesh; the flesh was stripped from the bones, possibly to be made into rissoles and sausages.

A timber building at Gloucester had meat waste round it, mainly scapulas and butchered femur fragments. This building had continued as a butcher's shop into the fourth century. Bakeries have been found at Silchester, Springhead (Kent) and Holditch (Staffordshire). In London a baker's shop was identified by the finding of a dough trough during the Poultry excavations (**colour plate 25**), but there would probably have been a large number of bakers' shops in London. The Vesuvius eruption destroyed at least 20 bakeries in Pompeii; Modestus' bakery in the Street of the Augustales still had 81 loaves in

88 Carbonised dates found at Colchester in a shop destroyed in the Boudiccan Rebellion, AD 60-1

the oven waiting for customers. Some might have brought their own dough to be baked in his oven, but these were his own products for they were stamped with his name. A baker's iron slice at Verulamium and a donkey mill at London identify other bakers' shops in Britain.

Dates were found in the remains of one shop burned down during Boudicca's rebellion at Colchester (**88**), and burnt seeds of dill, celery and poppy were in another. A shop in the east wing of the Caerwent forum seems to have sold oysters and other seafood. One building at Silchester has been tentatively identified as a dairy, with a milking parlour at the rear and a cool room where tall stones supported a cold slab on which butter and cheese could be placed. A shop in the corner of the Caerwent forum appears to have been more of a snack bar with a hearth for cooking or heating on one side. The customers played board games, judging by the counters found during the excavations. They may have idly plucked their eyebrows, cleaned their nails and scraped out their ears as they pondered their next moves, for tweezers, ear scoops and other toilet implements were also found. Shopping would provide an opportunity to gossip, meet friends and exercise consumer choice. As far as human nature was concerned, the inhabitants of Roman Britain would have the same attitude towards satisfying consumer habits as do inhabitants of present-day Britain (**89**).

89 *A poultry shop kept by women. Drawn from a relief in the Museo Torlonia, Rome*

90 *Apple market stall. Relief in the Musée Luxembourgeois, Arlon, Belgium*

Markets

Markets were also part of the wholesale and retail trades. In towns a market might take place in the forum, where temporary stalls would be set up on market days, or it might have its own separate building (*macellum*) generally selling a variety of goods, especially meat, fish and other foods (**90**). Wroxeter held a market in the forum. When the building was destroyed between AD 165-75, one of the traders was a pottery merchant. His stock of mortaria and samian dishes, together with a collection of Kentish ragstone whetstones, were thrown, still in their stacked condition, into a gutter. When the forum was rebuilt, they were not dug out but merely covered. In the countryside temporary markets might be allowed at religious sites on the festival days of certain deities. An example is Woodeaton (Oxfordshire) where so many small articles such as bronze letters, coins and small votive objects have been found, that it seems they must have been dropped by careless buyers.

The Romans shared a view held by British planners today, that a new market might take away custom from established shops; in the Roman case this might also reduce the taxes that a shopkeeper should pay. Therefore markets were closely controlled by the authorities, and permission had to be sought to hold one. In towns they were under the supervision of *aediles,* who had to police them, oversee the sale of animals, see that the consumer was protected from fraudulent traders and check that weights and measures were correct (**91, 92**). An inscription on a bronze steelyard weight from Pompeii, dated AD 47, indicates that it has been certified as correct by the *aediles* Marcus Articuleius and Gnaeus Turranius. Presumably they also had to oversee the collection of rents for market stalls, for stalls in markets were an obvious means of raising revenue. A gathering of large crowds was also an invitation to gossip and rumour, which might result in sedition and riot. Given the problems of unrest in Britain, especially in the northern areas during the first two centuries, a close control would have to be kept on all markets and no responsible authority could let them flourish unregulated.

Markets did, however, provide an economically efficient method of buying and selling goods. Yet transporting those to market was labour intensive and hard work. In the 1830s, 14 centuries after the Roman era ended, the unpublished diary of Thomas Venables, a Cheshire man, reveals the hardship of regularly going to a town market from his farm:

'It was a common thing to work hard all day preparing garden stuff and produce for the market and load up at night and start at midnight over dark and dangerous roads to Leek or Macclesfield and the Potteries, and in wet seasons the roads were so bad that it was a frequent occurrence to get stawed and stuck in a chock hole and occasionally to get warted (overturned) and having reached the market to stand with it (the produce) until sold. And then to load up with lime or coal or wood and come home in the following day or evening. And this was not a single experience of a summer but a matter of weekly occurrence'.

91 Bakers weighing bread. Part of the relief on the tomb of the baker, M. Vergilius Eurysaces, Rome

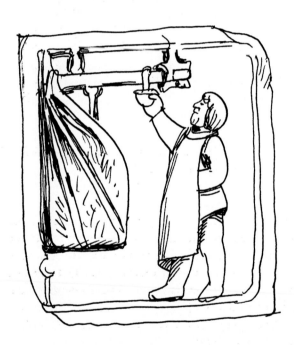

92 A steelyard in use in the market place. drawn from a relief in the Rheinisches Landesmuseum, Trier

Perhaps the needs of the military meant Roman roads were better maintained than those of William IV; none the less, this weekly task was a matter of sheer physical hard labour, but one necessary to make a farm or villa pay its way in a cash economy.

In the first century AD Verulamium had a *macellum,* which consisted of two rows of shops facing each other across an open courtyard. Later a Romano-Celtic temple was built opposite, which might have been dedicated to Mercury, god of trade and commerce. It seems to have been a successful move, for later a theatre was built nearby. This in turn justified the rebuilding of the *macellum* in the second century, which though reduced to half its size had an impressive frontage. Leicester built a

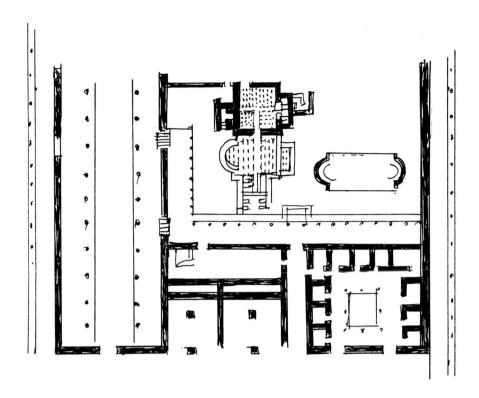

93 Detail of the south-west corner of the public baths at Wroxeter, showing the macellum inserted into it. After the plan in Wroxeter. Life and Death of a Roman City

separate *macellum* early in the third century in the form of a huge basilica placed close to the forum, with wings of shops on the east and west sides. At Cirencester a range of rooms was built in the AD 120s, each about 5.5m (18ft) square, with wooden partitions dividing them. Pits, dug at the edge of the street and in the rooms, were filled with cut and sawn animal bones. These remains from the preparation of joints identify the site as having butchers' shops An open space behind may have been the meat market and shops opposite, equipped with ovens and wells, may have prepared and sold cooked meats. The arrangement made efficient economic sense.

When the baths were redeveloped at Wroxeter after AD 150, a *macellum* was built into the south-west corner (**93**). About a dozen rooms were set round a courtyard and these would be hired out, either on a temporary or permanent basis, where goods could be set out on tables or on the ground. No doubt snack bars were included for those persons who patronised the adjoining baths and the baths' latrine would also be useful for the market traders and customers. Possibly Wroxeter also had a *forum boarium*, a livestock market, probably on the outskirts to prevent too many cattle being driven through the streets. The site may have been north of the baths, where a large enclosure, adjacent to a number of major routes, was situated near to the point where the aqueduct reached the city, thus providing ample fresh water for the animals. It was also downwind of the city so that any obnoxious smell would drift away from the inhabitants.

13 Army diet

Military demands

During the years following the Conquest, the army was an important agent in transmitting the Roman way of life to the provinces and, in so doing, it revolutionised the economy and provided new food for the native Britons. Its demands forced the natives to increase food production from subsistence farming to an agriculture which produced huge surpluses. Such success was demonstrated by the shipments of wheat sent to feed the Rhine army in the fourth century. Not only was food production affected. Fodder had to be supplied for horses, and materials provided for building. The army had an enormous demand for leather and possibly a tribute for leather was imposed on Britain like that which Tacitus records was imposed on the Friesians. Better breeding of cattle in turn, resulted in improved meat carcasses. The army also created a network of contacts, an efficient transport system and roads that allowed food products to be moved quickly throughout the province, as well as locally from country to town. This stimulated local trade, including the carriage of goods to market, hence encouraging the development of cash crops.

The military demand for wine, olive oil and liquamen encouraged long-distance traders to seek a market in Britain for their products. There were four legions in Britain during the first century AD, which meant the presence of about 21,000 men. Even if some men had a preference for native beer, there were numerous auxiliary troops and many civilians who developed a taste for wine as the Gauls and the Germans had done. Given the evidence for the import of wine into pre-Roman Britain, it would seem that the wine trade had preceded the flag and that contacts had already been initiated for a strong wine trade to develop. This was necessary as the army would need supplies as soon as the troops landed and established their bases.

This trade was partly directed by military officials, but civilians participated. Small-scale civilian trade would be carried on the back of a massive official supply system, making use of the roads, the *mansiones* which provided stopping places for a change of horses and for refreshment, and the *vici* of forts which gave shelter in safety for an overnight stay. One of the Vindolanda writing tablets mentioned Octavius, who supplied the garrison with grain, sinews and hides; he may have been a civilian trader or a serving soldier. If the latter, he is an early example of the numerous wheeler-dealers found in armies throughout history.

The overall supply of food would be the responsibility of the prefect of the camp (*praefectus castrorum*) and some troops, the *frumentarii,* had a full time role of procuring food. The quartermasters (*mensor, mensor frumenti, mensor tritici*) oversaw its distribution and the *horreanus* arranged its storage in granaries. Other troops were given the jobs of curing hams, brewing beer and making cheese. Food would be requisitioned from civilian sources, grown by the military themselves, bought locally or supplied under contract. It would be stored in granaries, each fort having one or several according to its needs. Tacitus said that Agricola insisted in having enough food stored in a fort to last the garrison a year. Calculations of the capacity of some fort granaries indicate that reserves were held beyond this annual requirement. This was done so that the soldiers could survive a siege or to avoid a failure of the harvest; the latter might lead to mutiny.

Army supplies

Granaries, usually grouped in pairs, were long buildings resting on pillars or transverse walls to raise them above the ground. Heavy stone flags supported the weight of the grain which, as it was in a semi-fluid state, exerted a thrust against the outside walls. To counteract this, buttresses were built and the grain divided into bins or sacks. An overhanging tiled or thatched roof forced rain to run off beyond the walls, and wooden louvres were placed between the buttresses under the roof for ventilation. Loading platforms at one end (**94**), like those provided at Corbridge and Rudchester, made the unloading of supplies much easier than if they had to be humped up a flight of steps, as was the case at Benwell and Housesteads. At Longthorpe, one stone building held the corn supply in bins 3.4m (11ft) wide and 3.1m (10ft) long, providing rations for 2,444 men for four months. A second stone building, smaller but wider, with rooms 4.6 x 5.5m (15 x 18ft) leading off a central corridor, has been provisionally identified as a store for barrels containing dried or salted meat and fish, amphorae containing olives, oil, liquamen, dried fruit and other items, some hanging from *carnaria* secured to the roof.

The commanding officers of forts had to be prepared to entertain fellow officers visiting from other forts, administrators and officials. During May AD 104 according to one of the Vindolanda writing tablets, Flavius Cerealis, Prefect of the Ninth Cohort of Batavians, seems to have entertained a legate, a governor and several visiting officers mainly on a diet of chicken. Many of the officers, including Flavius Cerialis, had their families with them. These had their own separate quarters and therefore could make their own arrangements for eating. On manoeuvres, however, or in war, they would have the same food as the men, as did certain Emperors. The Emperor Hadrian, following the example of his predecessor Trajan, ate bacon, cheese and hard tack and drank sour wine in camp.

The army in camp

A fixed sum (*in victum*) was deducted from soldiers' pay to cover the cost of their food, together with special stoppages for food on festive days; some of their salaries may have been given in the form of supplies. There does not seem to have been a common mess hall in the forts, so it would seem that rations were handed out to designated recipients

94 Simulated granary, built by a contingent of the Royal Engineers, in 1973, at the Roman Fort of The Lunt, Baginton, West Midlands. At the front is a loading platform, to which carts can be backed up

by the *mensor frumenti* or *mensor tritici*. The recipients were probably from each century in the legion, and in turn they would arrange for food to be given to, or cooked for, each *contubernium* or group of eight men. No mention is made of cooks or kitchen staff in the lists given by Vegetius and Paternus and kitchen duties are not mentioned in the rotas which have been found on sites in the empire. As a great number of duties had to be performed by the troops, probably those men who were not on duty had to cook for their group. The *contubernium* shared two rooms in a barrack block. The inner room was used as living and sleeping quarters and the outer one for storing gear, including cooking pots. Food was cooked here or under the shelter of the veranda outside the door (**colour plate 26**). At South Shields and Housesteads, sets of rooms in barrack blocks, both dating to the late third century, had hearths in the inner rooms for cooking and heating set against the central spine wall. Pottery ventilators had been set on the roof to allow the smoke to escape.

On the march soldiers usually carried their equipment on a *furca* or forked stick. This included a saucepan for cooking and eating, a bronze vessel which acted as a billy can, a string bag in which to put a water/wine container and a leather bag in which to put three days grain or any food obtained by foraging. Milecastle 21 at Swarthy Hill on Hadrian's wall had three buildings set within its walls. The central one had a substantial oven and

95 Bronze cooking vessels and gridiron, Newstead Fort

another had a central hearth. In the longer building there were four cubicle rooms, each of which had a hearth. Soldiers on patrol would be sure of shelter and had their own equipment to prepare a meal (**95**).

There may have been a common time for eating. In his *History of the Jewish War*, Josephus describes the Roman army on the march: 'The hour for supper and breakfast is not left to individual discretion: all take their meals together. This was done at the command of a trumpet, as were the hours for sleep, sentinel duty and rising.' He was speaking of marching camps, but it would be impractical not to have had fixed meal times in the fort. As Josephus said, 'Nothing is done without a word of command'. Both Josephus and Tacitus stated that there were two meals a day, on rising and in the evening, so any food in between would be snacks.

That the centuries in the permanent forts had their own cooking arrangements is suggested by inscriptions on equipment. The handle of a bronze *patera* found at Saham Toney (Norfolk) was marked 'century of Primus'. An *olla* at York has a series of inscriptions including the 'century of Attilius Severus' and the 'century of Aprilis', as if the pot had been handed on. An amphora sherd at Catterick was marked 'turma of Velox' indicating that an ala or *cohors equitata* stationed there had its own share of wine or olive oil delivered to it. A *patera* from Caerleon gives its history; stamped on the disc of the handle are the words 'Maturus made this', stamped on the upper surface is 'First Ala of Thracians', and incised below the handle is 'Lucca', possibly the man who did the cooking.

Soldiers may have milled their own corn. A fragment of quern found at Vindolanda is marked 'property of Victor' (or Victorinus), and emplacements for querns were found at that fort and at South Shields. The Emperor Caracalla prided himself on making and eating his own bread: 'With his own hand he would grind his personal ration of corn, make it into a loaf, bake it in the ashes and eat it'. Having each soldier mill a daily ration, however, seems an extravagant use of manpower. Some querns on Hadrian's Wall have on them the name of the man in charge of the century, like that of Lucius on a stone from Cawfields, so it is likely that each century had responsibility for grinding its own corn ration. This seems to be confirmed by part of a quern from Carlisle marked the 'fifth cohort, century of V...' and another from Maryport (Cumbria) marked the 'tenth mill of the century of ...'. Men would have a daily roster for the duty to grind corn, with the resulting flour delivered to, or collected by, each *contubernium*. A large mortaria from Usk marked 'mixing bowl for the *contubernium* of Messor' seems to indicate that Messor, the *caput contubernii*, had the bowl for mixing the dough.

Communal ovens were set into the ramparts of a fort to prevent danger from fire; three for example exist at Birdoswald in the rear of the rampart. Those at Caerleon (**96**), placed behind the south-west rampart corner, were small domed structures with slabbed floors aligned in pairs, reflecting the pairing of the centurial barracks. Probably there were originally 12 ovens, two for each century of the two cohorts in that part of the fort. They were rebuilt on a larger scale in the second century. A large oven at Birrens (Dumfriesshire) 1.8m (6ft) in diameter, dating from the late second century, had a neatly flagged stone floor, stone walls and a clay dome. Remains of bakehouses at Housesteads were found built against the north-east corner of the fort. Each had a raised stone flagged floor and would have been provided with a domed clay roof. The stoke hole would have been at waist height like that of a modern Italian pizza oven. Three more ovens were found in the south-east quadrant. These would have provided bread for two centuries, with probably one oven allocated to each. This hypothesis is supported by five ovens set in the back of a rampart of Fendoch (Tayside), one for each century. The best-preserved one consisted of a stone flagged floor surrounded by a low stone wall on which the clay dome had been erected. In front of two of the ovens was a large stone under which a fire could be lit; this formed the base of the oven. That bread could be baked in ovens for the whole legion is demonstrated by at least 50 ovens that had been cut into the ramparts of the German fort at the Saalburg. One of the groups of ovens was enclosed by timber posts, which supported the roof of an open shed. Something similar had been erected over three ovens at the Pen Llystyn fort in Wales.

In these ovens was baked the soldiers' bread, probably fresh loaves each day. Four lead dies from Caerleon and a terracotta one from Holt (Flintshire), the legionary out-base of the Twentieth Legion at Chester, were probably bread stamps used by the respective centuries to identify their bread baked in appropriate ovens. If this was the case, then Corellius Audax and Sentius Paulinus, soldiers of the Century of Vibius Severus, were at one time baking bread for their fellow soldiers at Caerleon. Experiments showed that if bread was made with an unleavened mix of wholemeal flour, oil and water, the stamp was clearly defined (**97**). If the bread was allowed to rise, the stamp outline became hidden. A bread stamp from Mainz (Germany) indicates

96 *Bases of circular ovens placed behind the ramparts at the fortress of Caerleon*

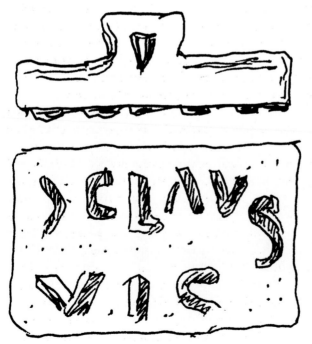

97 *Legionary bread stamp from Chester. The upper drawing shows the stamp in profile. The lower part shows the stamp as it would appear on bread. It reads: ⊃ CL(audii) AUG(ustani) VIC(toris)*

that two bakers and an assistant baked bread for their centuries at their own oven. There were two kinds of bread, the ordinary type *panis militaris castrensis* and another of superior quality *panis militaris mundus*, probably made from more finely refined flour. On manoeuvres or in times of war hard tack (*bucellatum*) was supplied. Soldiers did not like bread made from barley, as has already been mentioned. Vegetius reported that soldiers who did not fight efficiently during weapon training were given rations in barley not wheat. They were kept on these rations until they had demonstrated in front of their senior officers that they were proficient in weapon training.

Army diet

Individuals could make food purchases from shops in the *vici*. Legally married or cohabiting soldiers could supplement their rations in their off-duty visits to the *vici* by eating with their families living there or by buying food from shops and traders. Hunting trips would provide a bonus of wild boar, venison, hare and wild fowl. No doubt the odd chicken, duck or even cow would sometimes mysteriously disappear. Berries and nuts could be gathered locally. Soldiers would write for or be sent gifts. Letters written on *ostraca* found at Wâdi Fawâkhir in Egypt thank relatives for gifts — bread, vegetables, corn and fish feature amongst them. Others from Mons Claudianus in Egypt refer to buying food; Clemens writes to Antoninus, the centurion, that he has bought three suckling pigs for him. Essential elements of a soldier's diet would include meat, cheese, bread, vegetables, berries, olive oil (or lard if that was not obtainable), beer and wine. An amphora at Brough-on-Noe had seemingly contained plums and one at Caerhun (Gwynedd) cherries. This would fit in with Vegetius' remarks that in a satisfactory diet corn, wine and fruits of all kinds must be provided in abundance. The diet of the soldiers at Carlisle was similar to that on the Antonine Wall. Wild fruits included strawberries, raspberries, bilberry and sloes; celery, figs, coriander, and poppy seeds were noted. Henbane and hog's fennel were grown for medical purposes. Henbane and hemlock, both used as painkillers, were also found at the fort of Elginhaugh, near Edinburgh

At Vindolanda, which was occupied by *cohortes equitatum* at the beginning of the second century, one of the writing tablets gave the rations for June 19-25 in an unspecified year, but probably sometime between AD 92-105. No mention is made of corn, but there was a daily ration of barley. It was suggested that the soldiers were reduced to eating barley at the end of the season as a substitute for wheat and in particular wheaten bread. In a *cohors equitata*, however, eating barley bread might be no great hardship. Barley was part of the normal ration of animal fodder, and the soldiers might be accustomed in emergency situations to making the best use of what grain was available. These soldiers were provincials, and bread made from a mixture of rye and barley would be a normal part of their diet.

A more particular diet has been deduced at forts on the Antonine Wall. Here Vivien Swan has identified pottery akin to that made in North Africa. This included lid-seated casseroles and cooking-dishes, with rounded bases and rilled undersides like the Tunisian *tangine*, which prevented them from slipping when they were bedded on portable clay braziers (**98**). Experiments by Cohors V Gallorum re-enactment group showed that bread made with spelt flour could be baked in the dishes very satisfactorily, although there was some browning due to the intense heat (**colour plate 27**). It was suggested that reinforcements from Britain sent to the Emperor Antoninus Pius' troops in his war in Mauritania AD 146-49 returned with North African soldiers and Moorish levies. These brought with them their own cooking methods. Similar pottery has been identified at York and Caerleon but, in this case, the North Africans probably came to Britain as part of the Emperor Septimius Severus' army for his northern war in Britain in AD 208-11.

In most forts grain could be served as gruel or pottage. Pottage was sometimes made of ground beans or peas (**99**) and fortified with pieces of meat or fish, which added protein to the carbohydrates. Meat was eaten widely. At some forts local conditions might determine what was eaten. Soldiers at the fort of Hod Hill (Dorset), occupied in the first century, ate more mutton and lamb than any other meat which might imply not a preference, but the availability of sheep kept on the downs. At the Longthorpe fort the men ate beef, lamb, goat, and soup, made with expertly butchered bones. They hunted deer and hare and ate pork young; the soldiers liked suckling pig as much as civilians did. There also seemed to have been the occasional consumption of horse, although on the whole soldiers did not like the taste of that meat. Ducks, pigeon, widgeon, goose and woodcock added variety to their diet; domestic fowl were kept for meat and eggs. A curiosity was the discovery of crane bones, which had been disjointed as if for the pot. Vegetius had recommended that all sorts of poultry might be kept without any great expense and they are essential eating in the case of the sick. The fort was supplied with olive oil and liquamen from southern Spain. Fish-hooks indicated that fishing was done either individually or to order.

Fish bones have been found on some sites: perch at Chester, cod at Waddon Hill and Hod Hill and other bones at Brecon, Caerleon and Caernarfon. Oysters were very popular and oyster shells have been found on almost every military site together with less frequent finds of mussels, limpets, cockles and whelks. Edible snails were also consumed and soldiers at Papcastle fort (Cumbria) might have introduced a variety to the district. The debris discovered in a drain at the baths at Caerleon shows that soldiers were served chicken, lamb and mutton chops, pork ribs and trotters and oysters. Their snacks probably included sausages and stews. Later, by the third century, they seem to have eaten more beef and pork; those ribs were well chewed.

Some of the food had to be imported. Olive oil and liquamen were essential although the latter was often supplied in a cheaper variety, muria. Wine was equally popular. A graffito on the neck of an amphora at Richborough read *LYMP(A)*, a wine from the Mount Vesuvius region; soldiers at Caerleon got Aminean wine, those at Mumrills a sweet wine and at Exeter a sweet unmixed wine from Rhodes. The neck of an amphora found at Chester had an inscription relating to a spiced and flavoured vintage intended for the store cupboard; another at Newstead had the single word *vinum* on it. A flagon at Wallsend contained honey-sweetened wine, judging by the cursive lettering written on it. The officers would have the better type of wine but the majority of the soldiers would drink *acetum*, a low quality, vinegary wine diluted with water to form *posca*.

The wide variety of diet is revealed in the Vindolanda writing tablets. The list previously mentioned covering the payments and supplies over a period of eight days in

98 Unleavened bread and North African style brazier

June includes fish sauce (muria) and pork fat; other accounts mention roe deer, piglets, pigs' trotters, ham, lard, venison, olives, olive oil, plums, eggs, semolina, honey, twisted loaves, beans, lentils, salt and spices including garlic paste (*alliatum*). One buyer required two *denarii* of pepper, an expensive item, but known to have been used in an eye salve. It may have been connected with the item in another letter where ten men were noted to be suffering from inflammation of the eyes. Drinks include *acetum, vinum* and a native beer (*cervesa*); on 22 June 73 *modii* or 664 litres (146 galls) of wine were distributed to the garrison, possibly intended for the festival of Fors Fortuna which fell on 24 June. If so, it would have been remarkable if the troops had waited two days before drinking it.

One letter instructs the buyer to get good apples (*mala formonsa*) and eggs in large quantities, if they are on sale at a good price. Another refers to a *modius* of olives and two *modii* of ground beans. One personal letter refers to a friend sending 50 oysters from Cordonovi. A list, seemingly by a civilian tradesman, may refer to debts; Felicio, the centurion, owes for 45 Roman lb of bacon and 15½lb of bacon-lard, which cost 8 *denarii* and 2 *asses*. Atrectus, another soldier or perhaps a civilian as he is called a brewer, is in debt for pork fat worth 11 *denarii* and 2 *asses* (at 16 *asses* to one *denarius*).

The evidence of the tablets showed that adequate supplies continued to arrive. On the northern frontier it would seem that the soldiers could enjoy a varied and nutritious diet.

99 Pulverising food in a pestle and mortar. Re-enactment group of Cohors V Gallorum

If the evidence from the ditch at Bearsden and the sewers of York is taken into consideration, they also paid attention to bowel habits. Reasonable food, exercise and discipline produced an efficient fighting force and if anyone did go hungry in Roman Britain, it was not the army. Roy Davies in his analysis of army diet concludes that 'perhaps the best tribute to the army of the Principate, on campaign or in peacetime or even during the rare mutinies, is that there is no recorded complaint about the Roman military diet'.

Towards the end of the Roman period, the diet of the soldiers might have altered considerably. Recruitment from the northern provinces increased and the evidence for the African troops showed that men would have a preference for their own type of food. Supplies of olive oil and wine, which dwindled in the fourth century, could be replaced by beer and lard. By the fifth century barbarian soldiers were employed under contract. Roman central control, which had functioned so superbly, was giving place to local arrangements. Long-distance trade would still continue, but those persons who were locally self-sufficient would have considerable advantage over others who were reliant on regular supplies. Food preferences would become far more a matter of adhering to local customs.

14 Diet and nutrition

Food supply

Food is a priority. If supplies are scarce people will eat whatever they can; quantity not quality is the criterion. When food becomes more plentiful, consumer choice and discrimination are possible. So are self indulgence and gluttony, both of which were attributed to the Romans, not least because of Seneca's contemptuous comment that the Romans 'ate to vomit and vomited to eat'. There is no doubt that the Roman contact with Britain increased enormously the amount and variety of food which was available. This affected people's tastes. The pre-Roman population had already showed a liking for wine and for other products. New plants once introduced easily adapted to their new habitat and native wild plants were domesticated to give greater and more nourishing yield.

The evidence found during excavations shows that at least the soldiers in the forts and the urban population of the *colonia* and the larger towns could eat reasonably well with an increased variety of diet. This was not surprising, for many of the townspeople were Roman administrators or Romanised Britons, who were to provide role models for the civilised ways of Rome. These people ate more sophisticated food; they may have had the advantage of having one of the cooks who came to seek employment from other parts of the empire or who came in the service of the administrators. They might even have a cook who knew some of the recipes gathered in Apicius' book. Some of his recipes, for example, indicate that fish was eaten covered with heavy sauces, in the same way as meat. Meat was disguised as fish, equating with the Roman preference for eating one product masquerading as another. One Apician entrée was shaped like a fish, tasted like a fish, but was in reality well-salted liver; another — pounded cumin, pepper and liquamen with ground walnuts, poured into brine — resembled salt fish.

Food could be bought and sold in market centres, much being the product of the villas. Their owners would be only too eager to grow cash crops. They, their families and slaves could eat well, especially if they adapted to the more advanced Roman farming methods. The variety of crops is indicated by the rubbish used to fill a disused well at the Great Holt Farm villa, Boreham (Essex). It included cherry, plum and olive stones, walnuts, pine kernels, bones of geese, duck and woodcock, fish bones and oyster shells. The granary, which had burned down, produced evidence of charred grain, barley and peas. The addition of more meat and vegetables would have meant a varied and satisfying diet for at least part of the year.

Imported food added variety and nutritional value to personal diets and was distributed by an efficient transport system to other towns in Britain. It was in the more remote rural areas of the west and north that the diet would remain akin to that eaten in pre-Roman

Britain. There would be less acceptance in those parts of commodities such as olive oil and liquamen. This was not only because of tradition and anti-Roman feeling, but also because of the difficulties in storage and cooking. Cooking implements and tableware need storage places. Larger homes had cupboards where glass vessels could be placed or silverware locked up; these were generally lacking in round houses and long houses. Remote farms and isolated houses might have to be self-sufficient or exist on a diet which remained at subsistence level.

Diet

People living in the Highland regions would have a high protein diet based on animal products. This diet would be adequate in good summers yet less so in the winter. Lack of fodder entailed killing of cattle, ensuring a feast of meat in the autumn while the culling was taking place, but little thereafter. Presumably every part of the animals would be used. Offal, though lower in energy value because of its lower fat content, has a good protein content, and contains certain minerals and vitamin C. We are accustomed to thinking of meat in terms of joints. However, in Mongolia the entire carcass of a sheep is roughly cut up, put into a cauldron, covered with water and simmered. Everyone digs in and eats whatever comes out, be it a rib, part of a leg or the intestine. Nothing is wasted.

Food would be scarce in winter. Meat and soft cheese might be in short supply, but grain would be available, provided the storage pits had been well sealed, enabling a daily ration of bread to be baked. Barley and spelt, roasted, pounded and cooked with water in a cauldron, would make a thick pottage. Some foods would be preserved by salting, drying, smoking and steeping in brine, but survival might depend on the weather; a harsh winter meant hunger. Such a diet would be richer in fat and protein in summer. The carbohydrate content of the subsistence diet could be high in winter if its basis was the thick pottage, although meat and fish added to it would provide protein. This type of diet, though rich in fibre, could lack certain vitamins and be somewhat debilitating.

Though berry fruits, and rose hips in particular, can be used to make healthy syrups, rich in vitamin C, there would certainly be a lack of that vitamin in winter and scurvy would be a constant threat. Iron deficiency, which causes haemoglobin levels to fall resulting in anaemia, would probably be avoided if iron cooking pots and cauldrons were used and a diet contained pulses and cereals. Recent research has shown that a diet containing a large amount of indoles, present in the cabbage family, dried beans and lentils, inhibits the formation of tumours. If the lentils found at the Fishbourne villa are indicative of part of the diet, they would have provided a source of protein, together with iron, phosphate and potassium. Fat hen is particularly nutritious and the seeds can be ground to make pottage.

One problem with a mainly cereal diet is that as well as fibre it contains phytate. Its consumption interferes with the absorption of calcium thus predisposing individuals to osteomalacia, a disease found in Romano-British cemeteries. Vitamin D is essential for calcium absorption. Egg yolks, liver and fish oils provide vitamin D, but most vitamin D is created by the action of sunlight on the skin.

Plants and vegetables, if used quickly, would provide much-needed nutrients. Long transportation results in nutritionally depleted vegetables so the quicker the transfer of food from garden to table or from supplier to consumer the better. Food poisoning can occur through eating tainted food and fertilisation with sewage can lead to E.coli infection. Apicius gives advice on preserving food and preventing it from going bad. That people survived infestation has been revealed by the analysis of faecal remains from a cesspit at Carlisle and the York sewers. Whipworms and roundworms, both of which live in the intestines, were present in huge numbers. Heavy infestation, however, can lead to dysentery. Lack of good hygiene, especially with regard to foodstuffs, can lead to problems ranging from mild discomfort to chronic sickness and death. Yet the inhabitants of York had eaten a great variety of vegetables, including celery, radishes and beans, and fruit, including raspberries, blackberries, figs, mulberries, plums, grapes, dates, apples, cherries, crab apples and nuts, shellfish, river and sea fish, together with cereals cooked in different ways. A cesspit from the small salt town of Nantwich contained a wide variety of seed and fruit stones, and remains of vegetables, herbs, spices and bran, as well as the inevitable human parasites.

Calcium intake would be higher in summer than in winter because of the availability of green leafy vegetables and more fresh milk and cheese. Milk has a high calcium content essential for strong bones and teeth, small amounts of phosphorus and potassium and a significant amount of protein. Vitamin A content is greater in summer milk than winter milk; in the summer milk production in Britain would be most prolific. If milk has been carelessly handled or comes from an infected animal it can carry disease-causing organisms, especially tuberculosis and brucellosis. Several examples of tuberculosis of the bone have been found in skeletons excavated from Roman sites; three were noted at the Roman town of Poundbury (Dorset), which could have been caused by infected milk.

Fish needs to be transported, sold and consumed quickly. Growth of bacteria means that it deteriorates, becoming both smelly and dangerous to health. Fastidious eaters would avoid it and even those who were short of food would be wary of its nausea-producing effects. Pliny and Columella warned against eating fish that was anything less than fresh. Roy Davies draws attention to its danger, quoting a case in the second century AD. Terentianus, a soldier stationed at Alexandria, wrote to his father apologising for not meeting him. He, with almost all the garrison, was unable to leave the camp for several days because of 'so violent and dreadful an attack of fish poisoning'. Fish preserved in brine, however, kept for about a year and could be consumed during late winter and early spring, when food was scarce, or as a short-term response to famine.

The inhabitants of country regions would be aware of the abundance of plants and roots that would be useful and nourishing. Some crops would be crossbred with imported new varieties. Better breeding of sheep and cattle ensured finer animals. People knew nothing of nutrition, but they knew what they liked, what plants made them feel well and which were harmful to them. They produced their own palatable diet of foods associated with texture, smell, colour and taste — savoury, sweet and neutral. This food choice would, in general, give them a reasonable balance of protein, vitamins, minerals and calories.

In times of hunger, people could not be fussy. Many foods that tasted bitter, acrid or astringent would be eaten because they felt they were doing them good or were what are known a 'belly-fillers'. Recent work at the University of Washington Nutritional Sciences Programme at Seattle (USA) has determined that many people do not like vegetables, and the feeling is mutual. Plants protect themselves against being eaten by producing bitter-tasting phytochemicals that are often toxic. Children almost always dislike bitter flavours even if they develop more sophisticated tastes later. The prejudice against bitter flavours may protect people from poisoning themselves, but when food is scarce they may need to distinguish the toxic from the merely unpleasant. Roman adult taste was more sophisticated. The Romans disliked bland tastes and added contrived sour, spicy and bitter tastes by the use of herbs and spices. They countered these flavours by adding liquamen or olive oil. The oil blunted the bitter phytonutrients and, unknown to the Romans, had the added advantage of containing some vitamin E. Care had to be taken as the oil could easily deteriorate producing a rancid taste.

In towns, and at culling and harvest time in the countryside, the problem might not be lack of food but a surplus. The gorging of food and indulgence in wine can result in liver diseases and obesity. A rich diet, especially if laced with liquamen, can cause bad breath. Worse could occur. Juvenal gives the story of one woman who, arriving late for a dinner party in Rome, slakes her thirst with 'a couple of pints before dinner to create a raging appetite; then she brings it all up again and souses the floor with the washings of her insides'.

Cemetery evidence

Evidence from burials extends the picture. At Cirencester, out of 362 skeletons examined by the late Calvin Wells, 80 per cent revealed evidence of osteoarthritis, a similar number to those who had suffered from this disease in the Trentholme Drive cemetery at York. Ten out of 21 adults suffered from it in a burial place south of the Chignall villa (Essex). This is a 'wear and tear' disease, often the result of a lack of calcium in youth. It can cause immense pain and eventually disability. Those who had it could be a burden on the community. Pliny the Younger mentions that Domitius Tullus was crippled and deformed in every limb, so that he could not turn in bed without assistance and had to have his teeth cleaned for him. Female skeletons at Cirencester also revealed vigorous wear on the spinal column, probably due to humping heavy burdens and carrying buckets of water on yokes.

Some skeletons in the Cirencester and Poundbury cemeteries had a high bone-lead content. This could have been caused in a soft water area by the drinking water running in lead pipes. The lead levels at Poundbury, however, reflected a lifetime accumulation. Children had died of lead poisoning; the unborn may have absorbed it through their mothers' milk. Those persons surviving into middle age had ingested it from food cooked or resting in lead pans or through fruit juices and wine prepared in lead or pewter vessels. The acidity of the fruit caused traces of lead to dissolve. Fruit juices could be added to wine so that the amount of lead intensified in the solution. Persons suffering from lead poisoning develop a metallic taste in the mouth and experience lack of appetite; lead ingestion results in digestive trouble and diarrhoea. To counter lack of appetite, victims eat the more highly spiced and seasoned food which Roman cookery provides.

Skeletons found in a Roman cemetery at Dorchester (Dorset) have recently been examined to determine the protein composition of bone material. The carbon and nitrogen isotope ratios in bone can be measured to give average protein intake, and the proportion of shellfish, vegetable and meat protein consumed by a person over the last ten years of life. Two periods were studied. In the first century AD, when Roman influence was just beginning, people were buried in simple graves with few grave goods. The carbon isotopes ratio in their bones revealed that they had eaten average amounts of animal and plant protein. They were still eating food which could be hunted and herded or grown and gathered easily.

By the fourth century those buried in the cemetery had lived in the prosperous town of Durnovaria. Some people were being buried in stone coffins with more personal possessions and those in the higher social strata had stone tombs. This wealthier part of the community apparently had better food than those persons buried in wooden coffins. Shellfish had been eaten frequently and the diet was high in meat. The carbon isotope ratio of two people was, however, so high that it might imply they were recent immigrants or administrators from Rome or southern Gaul, the warmer Mediterranean regions where carbon is absorbed at a higher rate.

Teeth found in cemeteries at Chichester, Cirencester, York and Ilchester indicate a lack of dental caries. At Cirencester it affected about 5.1 per cent of the skeletons. At Trentholme Drive there was little evidence of dental disease until middle age, then dental caries increased. This was not because oral hygiene was better, although Pliny had advised that teeth could be cleaned with the toothpick and a mixture of ground up oyster shells and charcoal. As this was unpleasant, it was mixed with honey, which would undo the good work. Lack of dental caries was due instead a complete absence of sugar, and, in some areas, of fluoride absorption. A high fibre diet also protects the teeth because it is more abrasive and scours the teeth more than does a highly refined diet. The drawback is that grit in stone-ground bread could wear teeth down. The grinding surfaces on some teeth at Cirencester were almost completely worn down; at Trentholme Drive and Chignall, many of the skulls had teeth that showed evidence of abscesses in the alveolar bone. These would be painful and make chewing difficult.

In order to keep well, people would rely on folk remedies, which could provide additional nutrients to the diet, as in the case of fat hen. Food poisoning and dysentery could cause weakness or death, while the evidence from the York sewers suggests worms and bowel parasites were endemic. Lack of accurate medical records can only give rise to speculation regarding the fate of the population. It is impossible, for example, to say how many women died in childbirth from haemorrhages, puerperal fever or lack of nourishment after giving birth. The number of infants buried with females suggests that the risks of childbirth were great; out of 281 females at Poundbury, 51 had died soon after giving birth.

As in Britain 150 years ago and the developing world today, infectious diseases would have been major killers. Plague, cholera, acute dysentery, leprosy and other diseases would usually leave no trace, although one skeleton at Poundbury and two at Cannington (Somerset) provided evidence of leprosy. No traces of cancer have yet been identified in Roman Britain, but two Anglo-Saxon graves on a site at Edix Hill, Barrington

(Cambridgeshire) provided evidence of cancer. In both cases the bones were affected by cancers of soft tissues, which had spread through the bloodstream and produced secondary effects in the bone, known as metastic carcinoma. One adult male seemed to have suffered from lung cancer, the other from prostate cancer. He was a boy of 15 and the condition is rare at that age. Given this evidence, cancer would not have been unknown in Roman Britain, yet as the age of death was so low, many potential victims would die of something else first.

The large number of leg ulcers affecting the fibulas and tibias of skeletons in the Poundbury cemetery indicates a lack of vitamin C, probably arising when the inhabitants lacked fresh fruit and vegetables because of climatic conditions or deterioration in living standards. Infestation sometimes caused death as well as debilitation. A woman in the Orton Longueville cemetery (Cambridgeshire) died from drinking impure water. A calcified hydatid cyst, the size of a chicken's egg, caused by swallowing a tapeworm, had found its way into the thoracic cavity. Death was probably caused by the bursting of the abscess in the lung or the plural cavity. In the Chignall cemetery out of 36 burials, there were 11 cases of hypoplasia development of the tooth enamel showing lack of growth due to disease or malnutrition. Four cases of cribra orbitalia and four cases of porosity of the cranium indicated iron-deficiency anaemia.

Classical literature tells of plague sweeping through the empire in the fourth and fifth centuries. About AD 443 there is mention of a *pestilentia quae fere in toto orde diffusa est,* which probably reached Britain. Gildas, in the sixth century, also records a *pestifera lues.* The black rat (*rattus rattus*), whose fleas carried the bubonic plague bacillus, was known to have existed in Roman York and London. Pestilence, no matter in what form, would have had a debilitating effect on the population. Survivors would find it difficult to regain their strength and therefore would succumb through weakness or a secondary ailment. Famine would exacerbate the condition. Towards the end of the fourth century and into the fifth, when disease seems to have been commonplace, no amount of good food could provide immunity from endemic diseases. Excavators have recorded bodies seemingly lying unburied in the streets of Caerwent and Cirencester, as if the survivors had insufficient strength to bury the dead.

A nourishing diet could not have been achieved by everyone in Roman Britain. Evidence from skeletons shows the extent to which under-nourishment and a life of unremitting hard labour took its toll. This is seen in skeletal evidence for the heights and life expectancy of men and women. The average height for men was 1.69m (5ft 7in) and of women 1.63m (5ft 4in), but many men were about 1.5m (5ft) and women below that height. Out of 21 adults in the Chignall cemetery, the average age of death was 35 for males and 28 for female. Few in Cirencester had lived beyond the age of 50; the average age of 107 adult males over 21 was 40.8 years and of 44 females over 21, 37.8. The oldest male was 53 and the oldest female 58. At Ilchester (Somerset), out of 49 adults, the oldest male was 45 and the oldest female 50. The average age of death at the Lankhills cemetery, Winchester (Hampshire) was low; only 52 out of 284 adults seeming to have survived beyond the age of 36. The average age of death of persons in the Dorchester (Oxfordshire) cemetery was 33. At the Eastgate Needlemaker's cemetery, Chichester, the adult males had died in their mid-30s.

100   Adult skeleton with flagon, excavated in a Roman cemetery at Pepperhill, Gravesend, Kent, during construction works for the Channel Tunnel Link Railway

Tombstones, even allowing for the fact that the evidence of inscriptions may be unreliable, record that a few achieved a ripe old age. Julius Valens, a veteran of the Second Legion stationed at Caerleon, lived to be 100 and his wife to 75. Claudia Crysis was 90 when she died at Lincoln and Titus Flavius Natalis of Caerleon was 65. Even so, at York 14 out of 15 inscribed tombstones record ages below 40. This is higher than Keith Hopkin's comment on tombstone ages, which indicated that the average life expectancy at birth was between 20 and 30 years. The report on the Lankhills cemetery states that the evidence, 'is consistent with that of tombstones and other excavations in suggesting that life in Roman Britain was indeed short' (**100**). Out of a possible 290 burials in the Trentholme Drive cemetery 'a mere handful' lived beyond the age of 45. The excavators of that cemetery probably speak for the whole of Roman Britain: 'There is compelling evidence that the majority of the denizens of second-, third- and fourth-century York could not expect to survive their fortieth year. Indeed the sobering conclusion is that 77 per cent of them died before this event' (**101**).

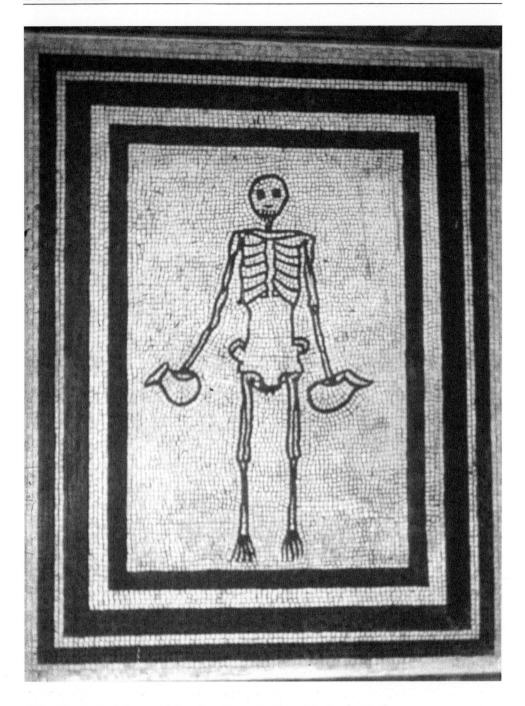

101 Mosaic of a skeleton with jugs from Pompeii. Museo Nazionale, Naples

Classical authors mentioned in the text

Anon. The *Periplus Maris Erythraei* is the work of an anonymous Greek traveller of the first century AD describing the coasts of the Red Sea and the Arabian Gulf, as well as showing a knowledge of parts of India.

Apuleius (active *c.*AD 155). *Metamorphoses* or the *Golden Ass* is the one Latin novel which survives in its entirety and gives many details of popular life. The hero is accidentally turned into an ass and undergoes a series of adventures.

Arrian (*c.*AD 85-after 145). A Greek, born in Bythinia, who followed a successful career in the Roman army and wrote books on customs and philosophy.

Athenaeus (active *c.*AD 200). Greek author of the *Deipnosophists* which is an imaginary tale of 16 men dining together in Rome and discussing a broad variety of topics including food and medicine.

Caesar (100-44 BC). Roman statesman, general and dictator. He subdued Gaul between 61 and 56 BC and invaded Britain twice in 55 and 54 BC. His *Commentaries* on the Gallic wars are written in the third person to indicate that this is an objective, truthful record of events.

Cato (234-149 BC). Roman statesman and moralist. His literary works included *Origines*, a history of the origins of Rome and the Italian cities, together with the more recent Punic wars. His *De Re Rustica*, also known as *De Agri Cultura*, is concerned mainly with the cultivation of fruits, olives and vines. He writes from his own experience and is mainly concerned with the practicalities of running an estate.

Cicero (106-43 BC). Roman statesman and orator, whose prolific writing includes poems, letters and speeches.

Claudian (died AD 404). Roman poet, one of the last to write in the classical tradition. He was a native Greek speaker who composed in Latin as a court poet to the Emperor

Honorius. He wrote a eulogy of the emperor and a three-book panegyric of the general and regent, Stilicho.

Columella (active AD 60-65). A Spaniard who served in the Roman army, he composed a treatise on farming, *De Re Rustica*. This covers all aspects of running an estate including livestock, cultivation, gardens and the duties of a bailiff and his wife.

Dio Cassius (*c.*AD 150-235). Also known as Cassius Dio. A Roman historian, born in Bythinia, and governor of Dalmatia and Africa. He wrote a history of the civil war of AD 193-97 (now lost) and a history of Rome in 80 books. This begins with the coming of Aeneas to Italy after the Sack of Troy and ends in AD 229. Much of the part after AD 9 has been lost, but what remains is useful, especially his contemporary comments on the third century.

Diodorus Siculus (active *c.*60-30 BC). A Greek historian who wrote a world history in 40 books centred on Rome. These are based on ancient sources and are a useful, but uncritical, compilation of legends, social history and mythology.

Dioscorides (active first century AD). A Greek physician who served with the Roman army, he wrote *De Materia Medica* in five books. The subject matter included the medicinal properties of plants and drugs.

Frontinus (*c.*AD 30-*c.*AD 104). After serving as consul in AD 73 or 74, he was Governor of Britain AD 74-78, during which time he subdued the Silures in south Wales. He wrote *Strategemata*, a manual on war strategies for the use of officers and *De Aquis Urbis Romae*, dealing with the history, technicalities and the regulation of the aqueducts of Rome.

Galen (AD 129-99), A Greek who was physician to the Emperors Marcus Aurelius, Commodus and Septimius Severus. He lectured, demonstrated and wrote on every aspect of medicine. His books had enormous influence and formed the basis of many later medical works.

Herodian (active *c.*AD 230). A historian born in Syria, who wrote the *Historia Augusta*, a history in eight books from the death of Marcus Aurelius (AD 180) to the accession of Gordian III (AD 238).

Hippocrates (*c.*460-*c.*370 BC). Probably the most famous figure in Greek medicine, his name is attached to the Hippocratic Corpus, 60 treatises dealing with medicine, surgery and health.

Horace (65-8 BC) Roman poet all of whose published work survives. The *Epodes* and the *Satires* were written about 30 BC and the *Odes* in 23 BC. He also wrote the *Epistles* and *Carmen Saeculare,* the latter dealing with the Secular Games of 17 BC

Josephus (AD 37-after 93). Jewish historian who wrote a history of the Jewish Revolt against Rome, which began in AD 66. The work contains one of the best descriptions of the Roman army.

Juvenal (active second century AD). He was probably the greatest of the Roman satirical poets, writing 16 bitter, humorous *Satires* portraying life in second-century Rome. He may have commanded the First Cohort of Dalmatians at Maryport about AD 90.

Libanius (AD 314-*c*.393). A Greek from Antioch, who studied at Athens and taught at Constantinople. He wrote an autobiography called *Orations*, a funeral oration of the Emperor Julian and several hundred letters.

Livy (59 BC-AD 17) He was born in Padua and is the author of the History of Rome in 142 books, the last 22 of which deal with events in his own time.

Lucretius (*c* 99-*c*.55 BC). Roman poet and philosopher. Author of *De Rerum Natura*, a poem dealing with the system of Epicurus and demonstrating that fear of the gods is groundless and that the world and everything in it is governed by the mechanical laws of nature.

Martial (*c*.AD 40-103). He was a Spaniard who worked in Rome after AD 64 and relied on his poetry for a living. Between AD 86 and 98 he wrote 11 books of *Epigrams*, short poems each of which pithily expressed a concept, with the subject matter ranging across the whole spectrum of Roman life.

Nemesianus (active late third century AD). He was a poet and the author of *Cynegetica*, a manual on hunting.

Oppian (active early third century AD). He was a poet in Cilicia in south-east Asia Minor, who certainly wrote the *Halieutica* (On Fishing) and may have written the *Cynegetica* (On Hunting).

Ovid (43 BC-AD 17). He was born in the valley of the Apennines, east of Rome and travelled round the Mediterranean. His poetry aroused the displeasure of the Imperial court and he was banished to Tomis on the Black Sea. His main poems are the *Ars Amatoria, Tristia, Fasti* and *Metamorphoses*.

Palladius (active fourth century AD). His treatise on agriculture, *De Re Rustica*, in 14 books contains general information on setting up and managing a farm and the work to be done each month.

Petronius (died *c*.AD 65). A satirical writer and author of the *Satyricon*, a novel of which the most well-known part is Trimalchio's feast, an ostentatious dinner party to which a motley crowd gain admittance.

Plautus (*c.*250-184 BC). A Roman dramatist born in Umbria, he wrote about 130 comedies of which 29 have survived. Although having many stock characters, the plays deal with contemporary life and social settings.

Pliny the Elder (AD 23-79). A prolific writer on natural history, his 37 books cover most aspects of natural history, ranging through natural phenomena, medicine, botany, zoology, geography and minerals. His death during the eruption of Vesuvius is recorded by his nephew (unless otherwise stated the references to Pliny in this book refer to Pliny the Elder).

Pliny the Younger (AD 61-113). He was adopted by his maternal uncle, Pliny the Elder, and became an administrator, holding several offices of state, including that of Governor of Bythinia-Pontus on the Black Sea, where he died. He wrote a large number of letters, which were published in ten books. These cover a wide variety of subjects, personal and official.

Posidonius (*c.*135-50 BC). He wrote 52 books on history covering the period 146-81 BC. These included the customs of barbarian races.

Strabo (64 BC-after AD 24). A Greek geographer who came to Rome several times after 44 BC and travelled widely round the Mediterranean. His *Geography*, in 17 books, covers the chief provinces of Roman world and other inhabited regions round the Mediterranean.

Suetonius (born *c.*69 BC). He wrote widely on antiquities and natural sciences, but the work that survives is his *Lives of the Caesars*, an account of Julius Caesar and the 11 subsequent emperors.

Tacitus (AD 56-*c.*117). Born in Gaul, he eventually became a Roman senator and Governor of Asia. He married Agricola's daughter and wrote a life of his father-in-law, published in AD 98, which gives a much-quoted description of Britain. In the same year he wrote the *Germania* dealing with the history and customs of the German tribes, north of the Rhine and the Danube. His major works, the *Histories,* dealing with the period AD 69-96, and the *Annals,* covering the period AD 14-68, are invaluable for events in the first century AD.

Varro (116-27 BC). A prolific writer who is said to have written over 600 books. Of these probably the most important are *De Lingua Latina,* a treatise on Latin grammar, and *De Re Rustica*, in three books, which was intended as a practical manual on running a farm for the benefit of his wife, Fundania.

Vegetius (active *c.*AD 379-95). A military writer who wrote a manual, *Epitoma Rei Militaris,* on military training and the organisation of the Roman Legion.

Virgil (70-19 BC). Roman poet born in Cisalpine Gaul, who studied philosophy in Rome. About 42 BC he began the composition of the *Eclogues*; he was then living in the Campania. This was followed by the *Georgics* and the *Aeneid*. After his death he was regarded as one of the greatest of the Latin poets and his works and his tomb, outside Naples, became the objects of a cult.

Zosimus (late fifth century AD). A Greek historian who wrote a history of the Roman Empire from Augustus to AD 410. He is an important source for the years AD 395-410.

Bibliography

Alcock, J.P. 1992. Flavourings in Roman culinary taste with some reference to the province of Britain, in Walker, H. (Ed.) *Spicing up the Palate, Studies of Flavourings Ancient and Modern*, 11-23.

Alcock, J.P. 1996. *Life in Roman Britain*. London: Batsford/English Heritage.

Allason-Jones, L. 1989. *Women in Roman Britain*. London. British Museum Publications.

André, J. 1961. *L'Alimentation et la Cuisine à Rome*. Paris: Libraire C. Klincksieck.

Andrews, A.C. 1948. Oysters as a food of Greece and Rome, *Classical Journal*, 43. 299-303.

Andrews, A.C. 1949. Celery and parsley as foods in the Graeco-Roman period, *Classical Philology*, 44. 91-9.

Andrews, A.C. 1949. The carrot as a food in the Roman period, *Classical Philology*, 44. 182-96.

Andrews, A.C. 1952. The opium poppy as food and spice in the classical period, *Agricultural History*, 26. 152-5.

Andrews, A.C. 1958. The turnip and the parsnip as food in the classical era, *Classical Philology*, 53. 131-152.

Aston, M.A. (Ed.) 1988. *Medieval Fish, Fisheries and Fishponds in England*. Oxford: British Archaeological Reports 182.

Basu, T.K. and Dickerson, J.W. 1996. *Vitamins in Human Health and Disease*. Wallingford. CAB International.

Bateman, N. and Locker, A. 1982. The sauce of the Thames, *London Archaeologist*, 4.8. 204-7.

Bestwick, J. 1975. Romano-British inland salting at Middlewich (*Salinae*), Cheshire, in De Brisay, K.W. and Evans, K. (Eds.) *Salt. The Study of an Ancient Industry*, 60-77.

Billiard, R. 1913. *La Vigne et La Vin dans L'Antiquité*. Lyon: H. Lardanchet.

Bingen, J. 1994. *Mons Claudianus. Ostraca Graeca et Latina Volume II*. Cairo: Institute Français d'Archéologie Orientale du Caire.

Bird, J., Graham, A. H., Sheldon, H. and Townsend, P. (Eds.) 1978. *Southwark Excavations 1972-1974*. London and Middlesex Archaeological Society and Surrey Archaeological Collections, Joint Publication No.1.

Bird, J., Hassall, M. and Sheldon H. (Eds.) 1996. *Interpreting Roman London. Papers in Memory of Hugh Chapman*. Oxford: Oxbow Monograph 58.

Birley, A. 1979. *The People of Roman Britain*. London: Batsford.

Birley, A. 1992. A case of eye disease (*lippitudo*) on the Roman frontier in Britain, *Documenta Opthalmologica*. 81. 111-19.

Birley, A. 2002. *Garrison Life at Vindolanda: a Band of Brothers*. Stroud: Tempus Publications.

Birley, A. 2009. *Vindolanda: a Roman frontier fort on Hadrian's Wall*. Stroud: Amberley Press

Birley, E. 1936. Marcus Cocceius Firmus: an epigraphic study, *Proceedings of the Society of Antiquaries of Scotland*, 17. 363-77.

Blagg, T.F.C. and King, A.C. (Eds.). 1984. *Military and Civilian in Roman Britain,* Oxford: British Archaeological Reports, 136.

Blagg, T.F.C. 1990. First-century Roman Houses in Gaul and Britain in Blagg, T.F.C. and Millett, M. (Eds.) *The Early Roman Empire in the West,* 194-204.

Blagg, T.F.C. and Millett, M. (Eds.) 1990. *The Early Roman Empire in the West,* Oxford: Oxbow Books.

Boon, G.C. 1958. A Roman pastrycook's mould from Silchester, *Antiquaries Journal,* 38. 237-40.

Boon, G.C. 1972. *Isca. The Roman Legionary Fortress at Caerleon, Monmouthshire.* Cardiff: National Museum of Wales.

Boon, G.C. 1974. *Silchester. The Roman City of Calleva.* Newton Abbot: David and Charles.

Bowman, A.K. 1994. *Life and Letters on the Roman Frontier. Vindolanda and its People.* London: British Museum Press.

Bowman, A.K. and Thomas, J.D. 1994. *The Vindolanda Writing Tablets.* London: British Museum.

Branigan, K. 1981. Celtic farm to Roman Villa, in Miles D. (Ed.) *The Romano-British Countryside,* 81-96.

Branigan, K. and Miller, D. (Eds.). 1989. *The Economics of Romano-British Villas.* Sheffield: Department of Archaeology, University of Sheffield.

Breeze, D. and Dobson, B. *Hadrian's Wall.* 2000. 4th edition. London: Harmondsworth.

Brown, A.G. and Meadows, I. 2000. *Roman Vineyards in Britain: finds from the Nene Valley and new research.* Antiquity, 74, 2000, pp. 197–198.

Brown, D. 1973. A Roman Pewter Hoard from Appleford, Berkshire, *Oxoniensia,* 38. 184-206.

Buckland, P.C. 1970. *The Environmental Evidence from the Church Street Roman Sewer System. The Archaeology of York. The Past Environment of York 14.1.* Council for British Archaeology for York Archaeological Trust.

Buckland, P.C. and Magilton, J.R. 1986. *The Archaeology of Doncaster, I. The Roman Civil Settlement.* Oxford: British Archaeological Reports 148.

Bulman, M.W. 1975. Honey as a surgical dressing, *Middlesex Hospital Journal,* 55.6.189-95.

Burn, A.R. 1953. Hic breva vivitur: a study of the expectation of life in the Roman Empire. *Past and Present,* 4. 25-36.

Burnham, B.C. and Johnson, H.B. (eds.) 1979. *Invasion and Response. The Case of Roman Britain,* Oxford: British Archaeological Reports, 73.

Butler, A.J. 1930. *Sport in Classic Times.* London: Benn.

Callender, M. 1965. *Roman Amphorae.* Oxford: Oxford University Press.

Casson, L. 1989. *The Periplus of the Erythraean Sea.* Princeton: Princeton University Press.

Castle, S.A. 1978. Amphorae from Brockley Hill, *Britannia,* 9. 383-92.

Charles, R.A. 1987. The Late- and Sub- Roman Cemetery at Queensford Farm, Dorchester-on-Thames, Oxfordshire. *Oxoniensia,* 52. 35-71.

Charlesworth, D. 1966. Roman Square Bottles, *Journal of Glass Studies* 8. 26-40.

Clark, J.D.G. 1942. Bees in Antiquity, *Antiquity,* 16 208-15.

Clarke, C.P. 1998. *Excavations south of Chignall Roman Villa, Essex, 1977-81. East Anglian Archaeological Report No 58.* Chelmsford: Essex County Council.

Clarke, G.N. 1979. *Pre-Roman and Roman Winchester. Winchester Studies 3. Part II. The Roman Cemetery at Lankhills.* Oxford: Clarendon Press.

Cool, H.E.M. 2006. *Eating and Drinking in Roman Britain*. Cambridge: Cambridge University Press

Crane, E (ed.) 1975. *Honey. A Comprehensive Survey.* London: Heinemann.

Crane, E. and Graham, A. T. 1985. Beehives of the Ancient World, *Bee World*, 66. 25-41.

Crocock, C. and Grainger, S. 2006. *Apicius. A Critical Edition with an introduction and an English Translation of the Latin recipe text* Apicius. Totnes: Prospect Books.

Croom, A.T. 2001. Experiments in Roman militray cooking methods. *The Arbeia Journal*, 6–7, (1997–1998), 34–37.

Crummy, P.J. 1984. *Excavations at Lion Walk, Balkerne Lane, and Middleborough, Colchester, Essex. Colchester Archaeological Reports 3*. Colchester: Colchester Archaeological Trust.

Cubberley, A.L., Lloyd, J.A. and Roberts, P.C. 1988. *Testa* and *Clibani*: the baking covers of Classical Italy, *Papers of the British School at Rome*, 56. 98-119.

Cunliffe, B.W. 1971. *Excavations at Fishbourne 1961-1969, Volume I. The Site.* London: Report of the Research Committee of the Society of Antiquaries of London No 26.

Cunliffe, B.W. 1975. *Excavations at Portchester Castle. Volume I Roman.* London: Report of the Research Committee of the Society of Antiquaries of London No 32.

Cunliffe, B.W. 1987. *Hengistbury Head, Dorset. Volume 3, The Prehistoric and Roman Settlement.* Report of the Research Committee of the Society of Antiquaries of London.

Curle, J. 1911. *A Roman Frontier Post and its People. The Fort at Newstead in the Parish of Melrose.* Glasgow: Maclehose.

Curtis, R. 1988. *Studia Pompeiana et Classica in Honor of Wilhelmina F. Jashemski. Volume I, Pompeiana,* New York: Orpheus Publishing.

Curtis R. 1991. *Garum and Salsamenta: Production and Commerce in Materia Medica.* Studies in Ancient Medicine 3. Leiden: E. J. Brill.

Dannell, G.B. and Wild, J.P. 1987. *Longthorpe II: The Military Works Depot: an Episode in Landscape History.* Britannia Monograph Series No 8. London: Society for the Promotion of Roman Studies.

Dannell, G.B. 1979. Eating and drinking in Pre-Conquest Britain: the evidence of amphora and samian trading and the effect of the invasion of Claudius in Burnham, B.C. and Johnson, H.B. *Invasion and Response: The Case of Roman Britain,* 177-84.

Darling, M.J. 1993. *Caistor on Sea. Excavations by Charles Green 1951-55.* East Anglian Archaeology 60. Norwich: Norwich Museum Services.

Davies, R.W. 1971. The Roman Military Diet, *Britannia* 2.122-42.

Davies, R.W. 1974. The daily life of a Roman soldier in the Principiate, in Temporini, H. *Aufstieg und Niedergang der Römischen Welt* II I Berlin and New York: W. de Gruyter.

De Brisay, K.W. and Evans, K.A. (Eds.) 1975. *Salt. The Study of an Ancient Industry.* Colchester: Colchester Archaeological Group Publications.

De Ligt, L. 1993. *Fairs and Markets in the Roman Empire. Economic and Social Aspects of Periodic Trade in a Pre-Industrial Society.* Amsterdam: J.C. Gieben.

De Ruyt, C. 1983. *Macellum. Marché Alimentaire des Romains.* Louvain: Publications d'histoire de l'Art et Archéologie de l'Université Catholique de Louvain, 38.

Dickson, C. 1989. The Roman army diet in Britain and Germany, *Archäobotanik Dissertationes Botanicae,* 133, 135-54.

Dickson, C., Dickson, J.H. and Breeze, D. 1979. Flour or bread in a Roman military ditch at Bearsden, Scotland, *Antiquity*, 53. 437-42.

Dobney, K.M., Jaques, S.D. and Irving, B.G. 1996. *Of Butchers and Breeds. Report on Vertebrae Remains from Various Sites in the City of Lincoln.* Lincoln Archaeological Studies 5

Down, A. 1988. *Roman Chichester.* Chichester: Phillimore.

Dunnett, R. 1975. *The Trinovantes.* London: Duckworth.

Du Plat Taylor, J. and Cleere, H. (Eds.) 1978. *Roman Shipping and Trade: Britain and the Rhine Provinces*, London: Council for British Archaeology Research Report 24.

Eckardt, H. 1999. The Colchester child's grave, *Britannia, 30.* 57-90.

Edwards, J. 1984. *The Roman Cookery of Apicius. Translated and Adapted for the Modern Kitchen.* London: Rider and Company.

Ellis, P. (Ed.), 2000. *The Roman Baths and Marcellum at Wroxeter.* London: English Heritage.

Ellmers, D. 1978. Shipping on the Rhine during the Roman period: the pictorial evidence in Du Plat Taylor, J. and Cleere, H. (Eds.). *Roman Shipping and Trade,* 1-14.

Étienne, R. 1970. Á propos du garum sociorum, *Latomus. Revue d'Études Latines,* 29. 297-313.

Farwell, D.E. and Molleson, T.I. 1993. *Excavations at Poundbury 1966-68, Volume II. The Cemeteries.* Dorchester: Dorset Natural History and Archaeological Society Monograph Series No 11.

Fielding, A.M. and Fielding, A.P. (Eds), 2005. *Salt. Proceedings of the International Conference on Traditional and Historic Salt making.* Northwich: Lion Salt Works Trust, Research report No. 2.

Flower, B. and Rosenbaum, E, 1958. *The Roman Cookery Book, a critical translation of the Art of Cooking by Apicius.* London: Harrop.

Fox, A. and Ravenhill, W. 1972 The Roman fort of Nantstallon, Cornwall, *Britannia,* 3. 56-111.

Foxhall, L. and Forbes, I.A. 1982. Sitometreia: the role of grain as a staple food, *Chiron,* 12. 41-90.

Frank T. 1940. *Rome and Italy of the Empire. An Economic Survey of Ancient Rome,* Volume V. Baltimore: John Hopkins University Press.

Frayn, J. 1978. Home baking in Roman Italy. *Antiquity*, 52. 28-33.

Frayn, J. 1993. *Markets and Fairs in Roman Italy.* Oxford: Oxford University Press.

Freezer, D.F. 1978. *From Saltings to Spa Town. The Archaeology of Droitwich.* Droitwich: Archaeological Committee of Hereford and Worcester County Council.

Frere, S.S. 1999. *Britannia. A History of Roman Britain.* Third edition revised. London: The Folio Society.

Frere, S.S. 1972. *Verulamium Excavations . Volume I.* Report of the Research Committee of the Society of Antiquaries of London, No 28.

Frere, S.S. and St. Joseph, J.K. 1974. The Roman Fortress at Longthorpe, *Britannia,* 5. 1-129.

Fuentes, N. 1991. The mule of the soldier, *Journal of Roman Military Studies,* 2. 65-114.

Gallant, T. 1985. *A Fisherman's Tale. An analysis of the potential productivity of fishing in the ancient world.* Miscellanea Graeca Fasciculus 7. Ghent: State University Press.

Garnsey, P. 1988. *Famine and Food Supply in the Roman World.* Cambridge: Cambridge University Press.

Gentry, A. 1976. *Roman Military Stone Built Granaries in Britain.* Oxford: British Archaeological Reports, 12.

Grant, A. 1989. Animal bones in Roman Britain in Todd, M. (Ed.) *Research on Roman Britain*, 135-147.

Grant, M. 1971. *Cities of Vesuvius*, London: Weidenfeld and Nicolson.

Green, C.E. 1989. *Excavations at Poundbury Volume I. The Settlements.* Dorchester: Dorset Natural History and Archaeological Society, Monograph Series No 7.

Grieg, J. 1983. Plant food in the past: a review of the evidence for northern Europe, *Journal of Plant Foods*, 5. 179-214.

Gunther. A.T. 1897. The Oyster Culture of the Ancient Romans, *Journal of the Marine Biological Association*, 4. 360-65.

Hall, A.R. and Kenward, H.K. 1990. *Environmental Evidence from the Colonia: General Accident and Rougier Street. The Archaeology of York. 14. 6. The Past Environment of York.* Council for British Archaeology for York Archaeological Trust.

Helback, H. 1964. The Isca Grain, a Roman plant introduction in Britain, *New Phytologist*, 63. 158-64.

Hinchliffe, J. 1980. *Excavations at Brancaster 1974 and 1977.* Norfolk Archaeological Unit: East Anglian Archaeological Report No 23.

Hopkins, K. 1966. On the probable age structure of the Roman population. *Population Studies.*20.2. 245-64.

Hurst, H.H.R. 1978. Viticulture at Gloucester, *Antiquaries Journal*, 58. 162.

Ireland, D. 2008. *Roman Britain: a sourcebook*. 3rd edition. Routledge: London.

Isenberg, M. 1975. The sale of sacrificial meat, *Classical Philology*, 70. 271-73.

Jackson, R. 1988. *Doctors and Diseases in the Roman Empire*. London: British Museum Press.

Jarrett, M.G. 1965. Roman officers at Maryport, *Transactions of the Cumberland and Westmorland Antiquarian and Archaeological Society*, 2. 70. 115-32.

Jarrett. M.G. 1966. The garrison of Maryport and the Roman army in Britain, in Jarrett, M.G. and Dobson, B. *Britain and Rome*, 27-40.

Jarrett, M. and Dobson, B. 1966. *Britain and Rome. Essays presented to Eric Birley.* Kendal: Titus Wilson.

Jesson, M. and Hill, D. (Eds.) 1971. *The Iron Age and its Hill Forts. Papers presented to Sir Mortimer Wheeler,* Southampton: University of Southampton.

Jones, D.M. 1980. *Excavations at Billingsgate Buildings 'Triangle', Lower Thames Street, 1974. Special Paper No 4.* London: London and Middlesex Archaeological Society.

Jones, G.B.D. 1984. Becoming different without knowing it. The role and development of *vici*, in Blagg, T.F.C. and King, A.C. (Eds.). *Military and Civilian in Roman Britain, 75-91.*

Jones, M. 1986. Agriculture in Roman Britain: the dynamics of change, in Todd, M. (Ed.) *Research in Roman Britain,* 127-34.

Jones, M, 1991. Food Production and Consumption — Plants, in Jones, R.F.J. (Ed.)1991. *Roman Britain: Recent Trends,* 21-27.

Jones, M.J. 2001. *Roman Lincoln*. Stroud: Tempus Publications.

Jones, R.F.J. (Ed.) 1991. *Roman Britain: Recent Trends*. Sheffield: J.R Collis Publications , University of Sheffield.

Jongman, W. 1988. *The Economy and Society of Pompeii.* Amsterdam: J. G. Gieben.

Junkelmann, M. 1998. *Panis Militaris*. Mainz: Verlag Philipp von Zabern.

Kenney, E.J. 1984. *The Ploughman's Lunch. Moretum. A Poem ascribed to Vergil.* Bristol: Bristol Classical Association.

King, A.C. 1984. Animal Bones and the dietary identity of military and civilian groups in Britain, Germany and Gaul in Blagg, T.F.C. and King, A.C. (Eds.) *Military and Civilian in Roman Britain,* 187-218.

King, A.C. 1991. Food Production and Consumption — Meat, in Jones, R.F.J. *Roman Britain: Recent Trends,* 15-29.

Knights, B.A., Dickson, C.A., Dickson, J.H. and Breeze, D. 1983. Evidence concerning the Roman military diet at Bearsden, Scotland, in the second century AD, *Journal of Archaeological Science* 10. 139-52.

Leach, P. 1982. *Ilchester. Volume I. Excavations 1974-75.* Bristol: Western Archaeological Trust Excavation Monograph, No.3.

Liversidge, J. 1955. *Furniture in Roman Britain.* London: Alec Tiranti.

Liversidge, J. 1957. Kitchens in Roman Britain, *Archaeological Newsletter,* 6. 82-5.

Luff, R.M. 1982. *A Zooarchaeological Study of the Roman North-Western Provinces.* British Archaeological Reports (International Series) 137.

McCance, R.A. and Widdowson, E.M. 1991. *The Composition of Foods,* fifth edition revised. London: Royal Society of Chemistry and MAFF.

McGee, H. 1986. *On Food and Cookery.* London: Allen and Unwin.

McWhirr, A., Viner, L. and Wells, C. 1982. *Romano-British Cemeteries at Cirencester. Cirencester Excavation II.* Cirencester: Cirencester Excavation Committee.

MacGregor, A. 1976. *Finds from a Roman Sewer System and an Adjacent Building in Church Street. The Archaeology of York. The Small Finds 17/1.* Council for British Archaeology. for York Archaeological Trust.

Maltby, M. 1989. Urban rural variations in the butchering of cattle in Romano-British Hampshire in Serjeantson, D. and Waldron, T. (Eds.). *Diet and Crafts in Towns,* 75-106.

Mann, J. 1984. A note on the *'Modius Claytonensis', Archaeologia Aeliana,* 5th Series, 12. 242.

Manning, W.H. 1985. *Catalogue of the Romano-British Iron Tools, Fittings and Weapons in the British Museum.* London: Trustees of the British Museum.

Marsden, P. 1980. *Roman London.* London: Thames and Hudson.

Mattingley, D. 2006. *An Imperial Possession. Britain in the Roman Empire, 54 BC–AD 409.* Allen Lane: Penguin Group.

Mau, A. 1899. *Pompeii: Its Life and Art.* London: Macmillan and Co.

May, J. 1996. *Dragonby. Report on the Excavation at an Iron Age and Romano-British Settlement in North Lincolnshire.* Oxford: Oxbow Monograph 61.

Mayeski, B.J. 1988. A Pompeian bakery in the Via dell'Abbondanza in Curtis, R. J. *Studia Pompeiana et Classica,* 149-66.

Meadows, I. 1996. Wollaston: The Nene Valley, a British Moselle? *Current Archaeology* 150, 212–215.

Meiggs, R. 1973. *Roman Ostia.* 2nd edition. Oxford: Clarendon Press.

Miles D. (Ed.) 1981. *The Romano-British Countryside.* Oxford: British Archaeological Reports 103.

Miller. J.L. 1969. *The Spice Trade of the Roman Empire.* Oxford: Clarendon Press .

Miller, L., Schofield, J. and Rhodes, M. 1986 *The Roman Quay at St. Magnus House, London.*

Excavations at New Fresh Wharf, London 1974-78. Special Paper No. 8. London: London and Middlesex Archaeological Society.

Milne, G. 1985. *The Port of Roman London.* London: Batsford. English Heritage.

Moffett, L.C. 1986. Gardening in Roman Alcester, *Circaea,* 5.2. 73-8.

Moritz, L.A. 1958. *Grain Mills and Flour in Classical Antiquity.* Oxford: Clarendon Press.

Moritz, L.A. and Jones, C.R. 1950. Experiments in grinding wheat in a Romano-British quern, *Milling,* June, 2-4.

Niblett, R. Verulamium, 2001. *The Roman City of St Albans.* Stroud: Tempus Publications.

O'Connor, T.P. 1988. *Bones from the General Accident Site, Tanner Row The Animal Bones. The Archaeology of York, 15.2.* Council for British Archaeology for York Archaeological Trust.

Ottaway, P. 1993. *Roman York.* London: Batsford/English Heritage.

Painter, K.S, 1977. *The Mildenhall Treasure. Roman Silver from East Anglia.* London: British Museum Publications.

Partridge, C.R. 1981. *Skeleton Green: a Late Iron Age and Romano-British Site.*:Britannia Monograph Series No 2. London: Society for the Promotion of Roman Studies.

Peacock, D.P.S. 1971. Roman amphorae in pre-Roman Britain, in Jesson, M. and Hill, D. (Eds.). *The Iron Age and its Hill Forts,* 161-88.

Peacock, D.P.S. 1974. Amphorae and the Baetican fish industry, *Antiquaries Journal,* 57. 232-43.

Peacock, D.P.S. and Williams, D.F. 1986 *Amphorae and the Roman Economy.* London: Longman.

Penney, S. and Shotter, D.A. 1996. An inscribed Roman salt-pan from Shavington, Cheshire, *Britannia,* 27. 36-65.

Perring, D. 2000. *The Roman House in Britain.* London: Routledge.

Pomey, P. and Tchernia. A. 1979. Le tonnage maximum des navires de commerce romain, *Archaeonautica,* 1978.2. 233-51.

Ponsich, M. and Tarradell, M. 1965. *Garum et Industries Antiques de Salsaison dans la Méditerranée Occidentale.* Université de Bordeaux et Casa Velàsquez. Bibliothèque Ècole Hispaniques Fasc.36.

Potter, T.W. 1984. The Roman Fenland: a review of recent work in Todd, M., *Research on Roman Britain,* 147-76.

Potter, T.W. and Johns, C. 1992. *Roman Britain.* London: British Museum Press.

Price, J. and Cottam, S. 1998. *Romano-British Glass Vessels: a Handbook. Practical handbooks in Archaeology, 14.* York: Council for British Archaeology.

Raftery, J. 1971. A bog butter find, *Journal of the County Kildare Archaeological Society* 15. 17-18.

Renfrew, J (Ed.) 1991. *New Light on Early Farming. Recent developments in Palaeoethnobotany.* Edinburgh: Edinburgh University Press.

Reynolds, P. 1979. *Iron Age Farm, The Butser Experiment.* London: British Museum Press.

Richardson, L. 1988. *Pompeii. An Architectural History.* Baltimore: John Hopkins University Press.

Rickman, G. 1971. *Roman Granaries and Stone Buildings.* Cambridge: Cambridge University Press.

Rickman, G, 1980. *The Corn Supply of Ancient Rome.* Oxford: Clarendon Press.

Roach, F.R. 1985. *Cultivated Fruits of Britain. Their Origin and History*. Oxford: Oxford University Press.

Rodwell, W.R. 1977. Iron Age and Roman Salt-working on the Essex Coast in Burnham, B.C. and Johnson, H.B. *Invasion and Response, 133-77*.

Rule, M. and Monaghan, J. 1993. *A Gallo-Roman Trading Vessel from Guernsey. The Excavation and Recovery of a Third-Century Shipwreck*. Guernsey Museum Monograph *No.5*. Guernsey: Museum and Art Galleries.

Sales, K.D., Oduwole, A.D., Robins. D., Hillman, G. and Holden, T.G. 1991. An analysis of the stomach contents of Lindow Man with ESR Spectroscopy, in Renfrew, J. *New Light on Early Farming*, 51-58.

Salway, P. 1982. *Roman Britain*. Oxford: Oxford University Press.

Sanquer, R. and Galliou, P. 1972. Garum, Sel et Salaisons en Armorique Gallo-Romaine, *Gallia* 30.199-223.

Schoff, W.H. (Ed.) 1912. *The Periplus of the Erythraean Sea*. London: Longman.

Sealey, P.R. 1975. Falernian wine at Roman Colchester, *Britannia*, 15. 250-4.

Sealey, P.R. 1985. *Amphorae from the 1970 Excavations at Colchester*. Oxford: British Archaeological Reports, 142.

Sealey, P.R. and Tyers, P.A. 1989. Olives from Roman Spain: a unique amphora find in British waters, *Antiquaries Journal*, 69.1. 53-72.

Serjeantson, D. and Waldron, T. (Eds.). 1989. *Diet and Crafts in Towns. The Evidence from Animal Remains from the Roman to the Post-Medieval Periods*. Oxford: British Archaeological Reports 199.

Severin, T. 1978. *The Brendan Voyages*. London: Book Club Associates.

Stallibrass, S. and Thomas, R. 2008. *Feeding the Roman Army: the archaeology of production and supply in N.W. Europe*. Oxford: Oxbow.

Stead, I. 1986. *Lindow Man. The Body in the Bog*. London: British Museum Press.

Stephens, G.R. 1985. Aqueduct delivery and water consumption in Roman Britain, *Bulletin of the Institute of Archaeology, University of London*, 21. 111-17.

Stephens, G.R. 1985. Civic aqueducts in Britain, *Britannia*, 16. 197-208.

Stirland, A. and Waldron, T. 1990. The earliest cases of tuberculosis in Britain. *Journal of Archaeological Science*, 17, 121–130.

Stobart, T. 1970. *Herbs, Spices and Flavourings*. Newton Abbott: David and Charles.

Swan, V.G. 1975. *Pottery in Roman Britain*. Princes Risborough: Shire Publications.

Swan, V.G. 1992. African Legionaries in Britain, *Journal of Roman Pottery Studies*, 5.1-34.

Swan, V.G. 1999. The Twentieth Legion and the history of the Antonine Wall, *Proceedings of the Royal Society of Antiquaries of Scotland*, 129. 399-480.

Symposium Vin et Histoire 1990. *Le Vin des Historiens: Acts du Première Symposium Vin et Histoire*. Suze-la-Rousse: Université du Vin.

Tassinari, S. 1993. *Il Vasellame bronzeo di Pompei. Soprintendenza Archeologica di Pompei Cataloghi 5*. Rome: L'Erma di Bretschneider.

Tchernia, A. 1986. *La Vin de l'Italie Romaine*. Rome: Ecole Française de Rome.

Tchernia, A. 1990. La vinification des Romains, in *Symposium Vin et Histoire*, 65-74.

Thompson, F.H. 1983. *Roman Cheshire. A History of Cheshire Volume II*, Chester: Cheshire County Council.

Thornton, M.D., Morgan, E.D. and Celoria, F. 1970. The composition of bog butter, *Science and Archaeology,* 10. 2-3.

Todd, M. (Ed.) 1989. *Research on Roman Britain 1960-1989. Britannia Monograph Series 11.* London: Society for the Promotion of Roman Studies.

Toynbee, J.M.C. 1982. *Art in Roman Britain.* London: Phaidon Press.

Tropical Products Institute. 1972 *Proceedings of the Conference on Spices held at the London School of Pharmacy April 10-14 1972.* London: Tropical Products Institute.

Wacher, J. 1998. *Roman Britain.* Revised edition. Stroud: Sutton Publishing.

Wacher, J. 1995. *The Towns of Roman Britain.* London: Batsford.

Waldron, H.A. 1973. Lead poisoning in the ancient world, *Medical History,* 17. 391-99.

Walker, H. (Ed) 1992. *Spicing up the Palate, Studies of Flavourings Ancient and Modern.* Totnes: Prospect Books.

Watson, G.R. 1969. *The Roman Soldier. London. Thames and Hudson.*

Webster, D., Webster, H. and Petch, D.F. 1961. A possible vineyard of the Romano-British period at North Thoresby, Lincolnshire, *Lincolnshire History and Archaeology,* 2. 55-61.

Webster, D. 1985.The Excavation of a Romano-British rural establishment at Barnsley Park, Gloucestershire, 1971-1979 Part III, *Transactions of the Bristol and Gloucestershire Archaeological Society,* 110. 73-100.

Wells, C. 1976. Romano-British pathology, *Antiquity,* 50. 53-5.

Wenham, L.P. 1968. *The Romano-British Cemetery at Trentholme Drive, York.* London: Ministry of Public Buildings and Works. Archaeological Reports No.5. H.M.S.O.

White, K.D. 1970. *Roman Farming.* London: Thames and Hudson.

White, R. and Barker, P. 1998. *Wroxeter. Life and Death of a Roman City.* London: Tempus Books.

Willcox, G.H. 1977. Exotic plants from Roman waterlogged sites in London, *Journal of Archaeological Science,* 4. 269-82.

Williams, D. 1977.A consideration of the sub-fossil remains of *Vitis vinifera L.*as evidence for viticulture in Roman Britain, *Britannia ,* 8. 327-34.

Williams, D. and Evans, J. 1991. A fragment from a probable Roman *clibanus* from Catterick, North Yorkshire, *Journal of Roman Pottery Studies,* 4. 51-5.

Williams, D.F. and Peacock, D.P. 1983. The importation of olive oil into Roman Britain in Blazquet, J. M. and Remesal, J. (Eds.). *Producción y Comercio del Aceite en la Antiqüedad II Congresso.* Madrid: Universida Complutense.

Wilkins, J., Harvey, D. and Dobson, M. (Eds.) 1995. *Food in Antiquity.* Exeter: University of Exeter Press.

Williams-Thorpe, O. and Thorpe, R.S. 1988. The provenance of donkey mills from Roman Britain, *Archaeometry,* 30. 275-89.

Woodward, P.J., Davies, S.M. and Graham, A.H. 1993. *Excavations at the Old Methodist Chapel and Greyhound Yard, Dorchester 1981-1984.* Dorchester: Dorset Natural History and Archaeological Society, Monograph Series No.12.

Wright, R.P. 1955. *Catalogue of the Roman Inscribed and Sculptured Stones in the Grosvenor Museum, Chester.* Chester: Chester and North Wales Archaeological Society.

Zeepvat, R.J. 1988. Fishponds in Roman Britain, in Aston, M.A. *Medieval Fish, Fisheries and Fishponds in England,* 17-26.

Index

Numbers in **bold** refer to illustrations

Abingdon, 40, 44, 93
Acheia 59
adipocere 58
aediles 145
Aelia Aeliana 122
Aelius Gallus 71
Aesernia 141, **85**
Africa, see North Africa
Agricola Julius 22, 120, 150
airag 58, **colour plate 7**
Alcester 21, 47, 54
Aldborough, North Yorkshire 43
allec 48, 80-1
Aminean wine 43
Amish community 110
amorino 51, **85**
amphorae 14, 47, 67, 73, 77, 80-1, 83-4, 93,
    104, 117, 141-2, 150, 155-6, **28, 29, 31, 32,**
    colour plate 10
anchovies 78-9
annona 21-2
Antipolis (Antibes) 80
Antonine Wall 29, 33, 68, 115, 155
Antoninus Pius, Emperor 156
Apennines 59
Apicius 13, 35, 43, 45-6, 55-7, 63, 65, 69, 71-3,
    76, 79, 102, 106, 110, 114-5, 118, 122, 161,
    163
Apollo 99
Appleford 106
apples 35, 66-7, 157, 163
    crab apples 66-7, 163
Appleshaw 106
Apuleius 25, 169
aqueducts 96, 148
Aquileia, Italy 37, **15**
Aquitania 88
Aristotle 86
Arlon Belgium 18, 20, 144, **12, 90**
army, see Roman army
Arrian 41, 169
artaba 21
asparagus 65

Asthall, 54
Athenaeus 12, 27, 34, 50, 77, 94-5, 169
athlete 127, **70**
Auchendavy 73
Augst 85
Augustus, Emperor 30, 51, 71, 88, 99
auxiliary troops 42, 45-6, 49, 152-5

Bacchus 90, 114, **59, 77, 78**
bacon 150, 157
Baetica 77,80, 87
Baginton fort, 151, **94**
bain-marie 110
Bainbridge, 60
bakers, bakeries 24, 26, 29-32, 142-3, 145, **10,**
    81, 82, 91, colour plates 5, 6, 25
baker's tomb, Rome see M. Vergilius,
    Eurysaces
baking pan **52**
balances 112-4
Ballyvourney, Co Cork 102
Bar Hill fort, Antonine Wall 68
barbarians 15, 33
barley 18, 20-1, 29-30, 43, 72, 93, 155, 161-2
Barnsley Park villa 18, 21, 46
barrack blocks 153
barrels 54, 88-9, 150, **33, 34**
Bartlow 122
basket chairs 122, 135, **68, 69, 79, colour**
    plates 17, 18
baskets, wicker 60-1
Batavians 15
Bath 43-4, 95, 110, 133, **19**
beakers 91, 129-30, **71, 72**
beans 29, 33, 35, 63, 65-6, 156-7, 163
Bearsden fort, Antonine Wall 28-9, 63, 67, 70,
    72, 159
Bede, Venerable 49-50
bee-keeping 76
beer (ale) 18, 28, 89, 92-4, 149-50, 155, 159
beets 63, 70
Belgae 57

Belgium 1, 20, 144
Beneventum, Italy 99
Benwell fort150
bikini 127, **70**
bilberries 66
Birdoswald fort 97, 153
birds see poultry
Birrens 153
Bishopstone 48-9
blackberries 66-7, 163
boars 38-40, 42-3, 155, **16, 18**
Bollihope Common, Stanhope 42
Bonn, Germany 35, 106
borage 69
Bordeaux 90-1, **35**
Boreham 43
Boscoreale villa, Italy **45**
bottles 89
Boudiccan rebellion 17, 67, 72, 140, 143
Bourton-on the Water 104
Boxmoor villa, Hertfordshire 90
Brading villa 20
Brancaster fort 43, 46, 49
bread stamps 153-5, **97**
bread wheat 17
bread 17, 27-32, 50, 72, 99, 126, 153-5, 157,
    162, **7, 8, 98, colour plate 25**
Brecon 48, 156
bream 48, 51-2
Bridgeness, Antonine Wall 38, **16**
brine, see salt
Broadchalk Down, Wiltshire 20-1
Brockley Hill, Middlesex 90, 118
Brough-on-Noe fort 155
bullaces 66
Burham villa 104
burials 164-7
butchers 137, 142 **colour plate 23**
butchery 37-8, 40, 45, **15**
butter 33, 58
    bog butter 58
Buzenol, Luxembourg 18, 20, **2**
Bythynia 80

cabbages 63, 70
Caerhun 155
Caerleon 17, 37, 40, 56, 65, 78, 97, 152-3 156,
    167, **96**
Caernarfon 48, 69, 156
Caerwent 20, 46, 56, 69, 72, 96, 143, 166
Caesar, Julius 43, 45, 89, 169

Caister-on-Sea 55
Caistor-by-Norwich 96
Caligula, Emperor 38
Campania, Italy 83, 87
cancer 165-6
Cannington 165
Canterbury 30, 77, 81, 84, 87, 95
Capheaton 134, **78**
Caracalla 33, 153
Carausius 78
caricature figurines 121, 126, **65**
Carlisle 88, 153, 155, 163
carnarium 103, 150
carp 48, 52
Carpow 88
carrots 63
Carvoran 22, **colour plate 3**
cassia 71
Castle Hill villa, Ipswich **colour plate 15**
Casterley Camp 76
Castleshaw fort 68
Castor, Northamptonshire 28
catfish 49
Cato 14, 17, 28, 33, 36, 40, 65, 67, 72-3, 86,
    121, 126, 169
cats 44
Catterick 20, 28, 88, 95, 152
cattle 14, 3, 40, 57-8, 144, 162, **12**
cauldrons, cauldron chains 100, 104, 119, 162,
    40, 47
caupone 137
Cawfields 153
celery 29, 65, 143, 155, 163
cellars 21, 104, 142
Celsus 56-7, 59, 76, 110
Celtic, Celts 14, 34-5, 41, 58, 83, 89, 94, 106,
    119, 127
cemeteries 96,103, 110, 164-7
cereals see grain, barley, oats, rye, wheat
Chalk villa 21, 104
Chanctonbury Ring 55
Charterhouse-on-Mendip 114
Chedworth villa 26, 43, 97, **20**
cheese 59-62, 69, 150, 155, 162
    cheese flavourng 62
    chcesc making 60-62, 150
    cheese presses 60-61, **23, 24**
    cheese, smoked 62
    cheese, types of, see cheese making
Chelmsford 54-5
Cherchel, (Caesarea), Israel 37
cherries 66-7, 155, 161, 163

Chester 51, 77, 80, 152, 156, **21, 66**
Chesters fort 26, 97
chestnuts 43, 67
Chew Park villa 66
Chichester 165-6
chickens 45-6, 155, **85**
Chignall villa 164-6
chives 69
Chollerford 26
Chrysippus of Tyre 13
Cicero 102, 169
cider 94
cinnamon 71
Cirencester 30, 95, 110, 119, 126, 147, 164-6
Claudis Crysis 167
Claudian 41, 169
Claudius, temple of 40, 71
Claudius, Emperor 71, 87
cleavers 37, 111
cockles 54, 156
cod 47-8, 51, 156
Cohors V Gallorum Re-enactment Group
    155-6, **99, colour plates 12, 27**
colanders 117, **62**
Colchester 17,40, 43, 46, 50, 54-5, 60, 65-8,
    72, 78, 80, 87, 90-1, 93, 100, 114, 118, 121,
    126, 129-31, 142-3, **65, 74, 88**
Cologne 89, 129, 133,
Columella 14, 17, 18, 33, 35, 46, 53, 57-9, 61-3,
    65, 67, 69, 75-6, 78, 85, 87, 90,163, 170
conditum 86
contubernium 151, 153, **colour plate 27**
cookery, cooking 13, 164
cookery books 13
cooking pots, vessels 115-6, 151-3, **95**
cooking utensils 106-10
cooks 102, 151, 161
coprolites 18
Corbridge 48, 51, 60, 97, 150, **39**
Cordanum 56
Corfe Mullen 25
coriander 26, 69-70, 155
Corinth 39
corn measure 21-2, **3, colour plate 3**
cows, see cattle
crab 54
crane 46, 156
cucumbers 63
cumin 50, 70, 79, 119, 161
Cunobelin 94
cupids 92, **36**
Curatia Di(o)nysia **66**

dace 48
Dagda 106
dairy products 57-62, 143
damsons 66-7
dancing girls 127, **70**
dandelion 66
dates 67, 143, 163, **88**
deer 43, 156-7
defrutum 87
dental caries 165
Denver 74
desserts 126
Dijon 137, **80**
dill 69, 72, 143
dining, dining habits, dining rooms 119-135,
    64, colour plates 16, 17
Dio Cassius 170
Diocletian, Emperor, price edict 34, 41, 49, 54,
    72-3, 80, 94
Diodorus Siculus 18, 34, 83, 119, 169
Dioscorides 29, 37, 86, 94, 170
Ditchley villa 19
dogs 36, 38, 40-4, **17, 19**
dolia 104, 139, **45, 46, 83**
Domburg 90
Domitian, Emperor 90
Doncaster 47, 66-7, 94
donkeys 21
Dorchester on Thames, Oxfordshire 54, 91,
    166
Dorchester, Dorset 44, 48, 95, 122, 165
dormice 43
Dorn farm, Moreton in Marsh 112
doves 46
Dragonby 49, 55
Dresden, Germany 35, 137, **colour plate 23**
Droitwich 74
ducks 46, 155-6, 161
Duntocher 114

East Huntshill 74
East Coker villa 43, **cover**
Eccles villa 60
Edix Hill, Barrington 165
eels 48-50
eggs 29, 46, 52, 55, 69, 71-2,110, 126, 157
Egypt 21, 46, 52, 55, 69, 71-2,110,126, 157, **48,
    49, 50**
einkorn 17
elderberries , elderflower 66
Elginhaugh 155

emmer 17, 28-9
endive 63
entertainment 126-7
Etruria 59
Exeter 96, 159
Exsuperius 110

Fabricius 14
Falernian wine 87
fat hen 162, 165
Faversham 118
Fendoch fort 153
Fenland 40, 73-4
fennel 69-70
figs 29, 67, 155, 163
figurines, bronze 34, 36, 42-3, **14, 18**, silver,
    34, **14**, terracotta 121, 126, **64**
Finn 50
fires 99
fish sauce, see liquamen
fish, fishing 15-6, 47-54, 119, 150, 156, 161,
    163, **21, 22, 85**
fish farming 53-4
Fishbourne 30, 46, 51, 65, 97, 162, **38**
Flavius Cerealis 45-6, 150
flounder 47-9
flour 23-6, 28-9
Folkestone villa 102
food poisoning 163
Fors Fortuna, festival of 157
forum boarium 147-8
fountains 96, 98, **37, 39, colour plate 11**
fowls, see chickens, poultry
France 35, 57, 61, 63
frescoes 32
Frocester villa 26
frogs 44
Frontinus 71, 170
fruit 59, 66-7, 126, 163, 166, **colour plates
    17, 19**
frumentarii 149
frying pans 106-8, **48, 49, 50**
furca 151

G Antonius Quietus 77
Gaetae 57
Gaius Asicius Probus 80
Gaius Tetius Veturius Micianus 42
Galen 170
game 41-3, 59

game birds, see poultry
garfish 48
garlic 70, 157
garum, see liquamen
Gaul, Gauls 14-5, 28, 33, 49, 51, 83, 88, 90,
    112, 118, 149, 165
Gaza 87
geese 45-6, 156, 161
Geoponica 80
Germania 59, 94
Germans, Germany 15, 59, 63, 94, 149
Geta 31
Gildas 166
gilthead 49
ginger 71
gladiolus 65
glass, glassware 117-8, 130-3, **63, 73, 74, 75,
    colour plate 22**
Glastonbury 27
globi 72
Gloucester 80, 87, 91, 142
goats 34, 57, 156, **14**
Godmanchester 72, 95
Good King Henry 66
Gorhambury villa 48
gout 126
graffiti 14, 25, 141, **86**
grain 15, 17-26, 35, 99, 149-50, 153, 161-2, **1**
granaries 17-8, 20-1, 150, 161, **94**
grapes 91, 163
graves 164-7, **colour plate 10**
Great Witcombe villa, 42, 52
Great Bedwyn villa 35, 49
Great Chesterford 18, 26, 54, 106-7, 110-11,
    47, 54
Great Chesters 98
Great Holt Farm, villa, Boreham 161
Great Lea, Binford 107
Great Northern Diver 46
Greta Bridge 99
gridirons 100, 110, **26, 40, 41**
Guadalquivir Valley, Spain 77
Guernsey 51
Guilden Morden 42,
guilds 21, 99

Hacheston 112
Hadrian, Emperor 60, 150
Hadrian's Wall 26, 97, 115, 153
hallec, see liquamen
hallibut 48

Halstock villa 55, 94
Haltwhistle Burn 26
Hambleden villa 20, 94
hams 151
Hamworthy 26
hardtack (*bucellatun*) 155
hares 43, 155, **19, 20**
Hartlip villa 21, 104
Hayling Island 55
hazelnuts 68
hearths 101, 104, 106, 151-2
hemlock 70, 155
henbane 70, 155
Hengistbury Head 77, 83
herbs 69-70, 163
Herculanium 96, 140-2, **83, 84, 87, colour plates 11, 24 & 25**
Herodian 170
herrings 16, 47-9, 81
Hippalus 71
Hippocrates 59, 63, 95, 170
Hochdorf, Germany 106
Hod Hill fort 156
hog's fennel 155
Holborough 78, 122
Holditch 30, 142
Holt fort 60, 68, 153
honey 43, 55, 71-2, 75-6, 79, 93-4, 119, 122, 157
Horace 73, 80, 99, 103, 140, 170
horehound 88
horses 8-9, 36, 149, 156
Hortensius 93
Hounds, see dogs
Housesteads 97, 134, 140, 150-1, 153
Hunsbury 24
hunting 41-3, 51, 156
Hyrieus 103

Iatrocles 13
Icklingham 100, 107, 112
Igels column, Moselle Valley **42, 68**
Ilchester 45, 91, 165-6
India 23, 71
Ireland 28, 33, 35, 41, 558, 106, 119
Iron Age 18, 20, 27, 33-5, 37, 45, 77, 83, 103-4, 106
Iwerne 21

Josephus 152, 170
Julia Velva 122, **67**

Julia Domna 31
Julian, Emperor 15, 67
Julius Verecundus 46, 81
Julius Verens 167
Julius Secundus 42
Juno 38
Jupiter 38, 103
Juvenal 49,54-5, 103-4, 164, 171

Keynsham villa 51
Kimmeridge Bay 122
Kingsnorth 81
Kingscote villa 26, 100
Kingsholm 87
kitchens 38, 99-118, **26, 40, 42, colour plate 13**
knives 37, 111-2, **55**

L Junius Melissus 87
L Viducius Placidius 90
L Solomarius Secundinus 90
lac concretum 59
lactantia 57
ladles 110-1, **54**
lamb 38, 40, 61, 104, 137-8, 142, 156, **80**
Lancaster 18, 30, 72
Langton villa, 19
lard 157, 159
lead poisoning 87, 96, 110, 164
Lechlade 102
legions see Roman army
Leicester 60, 96, 146
lentils 29, 65, 157, 162
lettuce 63
Libanius 15, 171
Lincoln 36, 38, 40, 43, 48, 81, 90, 95, 99, 167
Lindow Man 18, 29
liquamen 55, 79-83, 110, 149-50, 156-7, 161-2
Little Butser 76, 103-4, **12, 43, 44**
Livy 77, 102
loaves, see bread
London 17, 26-7, 31, 33, 37-8, 41, 43, 47-8, 51-2, 55-6, 60, 65-9, 72, 77-8. 80-1, 87-91, 95-7, 99, 107, 111-2, 114-5, 118-9, 127, 30, 140, 142-3, 166, **56, colour plates 13, 18, 23 & 25**
Longthorpe fort 55, 60, 150, 156, **25**
lovage 55
Lower Halstow 60, **24**
Lucretius 40
Lucullus 55, 66, 93

Lufton villa 52, **22**
Lullingstone villa 61, **25**
Lydney 42, 50, **17**
Lynch Farm, Water Newton 53
M Vergilius Eurysaces 30-1, 100, **10, 11, 91**
M Aurelius Lunaris 90-1, **35**
macellum 145-8, **93**
mackerel 47-8
Macrobius 54
Madrague de Giens shipwreck 93
Mainz 153
mallow 70
Mancetter 118, 130
mansiones 149
Marcus Cocceius Firmus 73
marigold 70
marjoram 69
markets 143- 8
marrubiin 88
Mars 38
Mars Braciaca 94
Martial 13, 25, 44, 51, 55, 57, 59, 62, 65, 69,
  79, 87, 102-3, 122, 126, 137, 171
Maryport 48, 54, 153
mead 93, 106
meals 14, 122, **colour plate 16**
meat 33-41, 43, 50, 76, 126, 150, 155-6, 161-2
medical problems 57
medicine, medical usages 56-7, 65
medlars 66
melca 57
Mercury 99, 146
metalware 133-5
Metz 137
Middlewich 62, 74-5
Mildenhall treasure 133-4, **78**
milk 30, 33-4, 57-9, 71, 119, 136, **colour
  plate 7**
mills, milling 23-7, 30, 143, **5, 6, colour plate 5**
Minerva 103
mint 55, 69-70
modius, see corn measure
Mongolia 58, 162, **colour plate 7**
Mons Claudianus fort, Egypt 156
Moretum 24, 27
mortaria, see pottery
mortars 23, 63, 69, 72, 117, **99, colour plate 3**
mosaics 43, 50, 52, 119, **20, 22, 100, cover
  photo, colour plate 15**
Moselle 90, 129
Mount Bures 77, 83
mulberries 66-7, 163

mules 19
mullet 48, 52
mulsum 87,
Mumrills 156
muria, see liquamen
Murrell Hill 122
mushrooms 65
mussels 54, 56
must 62, 87, 91
mustard 70-2

Nantstallen fort 77
Nantwich 62,75, 163
Neatham 40-1
Nehalennia 90
Nemesianus 41, 171
Nepal 19, **colour plates 1, 2**
Neptune 52, 103
nettles 65
Neumagen, Germany 88, 122, **34, 69**
Neusse, Germany 72
Newport, Isle of Wight 102
Newstead fort 18, 43, 68, 110, 156, **95, colour
  photos 8, 19**
Nîmes 59
North Thoresby 90
North Africa 52, 77-8, 81, 87, 155-6
Northwich 62, 75
nutrition 14, 16, 161-4
nuts 35, 50, 67-8, 155, 163

oats 18, 117
Oconea 110
Odell villa, 65
Old Carlisle **58**
olives 63, 157, 161, **28, colour plate 9**
olive oil 72, 77-8, 149, 156-7, 159, 162
olla 115, 152
Oppian 41, 51, 171
Orton Longueville 166
Ospringe **colour plate 22**
osteoarthritis 164
Ostia 84, 86, 103, 137, **46**
ovens 27, 30-1, 99-101, 104, 147, 153, **10, 11,
  96, colour plates 5, 12**
Ovid 27, 47, 103, 171
Owslebury 63, 77
oxen 19, 36-7
oxygala 57
oysters 13, 47, 54-6, 70, 126, 143, 156, 161

Pakistan 23, **colour plate 3**
Palladius 18, 61, 87, 171
Palmyrenes 15
pans 87, 100, 110, 164, **52,** see also frying pans
    salt pans 73, 75, 156, **27**
Papcastle fort 156
Park Street villa 20-1, 104
parsley 55, 69-70
parsnips 63
partridge 46
pastrycooks's mould 31
patellas 110
paterae 108, 110, 152, **51**
patinae 110
Paturnus 151
peacock 141
pearls 56
pears 66,79
peas 65, 156, 161
Pen Lystyn 153
pennyroyal 69
pepper 55, 71-2, 79, 157, 161
Pepperhill cemetery 166, **100**
perch 48-9, 156
pestles 23, 63, 69, 72, 117, **99, colour plate 3**
Petronius 29, 43, 111, 171
pheasant 46
Philemon 59
Piddington villa 106
Piercebridge 36, 43
pigeon 46
pigs, pork 34-8, 40, 106, 137, 156, **15,** see also
    boars
pike 48, 52
Pimperne, Dorset 103-4
pine kernels 62, 118, 161
pipkins 103
pitch 55, 61-2, 73, 86, 104, 115
Pitney villa 36
pits 20-1, 102
plaice 48-9, 51
Placidus 90
plague 165-6
Plautus 51, 70, 111, 171
Pliny the Elder 14, 18, 21, 23, 25, 28-9, 32-3,
    44, 46, 53-4, 56-9, 61-3, 65-72, 76-7,
    79-81, 83, 87-8, 90, 94, 97, 131, 163, 165,
    171
Pliny the Younger 51, 163, 171
plums 66-7, 155, 157, 161, 163
pomegranate 67
Pompeii 26-7, 30, 32, 52, 83, 96, 100, 104, 107,
    109-10, 137, 140-2, 145, **37, 52, 53, 81, 82,**
    101, colour plate 5
Pompeius 60
Pontus 66
popinae 137, 140
poppy seeds 29, 43, 72, 143, 155
pork, see pigs
Portchester 38, 40,49
Posidonius 50, 77, 119, 171
potboilers 102
pottage, porridge 17, 28, 156, 162
pottery 20, 115-8, 145, 155-6. **30, 71, 98,**
    colour plates 8, 21
    Alice Holt 116
    black burnished 115-6, **60**
    Castor ware 42, 129
    Cranbeck 129
    Dales ware 116
    Derbyshire ware 116
    Glevum 61
    mortaria 30-1, 61, 63, 67, 69, 77-8, 117-8,
      145, **25, 62, colour plates 8, 13**
    Nene Valley 60,118, 122, 129, **25**
    Oxford 118, 129
    Rhenish **25, 72**
    samian 145, **25, colour plates 19, 20**
    Savernake 116, **61**
    Severn Valley ware **61**
    Trent Valley 116
poultry 45-6, 126, **89**
Poundbury 40-1, 43, 57, 60, 77-8, 104, 110,
    163-5
Pozzuoli, Italy 112
Prae Wood 77
praesion (horehound) 77
Preston villa 122
Prestwick Carr 106
Probus, Emperor 90
puffballs 65

Queen of Sheba 71
querns, quernstones 23-4, 99, 153, **4**

radishes 63, 65, 163
Radnage 130
raspberries 15, 66-7, 155, 163
Redlands 26
rennet 61
Rhineland 88-9, 122
Rhodes 83, 87, 156

Richborough 51, 54, 156
roach 48-9
Rockbourne villa 76
rocket 69
Roman army 17, 33, 90, 149-59, **1, 26**
Rome 31, 46, 52, 54, 56, 59-60, 62, 71, 99, 122
rosemary 69
rotary quernstones, see querns
Rotherly 68
Rouen 90
round houses 103-4, 119, **43, 44**
Rudchester 150
Rudston villa 52
rue 18, 29, 69
Rushall Down 107
Rustius Barbarus 60
rye 18, 69

St Brendan 49
St John's Wort 70
Saalburg fort 153
sacrifices, sacrificial meat 38, 39-40, **16**
saddle querns, see querns
saffron 70-2
sage 69
Saham Toney 152
salmon 48-50, 52
salt 29, 47, 72-5, 79-80, 157, 162, **27**
saltern sites 74
Sarcina 59
Sardinians 15
sarcophagus 133, **79**
Satyricon 29, 111
sauvetaurila 38, **16**
savory 69
Scargill Moor 42
Scole 68
scythes 18
Sea Mills 112,
Seneca 14, 53, 82, 122, 137, 164
Septimius Severus, Emperor 31, 77, 156
Sevir Augustalis 90, **35**
sextarii 22, 81
Sextus Pomponius 73
Shakenoak 53
shale 122
Shapwick Heath 94
Shavington 53
Sheep 33-4, 37, 40-1, 57-8, 156, **13**
Sheepen 77, 83
shellfish 54-6, 79, 126

shops, shopping 137-44, **80, 81, 82, 83, 84, 87, 89, colour plate 24**
shutters 140, **colour plate 24**
sickles 18
silago 29
Silchester 18, 20, 24, 30-1, 36-8, 40, 44, 46-8, 54, 60, 63, 65-7, 69, 72, 76, 86-9, 91, 97, 100, 104, 106-7, 111-2, 117-9, **33, 47, 55, 57, 59**
silphium 118
Silvanus 42
silverware 162
Simpleveld, Holland 133, **79**
Simulus 27, 103
Simus 13
Skeleton Green 49, 77
skeletons 14, 166-8, **100, 101**
skillets 134, **77**
Slack fort 68
sloes 66, 155
smelt 48
smoking, meat, cheese 40
snails 44, 156
Snailwell 83
snipe 46
sorrel 70
South Shields 43-4, 151, 153
Southwark see London
Spain 28, 47, 87-8, 90, 142, 153
Spaniards 15
sparrowhawk 42
spelt 17, 19, 20, 28-9, 162
spice trade 71
spices 70-2, 20, 28-9, 162
spoons 52
sprats 51, 81
Springhead 30, 39, 142
stalls, market **90**
Stanfordbury 77, 83
Stanwick, Northamptonshire 55, 107
steelyards 112-4, 145, **57, 91, 92, colour plate 12**
steelyard weights 112-4, **58, 59**
Stockton 51
Stonea 56
stools 122, 137
stoves 100-2, 104, **40, 42**
Strabo 34, 41, 54, 71, 88, 94, 171
strainer 133, **76**
strawberries 66-7, 155
Suetonius 30, 38, 71, 88, 94, 171
Sulis Minerva 119
Symmachus 41
Syrians 15

tabernae 137
tables 120, 122, **67, 68, 69, colour plate 17, 18, 21**
tableware 128-30, 161
Tacitus 20,22, 56, 63, 94, 120, 127, 149-50, 152
tanneries 41
Tarraconensis 77-8, **28, colour plate 9**
Templeborough fort 60, 76
temples 40, 50, 146
tench 49
testa 28, **9**
thermopolia 137
threshing 19
thrush 43
thyme 62, 69
Tiberius, Emperor 13, 63
Tibet19, 58, **colour plate 14**
Titus Flaminius 90
Titus Flavius Natalis 167
Tolosa (Toulouse) 59
tombstones 43, 122, 167, **66, 67, 69, 80, 91, colour plate 17**
Tottenhoe, villa 55
Trajan, Emperor 56, 150
Trajan's Column 18, **1**
Trawsfynydd 94
Trebula 62
Trentholme Drive cemetery, see York
tribulum 19
triclinium 120, **64**
Trier 89, **34, 92**
Trimalchio 29, 43, 121, 126
tripod 100,
trivet 100, **41**
trout 48-9, 52
tuberculosis 163
Tungrians 15
turbot 48
turnips

Uley 48
Umbria 59
urine 63, 117
Usk 60, 153

vallus 18, **2**
Varro 14, 17, 19, 33, 35, 44, 53, 57, 59, 61-3, 67, 70, 75, 87, 95, 171
vegetables 63-5, 126, 155, 161, 163, 166
Vegetius 151, 155-6, 171
Venables, Thomas 145

Venison 43, 155, 157
venus 38
Vergil 57, 75, 103, 171
Verulamium 17-8, 31, 36, 48, 56, 67, 90, 94-5, 99, 101, 116, 140, 142-3, 145, **62, 71, 72**
vetch 33
vici 149, 155
Vidinarius 13
vigiles 99
villas 15, 30, 40, 99, 102, 119, 146, 161
Vindolanda 27, 33-4, 36, 43-6, 48, 56, 58, 65, 68, 71, 77, 81, 88-9, 133, 149-50, 153, 155-7
vinegar 50, 55, 61, 65, 69-70, 72, 119, 126
vines, vineyards 63, 84, 90, 93, **36**
vitamins 17,23, 29-30, 162-4, 166
Vitruvius 21, 24, 95-6

Waddon Hill fort 46, 48, 94, 156
Wâdi Fawâkhir fort 60, 156
walnuts 68, 161
wasp, caprificatory 67
water pipes 95-7, **38**
water supply 95-8
Wattisford 43
weeds 65-6
wells 88, 96, 147
Welwyn 130, **10**
Welzheim, Germany 72
whales, whalemeat 48
wheat 17, 23-5, 43
whetstones 145
Whitton 94
Wickford 21, 54
wigeon 156
Wiggenholt 68
Wilcote 54
Wilderspool 18, 118, 130
William of Malmsbury 49
Willowford 26
Winchester 68, 96, 166-7
wine, wineshops 55, 76, 83-93, 110. 137, 139, 142, 149, 155-7, 159, 161, **34, 80, 83, 85, 87**
winnowing 19, **colour plates 1, 2**
Wint Hill 131-2, 75
Winterton villa 91, 119
Wollaton 90
Woodchester villa 119
woodcock 156, 161
Woodeaton 39, 145
wool 34, 40
Woolaston Pill villa 26, 36

wormwood 86, 93
wrasse 48
writing tablets, London 140, Vindolanda 45, 58, 81, 133, 149-50, 156-7
Wroxeter 51, 90, 95-6, 118, 145, 147-8, **93**

York 15-7, 21, 36-8, 49, 44, 46, 48, 54, 63, 65, 67, 69, 72, 78, 80, 88, 90-1, 95, 101, 103, 122, 152, 159, 163-7

Zosimus 15, 171